KEYNES AND PUBLIC POLICY AFTER
FIFTY YEARS
VOLUME 2: THEORIES AND METHOD

Keynes and Public Policy After Fifty Years
Volume 2: Theories and Method

Edited by
Omar F. Hamouda
John N. Smithin

EDWARD ELGAR

Published by
Edward Elgar Publishing Limited
Gower House
Croft Road
Aldershot
Hants GU11 3HR
England

British Library Cataloguing in Publication Data

Keynes and public policy after fifty years.
  1. Keynes, John Maynard.   2. Keynesian economics.
  I. Hamouda, O.F.   II. Smithin, John N.
  330.15′6   HB99.7

  ISBN 1-85278-003-7 v.1: Economics and policy
  ISBN 1-85278-004-5 v.2: Theories and method

Printed and bound in Great Britain

Contents

Foreword   *G.C. Harcourt*   vii
Acknowledgements   viii
Introduction   *O.F. Hamouda and J.N. Smithin*   x
Contributors   xvii

PART I   KEYNES AND ECONOMETRIC METHOD

 1 Keynes and the origins of macroeconometric modelling
    R.G. Bodkin, L.R. Klein and K. Marwah   3
 2 Keynes's vision and econometric analysis   *I.H. Rima*   12
 3 The Keynes–Tinbergen exchange in retrospect
    J.C.R. Rowley   23

PART II   THE THEORY OF INVESTMENT

 4 Keynes's view of investment   *C.L. Barber*   35
 5 The q-ratio and replacement investment: an extension of
    Keynesian theory   *M. Perelman*   41
 6 Keynesian microeconomics and the microeconomics of Keynes
    in public sector investment decisions.   *A. Abouchar*   49

PART III   ASPECTS OF THE LABOUR MARKET

 7 Wage flexibility and employment   *P. Howitt*   61
 8 The aggregate supply function and the share economy: some
    early drafts of the *General Theory*   *A. Asimakopulos*   70
 9 Weitzman's share economy and the aggregate supply function
    P. Davidson   81
10 Hicks's wage-theorem and Keynes's *General Theory*
    C. Marme and P. Wells   93
11 Unemployment resulting from preferences on wages or prices
    S.-C. Kolm   102

PART IV   MONEY AND INTEREST RATES

12 Keynes's treatment of interest   *B.J. Moore*   121
13 Keynes and stable money   *T.K. Rymes*   130
14 Money, interest and rentiers: the twilight of rentier capitalism
    in Keynes's *General Theory*   *M. Lavoie and M. Seccareccia*   145

15 Money and interest rates: a comment   *N.J. Wulwick*   159
16 Keynes and money: a comment   *M.L. Burstein*   162

PART V   INTERNATIONAL TRADE AND FINANCE

17 Keynes and the question of tariffs   *B.M. Wolf and
   N.P. Smook*   169
18 The international debt of the LDCs   *L. Tarshis*   183
19 The international debt problem and the 'Clearing Union'
   B. Schmitt   194

PART VI   POSITIONAL GOODS AND GROWTH:
          ANALOGIES TO KEYNESIAN ECONOMICS

20 Stagflation for our grandchildren   *O.F. Hamouda and
   L. Tarshis*   205

Name index   209
Subject index   214

Foreword

The conference of which these volumes are the fitting outcome could not have been held at a more appropriate time: fifty years after the publication of the *General Theory*, and in honour of Lorie Tarshis's seventy-fifth birthday. Keynes's contributions, and especially the *General Theory*, are experiencing a proper reappraisal and revival following those lean years in which the modern purveyors of classical theory (in Keynes's sense) celebrated prematurely both his demise and their own ascendancy. Lorie Tarshis is a most distinguished expositor of Keynes's theories and their extensions, to which he himself has made substantial contributions. He has also always placed his own eminently sensible policy proposals on a secure Keynesian base, drawing on his thorough grounding in Keynesian principles, first, at the University of Toronto, and then at Cambridge itself when Keynes was lecturing from the proof-sheets of the various stages of the development of the *General Theory* embryo.

Thanks to the energy and enthusiasm of Omar Hamouda, John Smithin and Bernard Wolf, a friendly and happy band were gathered together in the fine surroundings of Glendon College of York University in Toronto for an exhausting but exhilarating few days. It is splendid that the papers presented there should be preserved in more permanent form in these two volumes. And it is especially good that Richard Goodwin and Robert Skidelsky, those intrepid travellers on People's Express, should have their addresses – one after lunch, the other after dinner – printed in the volumes. Both were great occasions. The addresses were fitting climaxes to the fine meals and ample wines (for Canada) which preceded them. They will serve to recall to those who were there the standing ovation which Lorie Tarshis received when after dinner he was presented with the first published copy of the book of essays in his honour.

There is a wide range of topics and approaches covered in these volumes. I hope that the small band of original Canadian Keynesians who were present will be cheered to see in what capable hands their tradition is being carried on.

G.C. Harcourt, *Cambridge*

Acknowledgements

The editors of these volumes wish to express their thanks to Bernard M. Wolf, who played a leading role on the organizing committee of the original Glendon Conference (and is also the co-author of one of the contributed papers).

The organizing committee, *in toto*, would also like to thank the following individuals and organizations, all of whom have given invaluable support and encouragement in various ways, both for the Conference and the preparation of these volumes: President Harry Arthurs, York University; Principal Phillipe Garigue, Glendon College; Mr John Crow, Governor of the Bank of Canada; the Hon. Robert Nixon, Treasurer of Ontario; Mr Bryne Purchase, Ministry of Treasury and Economics, Government of Ontario; Professor Jon Cohen, University of Toronto; Dr Geoff Harcourt, University of Cambridge; Vice-President Ken Davey, York University; Associate Vice-President Paul Lovejoy, York University; Associate Principals Ian Gentles and Beth Hopkins, Glendon College; Dean David Bell, York University; Dean Yvette Szmidt, Glendon College; Ms Noli Swatman, Office of Research Administration, York University; Mr Tim Nau, Office of the Principal, Glendon College; Ms Danielle Comarmond, Budget Office, Glendon College; Professors John Buttrick, John Evans and Charles Plourde, Department of Economics, and Professor Bryan Massam, Department of Geography, York University; Professors Ian McDonald and David McQueen, Department of Economics, Glendon College; Glendon College Students' Association; and the Economics Graduate Students' Association, York University.

Financial support for the Conference was provided by the Ministry of Treasury and Economics, Government of Ontario; Office of the President, York University; the York University Ad Hoc Research Fund; and the Glendon College 20th Anniversary Celebration Committee.

First-class secretarial support has been provided by Mrs. Paule Cotter, Research Office, Glendon College; Mrs Azi Subrahmanyam and Christine Goary, Department of Economics, Glendon College; and Ms Svatka Hermanek, Faculty of Administrative Studies, York University.

Special mention must be made of the hard work put in during the Conference by M. Franque Grimard and his fellow undergraduate students in Economics at Glendon College; Louise Laliberté, Joanne Castonguay-McNamee, Milos Kostich, Michéle Rioux, Todd Smyth, Charles Rouyer, David De Wees, Jim Lauer, Robert Najm and Eric Armour. It was largely thanks to their efforts that the meetings, out of which this collection of papers developed, were conducted so smoothly. Finally, we would like to express our appreciation for the enthusiasm and vision of our publisher, Edward Elgar, in guiding these volumes through to publication.

Introduction

Omar F. Hamouda and John N. Smithin

This collection of papers originated in a Conference on 'Keynes and Public Policy after Fifty Years', which was held in September 1986 at Glendon College, York University, Toronto, to mark the fiftieth anniversary of the publication of Keynes's *General Theory* (the actual date of publication being February 1936).

As well as commemorating the *General Theory*, the Conference participants were also able to honour Professor Lorie Tarshis, who is currently chairperson of the Economics Department at Glendon College and was celebrating his seventy-fifth birthday during 1986. Lorie was a pupil of Keynes at Cambridge during the crucial period 1932–6 in which the *General Theory* was being elaborated, and has since gained an international reputation for his many contributions to Keynesian economics. At the Conference dinner on the evening of 26 September Geoff Harcourt presented Lorie with the first copy of a Festschrift, edited by Jon Cohen (University of Toronto) and himself, containing contributions by many of Lorie's old friends and admirers in the economics profession. Lorie received a standing ovation from the Conference.

We are also pleased to record the participation of two other students of Keynes, Robert B. Bryce and Walter S. Salant, who were classmates of Lorie Tarshis fifty years ago, and like Lorie, have gone on to distinguished careers: Bryce at the Ministry of Finance in Ottawa, and Salant in Washington, DC, latterly at the Brookings Institution. These volumes contain contributions by all three former pupils of Keynes: Bryce, Salant and Tarshis.

The anniversary happened to fall at a time of more than usual uncertainty in the realm of macroeconomic theory and policy. During the 1970s and early 1980s it seemed that Keynesian economics was rather out of fashion, and with the rise first of monetarism, and then the so-called 'new classical' school, more than one economist could be found to assert that the insights of Keynes into the functioning of the capitalist market economies of forty and fifty years ago were no longer relevant to the modern world. By 1986, however, things seemed to be much less clear-cut. The worldwide recession of 1981–2 (which some economists have blamed, at least partly, on monetarist policies designed to cure inflation) and the subsequent return to prolonged mass unemployment in many of the industrialized countries, have naturally evoked memories of the 1930s. Rising protectionist sentiment, particularly in the USA, reinforces this impression. Of course, circumstances are different, but it is hardly surprising that there has been renewed interest in the diagnosis and solutions offered by Keynes for an apparently similar set of problems.

In this situation the objective of these essays is not merely, or not only, commemorative, but also to take the opportunity suggested by the anniversary to inquire to what extent we can learn from the past and to place Keynes's ideas in a present-day context. The contributors are a diverse group of scholars, practitioners and theorists, some of whom participated in the original Keynesian revolution, some who have established reputations in the development and interpretation of ideas originally suggested by Keynes, and a younger generation who feel that the study of Keynes remains relevant to the macroeconomics of the 1980s. The emphasis on public policy is natural, as Keynes was, *par excellence*, the economist for whom economic theory was only valuable in as far as it contributed to a sound basis for public policy.

Taken as a whole, these papers testify to the fact that Keynes's ideas continue to provide an intellectual challenge to the contemporary economist, and to an extent that would have seemed surprising at the zenith of the 'rational expectations revolution' only a few years ago. It is perhaps too soon to talk of a 'Keynesian recovery', to borrow Peter Howitt's (1986) phrase, but such a development no longer seems impossible.

The real reason for the continuing relevance of Keynesian ideas, we would argue, lies not so much in the text of the *General Theory*, or even the personality of Keynes himself, remarkable though that was in the testimony of those who knew him, but rather in the perennial and fundamental nature of the issues being discussed. These concern the deeply controversial questions of the nature and functioning of capitalist market economies, and the extent to which state intervention in economic affairs, particularly at the macroeconomic level, is necessary and desirable. As long as the real world economy fails to replicate the smooth functioning of an Arrow–Debreu type general equilibrium model, these issues of policy will continue to be debated. This is inevitably so, even if one takes the Hayekian view that it is (misguided) government intervention which causes macroeconomic problems in the first place.

At this date, it is possible to see that Keynes's original contribution was not so much in any specific policy proposal or theoretical construct, but in the notion that policy problems may be capable of rational thought and management. Before Keynes (and in many quarters after him), both the defenders of the economic system and its critics – the political forces of the right and the left – took what can only be described as an *alienated* view of macroeconomic problems. That is to say, that the economy is seen as an external force which determines the fates of those who live under it but is not amenable to conscious control by them. For the believers in *laissez-faire* this is not disturbing, because the market economy, while sometimes harsh in its judgements on individuals, is ultimately benign from the point of view of society as a whole. It is a natural organism which only has to be left alone to provide the best of all possible worlds, in a material sense, for its powerless participants. To the political left, the capitalist economy is equally an uncontrollable natural force, but in this case a demonic one, which leads only to misery and suffering for most of those in its power, and is proceeding via ever worsening crises to inevitable breakdown.

Keynes, who lived through World War I, Britain's economic stagnation and political crisis in the 1920s, and the worldwide depression of the 1930s, was certainly not able to believe in *laissez-faire*; but at the same time, he was not prepared to contemplate the ultimate collapse of the economic system and a totalitarian future, which would destroy the basis and values of civilization as he knew it. He came to believe that a third alternative was possible, that the system could be managed in order to retain the benefits and material standard of living that capitalism and the market system had made possible, and yet avoid its abuses. Not even the most ardent Keynesian could claim that Keynes fully spelled out the details of how this could be achieved in practice, and it is no doubt the case that Keynes's faith in governments was influenced by his position in the élite of British society, with its deeply ingrained paternalistic sense of public duty. It is also possible that observation of some attempts at economic management in the past fifty years would have made him more sceptical. None the less, the idea that society is not powerless in the face of the impersonal tides of the economy is Keynes's great contribution to the history of ideas.

Very clearly, after a period between World War II and the early 1970s, in which society and governments in the industrialized democracies seemed to accept something like Keynes's vision of the relationship between the public and private sectors, the later 1970s and early 1980s witnessed a strong revival of what we are calling here the 'alienated view.' Symptomatic of this was the prominence among theoretical economists of the famous 'policy irrelevance' proposition of the new classical school and, in the real world, the election to power in many jurisdictions of governments which explicitly rejected the apparent post-war consensus about the role of government in the management of the economy; in particular, the responsibility to maintain full employment.

As it has turned out, however, the events of the 1980s, including the 1981–2 recession, have rather seriously damaged the credibility of the view that government policy is powerless to influence (for good or ill) the course of the economy. It is simply not plausible to argue, for example, that there is no link between the monetary and fiscal policies of the British government since 1979, and the double-digit unemployment rate which has persisted in that country throughout the decade thus far. Or similarly, that the unbalanced US fiscal/monetary policy mix of the 1980s was not connected with the unwelcome rise of the exchange value of the dollar to late 1985, and the ensuing trade difficulties. Nor is it persuasive to invoke the rational expectations distinction between 'unanticipated' and 'anticipated' policy actions in an environment in which the break with traditional macroeconomic policy was much heralded, and actually a major plank of the political platforms of the governments concerned.

One potential response to recent events, of course, is that they reinforce the view that governments themselves are the source of the problem, and that the authorities should somehow disengage themselves from the economy, pursue a 'neutral' policy, adhere to 'rules rather than discretion', etc. But this view itself is not exactly 'policy irrelevance', and glosses over the fact that at least some of the responsibility for the dramatic policy shifts of recent years lies with the confident rational expectations arguments of the 1970s that there could be 'disinflation without tears' if only the committment to reduce inflation was sufficiently credible. More fundamentally, the mere observation of policies that increase unemployment, or cause trade difficulties, leads one to suspect that the other side of the coin may be that policies are indeed possible.

Hence it is another rather natural corollary of the dislocations of the past few years that some economists are willing to take another look at Keynes's fundamental ideas. Few would argue that there are any ready-made formulas from the 1930s or 1940s which can be removed from the shelf, dusted off and applied without modification to contemporary problems. Each generation will clearly have to grapple with the issue of the extent to which conscious macroeconomic control of the economy is possible and desirable in the particular historical circumstances of its time. However, the widening gap between much contemporary economic theory and the 'facts of experience' does suffice to explain why Keynes's pragmatic and undoctrinaire approach to macroeconomic policy problems once again seems attractive and worthy of attention.

This collection of papers has been grouped into two volumes: Volume I contains three sections entitled 'Keynes and Public Policy in Britain and North America', 'Keynesian Economics Past and Present', and 'Impressions and Recollections of J.M. Keynes'. The first section, with contributions by Elizabeth Durbin, Susan Howson, Don Moggridge, Walter Salant and Robert Skidelsky, deals with both the immediate and more lasting impact of Keynes's ideas on public policy, political parties and political programmes on both sides of the Atlantic. We have also included here a brief comment by Alexander Dow on these issues. Part 2 contains papers by Brian Bixley, David Colander, Robert Clower, Sheila Dow and David McQueen, each of which from different points of view attempts to assess the current state of Keynesian economics and suggest directions for the future. Robert Dimand's chapter in this section has a more historical theme and traces the actual development of Keynes's original theory from 1932 to 1936 using the lecture notes of Keynes's students, including those taken by Bryce, Salant and Tarshis.

The final section of Volume I, 'Impressions and Recollections', includes Robert Bryce's paper and also a contribution by another distinguished Canadian public servant, Louis Rasminsky, a former Governor of the Bank of Canada, who came into contact with Keynes at an earlier stage in his career during the historic negotiations leading up to the Bretton Woods agreement in 1944. The chapters by Robert Skidelsky and Richard Goodwin in this section originated as dinner and luncheon speeches at the Conference respectively. Skidelsky's paper drew on his authoritative biography of Keynes, and Goodwin's on his participation in the Keynesian revolution on both sides of the Atlantic: first, as the pupil of Keynes's close colleague and disciple (and first biographer), Sir Roy Harrod, at Oxford, and later at Harvard.

Volume II contains chapters which focus on particular specific issues and is divided into six parts, including 'Keynes and Econometric Method', 'The Theory of Investment', 'Aspects of the Labour Market', 'Money and Interest Rates', 'International Trade and Finance' and 'Positional Goods and Growth: Analogies to Keynesian Economics'. The first of these, with contributions by Ingrid Rima and Robin Rowley, and the joint paper by Ronald Bodkin, Lawrence Klein and Kanta Marwah, is addressed to the current debate about Keynes's influence on the development of macroeconometric models. The authors take different positions on this issue, and the extent to which Keynes anticipated the criticisms of econometric methodology which are troubling today's practitioners. The chapters by Clarence Barber and Michael Perelman in Part 2 both deal with aggregate investment spending, the behaviour of which was a key element in the original Keynesian system. Alan Abouchar's chapter in this section has a more microeconomic focus and explores the implications of Keynesian ideas for the optimal level of public sector investment.

The third section of Volume II contains a number of contributions which address labour market issues. The chapters by Tom Asimakopulos and Paul Davidson are both critical of the recent widely publicized proposals put forward by M.L. Weitzman for the reform of labour market institutions (the 'share economy'). Both authors point out that the basic concepts were explored, and apparently discarded, by Keynes himself even before the publication of the *General Theory*. In the other contributions in Part 3 Peter Howitt's chapter, using contemporary analytical techniques, revives the controversial argument of chapter 19 of the *General Theory* that a 'flexible wage policy' will not necessarily improve employment performance, while the contribution by Christopher Marme and Paul Wells criticizes Sir John Hicks's 'Wage Theorem' interpretation of the ch. 19 arguments. The final chapter in this part, by Serge-Christophe Kolm, explores the implications for employment of concern over relative wages and wage norms, a question originally broached by Keynes in ch. 2 of the *General Theory*. Various controversial topics involving monetary and interest rate policy are discussed in the contributions in Part 4 by Basil Moore, Thomas Rymes and Marc Lavoie and Mario Seccareccia. As there was considerable discussion of these issues at the original Conference, we have also included here written comments by Meyer Burstein and Nancy Wulwick.

Part 5 deals with various aspects of international trade and finance. Bernard Wolf discusses Keynes's attitude towards free trade and the tariff question and attempts to put into perspective Keynes's famous volte-face on the issue of tariffs in the 1930s. Lorie Tarshis's contribution addresses a policy issue of great current concern in the international debt crisis of the less developed countries (LDCs), and suggests a number of alternative methods of dealing with the problem. Bernard Schmitt, in a chapter which perhaps reflects the spirit rather than the letter of Keynes's approach to the problem of international monetary settlements, claims to find a major flaw in the current system, and suggests far-reaching reforms.

Finally, Part 6 in Volume II contains just one contribution, prepared by Omar Hamouda and Lorie Tarshis, which is a summary of Tibor Scitovsky's contribution to the conference. It is suggested that Hirsch's concept of 'positional goods' may in some sense be regarded as a generalization of Keynes's 'liquidity preference', and that an increase in the demand for such goods in an affluent society may have effects in retarding output and employment growth similar to those of an increase in liquidity preference in the Keynesian system.

The two volumes deal with a number of diverse topics, each of which is of intrinsic individual interest, but are also unified by the theme of the general approach to macroeconomic problems and policies pioneered by Keynes fifty years ago.

References

Howitt, P., 'The Keynesian Recovery', The Innis Lecture 1986, *Canadian Journal of Economics*, **XIX**(4), November 1986, pp 626–41.

Contributors

Alan Abouchar, University of Toronto, Canada
Athanasio Asimakopulos, McGill University, Canada
Clarence L. Barber, Professor Emeritus, University of Manitoba, Canada
Brian Bixley, York University, Canada
Ronald G. Bodkin, University of Ottawa, Canada
Robert B. Bryce, Ex-Deputy Minister of Finance, Government of Canada
Meyer L. Burstein, York University, Canada
Robert W. Clower, University of South Carolina, USA
David Colander, Middlebury College, USA
Paul Davidson, University of Tennessee, Knoxville, USA
Robert W. Dimand, Carleton University, Canada
Alister Dow, University of Sterling, Scotland
Sheila C. Dow, University of Sterling, Scotland
Elizabeth Durbin, New York University
Richard Goodwin, Professor Emeritus, Cambridge (UK) and Siena University, Italy
Omar Hamouda, York University, Canada
Geoffrey C. Harcourt, University of Cambridge, UK
Peter Howitt, University of Western Ontario, Canada
Susan Howson, University of Toronto, Canada
Lawrence R. Klein, University of Pennsylvania, USA
Serge-Christophe Kolm, ENPC, Paris, France
Mark Lavoie, University of Ottawa, Canada
David McQueen, York University, Canada
Christopher Marme, University of Illinois, USA
Kanta Marwah, Carleton University, Canada
Don E. Moggridge, University of Toronto, Canada
Basil J. Moore, Wesleyan University USA
Michael Perelman, California State University, Chico, USA
Louis Rasminsky, Ex-Governor of the Bank of Canada
Ingrid H. Rima, Temple University, USA
Robin Rowley, McGill University, Canada
Thomas K. Rymes, Carleton University, Canada
Walter S. Salant, Senior Fellow Emeritus, Brookings Institution, USA

Bernard Schmitt, Fribourg University, Switzerland
Tibor Scitovsky, Professor Emeritus, Stanford University, USA
Mario Seccareccia, University of Ottawa, Canada
Robert Skidelsky, Warwick University, UK
John Smithin, York University, Canada
Nicholas P. Smook, York University, Canada
Lorie Tarshis, York University, Canada
Paul Wells, University of Illinois, USA
Bernard M. Wolf, York University, Canada
Nancy Wulwick, LeMoyne College, USA

PART I

KEYNES AND ECONOMETRIC METHOD

1 Keynes and the origins of macroeconometric modelling

Ronald G. Bodkin, Lawrence R. Klein and Kanta Marwah[1]

Econometric models have already had a long and interesting history, now spanning more than half a century. For this reason it is interesting to return to the origins, to note some of the important antecedents of this intellectual construct. In our book we examine four major antecedents of current-day macroeconometric models: Walrasian-Paretian models of general equilibrium; work on classical statistics around the turn of this century, John Maynard Keynes's *General Theory*, and the subsequent development of this approach; and finally, the empirical literature on Keynesian macroeconomic concepts (particularly on consumption functions) which flourished between the publication of Keynes's *General Theory* (in 1936) and the outbreak of World War II (or the publication of Tinbergen's *Business Cycles in the USA, 1919–1932*), late in 1939. In this chapter we are going to examine only the third major antecedent, namely, Keynes's *General Theory* and the subsequent development of this approach. This narrowing of the focus may be justified by the current interest in a half-century retrospective look at Keynes's monumental work, as the operational heritage of this book has been enormous. Indeed it is no exaggeration to say that, originally, macroeconometric models were designed to implement the Keynesian system, however much these models may have evolved in the succeeding half-century.[2]

Thus it is reasonable to argue that the most important single antecedent for the construction of macroeconometric models is John Maynard Keynes's *The General Theory of Employment, Interests and Money* (1936). Moreover, this would appear to be a point that would command wide agreement. Thus Richard Stone asserted, in his Keynes Lecture in Economics of 1978, 'For there is no doubt that in its day Keynes' book had done probably more than any other to encourage the systematic estimation of national accounts magnitudes and the construction of econometric models' (Stone, 1980, p. 62). Similarly, Don Patinkin argues:

Furthermore, and most important in the present context, the desire to quantify the *General Theory* provided the major impetus for the exponentially-growing [*sic*] econometric work that began to be carried out in the late 1930's on the consumption, investment, and liquidity-preference functions individually and, even more notably, on econometric models of the Keynesian system as a whole. (Patinkin, 1976, p. 1092)

Indeed we have already asserted that, for many years, macroeconometric models have been constructed as essentially empirical counterparts to the Keynesian system; only in recent years have econometric models based on alternative paradigms (monetarist, radical or post-Keynesian) appeared.[3]

Keynes's *General Theory* itself is worth a cursory review in this context. After six chapters of introductory material, there follow three chapters (grouped together in a section called Book III, 'The Propensity to Consume'), which treat the consumption function and an associated concept, the multiplier. The notion of consumption as a relatively stable function of a few explanatory variables, including community income, appears to cry out for empirical verification and Keynes himself made some preliminary attempts, using early national income data for the UK developed by Colin Clark, and for the USA developed by Simon Kuznets, to verify his hypotheses.[4] However, it must be admitted that the bulk of the work of the empirical testing of the Keynesian system was left for others, particularly after Keynes's severe heart attack in 1937.

Other parts of the *General Theory* contain concepts that are easily put into theoretical formulation susceptible to econometric testing and estimation without much difficulty. Thus Book IV, entitled, 'The Inducement to Invest', contains an extended discussion (in chapters 11 and 12) of a concept called 'the marginal efficiency of capital'. Without too much manipulation, this discussion can be recast in the form of an investment demand function and so be confronted with statistics on business fixed investment and some of its hypothetical determinants. Book IV also contains an extended discussion of what Keynes called 'liquidity preference' generally, scattered through five chapters (chapters 13–17); again, one could attempt to render the liquidity preference function operational and then to estimate its parameters, which indeed was done by A.J. Brown (1939) and in the immediate postwar period. Finally, Book V, 'Money-Wages and Prices', contains three chapters (chapters 19–21) and concludes the central theoretical corpus of the work. Depending upon one's preferences, this portion of the *General Theory* could be formulated as an aggregate supply function relating real national product to the price level or its rate of change; alternatively (and corresponding to the breakdown of Book V into three separate chapters), this portion could be represented as an employment function (an inverted short-period production function), an equation for the determination of the money wage rate and an equation for the determination of the aggregative price level.[5] It should be noted that Keynes attempted empirical verification of none of these other relationships, although his theoretical discussion and his example with regard to the consumption function would appear to have pointed the way.

But would Keynes himself have approved of this use of his theoretical apparatus? The apparent answer would appear to be 'no', on the basis of two important pieces of evidence: the strictures in the *General Theory* against the representation of his macroeconomic theory as a set of mathematical relationships ('mathematical economics', as he called it), and his September 1939 review of Tinbergen's study for the League of Nations.

About Keynes's attitude towards mathematically formulated economic theory (which is so essential for econometric modelling of any type, not just macroeconometric models), little need be said.[6] However, his review of Tinbergen warrants some comment. Keynes was quite critical of this approach to macroeconomic research,[7] and the tone of his comments suggested that Tinbergen was largely wasting his and the profession's time, if not practising alchemy. The specific criticisms are, in general, reasonably taken, although Keynes enthusiasts have to be embarrassed by the suggestion that linear difference equations may be incapable of generating cyclical fluctuations in themselves, so that (according to Keynes) Tinbergen may be engaged in the task of explaining cycles (in the endogenous variables) by cycles (in the exogenous variables). The other criticisms seem quite reasonable in themselves and appear to have stood the test of time; thus Keynes's various remarks could be interpreted as pointing to single equation bias, the bias of omitted variables, measurement errors in the explanatory variables,[8] the possible mis-specification entailed in assuming linearity throughout the full range (and beyond) of the dependent variable and (especially) problems of structural change (i.e. the possibility that all the past data utilized for parameter estimation may not be homogeneous or may emanate from different universes). Keynes's remarks may also be taken to be a criticism of crude empiricism that may be entailed in the determination of time-lags without a suitable theoretical foundation or in the introduction of time trend variables to capture ill-defined secular forces. Keynes also points to the difficulties of an econometric estimation of the effects of an explanatory variable, in the case in which this particular variable has very little movement during a particular historical episode (the influence of the rate of interest on investment expenditures during the 1930s comes to mind as an example). While nearly all of these points are reasonable in themselves,[9] and most would be incorporated into econometric textbooks today, Keynes certainly seems to have had relatively little appreciation of the difficult nature of the problems that Tinbergen was attacking and of the generally unsatisfactory nature of non-econometric solutions to this class of problems. Indeed it can be asserted without too much fear of controversy today that intuitive estimates of concepts such as the multiplier or the effect of a certain fiscal policy on the economy are even more likely to be misleading than the econometric estimates, despite the limitations of the latter.[10]

Beyond the specific issues of econometric technique, there is a more general position regarding methodological approach, as Klant (1985), Lawson (1985) and Pesaran and Smith (1985) have pointed out. One can argue that, due to instability of structures in the social universe, no econometric test is possible; the best that econometricians can do is to *measure* or estimate, as (in this view) testing is a technical impossibility. Klant, Lawson, and Pesaran and Smith argue (with differing degrees of emphasis) that this indeed was Keynes's position and this is why Keynes reacted so vehemently against Tinbergen's League of Nations study, which was attempting to test alternative theories of the business cycle. By contrast, it is claimed (by Pesaran and Smith) that Keynes would have been far more sympathetic to Tinbergen's earlier work (1937), which put the emphasis on estimation and solution of practical policy problems.[11] A secondary reason why econometric technique can never test critically a received theory (in this view) is that most (or even all) theories are underidentified or at least ambiguous. Accordingly, for econometric testing, supplementary hypotheses must be provided. But if a theory fails a given econometric test, an ardent proponent of that theory can always claim that the fault lies in the supplementary hypothesis furnished for testing purposes rather than in the central core of the theory. This critique resembles the 'post-Keynesian' critique of deterministic or econometric models, where it is held that no coherent model, macroeconometric or otherwise, can capture the essential message of Keynes, which in this view is held to be an emphasis on the important role of uncertainty, the uniqueness of particular historical episodes and the underdetermination or the indeterminacy of the macroeconomic system, among other points.[12] Nevertheless, it would appear that Klant and Pesaran and Smith (but not Lawson) agree that building forecasting models and econometric research are useful things to do, in the face of serious policy problems. Pesaran and Smith even argue that Keynes would not have been unsympathetic to this approach and that he did something similar in his approach to the practical problems of the day, e.g. in 'How to Pay for the War' and 'Can Lloyd George Do It?'.

This, however, should not be regarded as the end of the matter. Richard Stone (1980) argues that under the pressure of economic policy-making under wartime conditions, Keynes changed his attitudes towards economic statistics ('political arithmetic') and even towards econometric modelling. Moreover, Keynes was associated with the 'Cambridge Research Scheme' of the National Institute of Social and Economic Research during the period just before World War II (1938 and 1939), and much of this research had a strong quantitative and econometric flavour. Stone feels that, in light of the timing of these activities, 'the Tinbergen episode seems even more bizarre'. Moreover, both Patinkin (1976) and Stone note that when Alfred Cowles first proposed to Keynes to be President of the Econometric Society, he first protested that 'whilst I am interested in econometric work and have done something at it at different times in my life, I have not recently written anything significant or important along these lines, which would make me feel a little bit of an imposter'.[13] Thus, as Patinkin rightly points out, we are entitled to infer that Keynes saw himself as someone who had made important contributions to econometrics at one stage of his life; we are also probably entitled to infer that his critical views on econometric modelling had moderated somewhat by that date (1944). This inference is also indirectly corroborated by the fact that Stone reports that Keynes delighted in his personal reunion with Tinbergen right after the end of World War II in Europe (in July 1945), speaking enthusiastically not only of Tinbergen's personal qualities, but also of his work.[14]

Ultimately, however, the issue of Keynes's final views on the econometric developments that his macroeconomic theory stimulated to a very large extent is a secondary issue.[15] It now seems clear that the *General Theory* was a tremendous stimulus not only to macroeconomic theory in general, but to macroeconometric model-building in particular. Indeed, as asserted above (and as detailed in our book), for nearly a generation and a half after the publication of the *General Theory* macroeconometric models constructed in the spirit of Keynesian theory dominated the model-building process; only around the beginning of the 1970s did alternative paradigms of macroeconomic theorizing begin to be incorporated into macroeconometric models. Moreover, Keynes's theorizing completed a small step that Pareto had taken away from Walras's microeconomic analysis, allowing researchers to deal with global concepts and quantities that were much easier to measure in practice. This, in turn, permitted a return to the sweeping, aggregative concepts of François Quesnay's *tableau économique*[16] with, however, a much higher degree of precision. In summary, then, this aspect of the 'Keynesian revolution' opened the field to macroeconometric model-building.

Notes

1. This paper is drawn from chapter 1, 'Antecendents of Macroeconometric Models' of our prospective book, *A History of Macroeconometric Model-Building*. A preliminary version was presented to the Twelfth Annual Convention of the Eastern Economic Association in Philadelphia, in April 1986. For helpful comments on that occasion we should like to thank Eric G. Davis and Thomas K. Rymes. For helpful comments on the occasion of this Conference we should like to thank Robert Dimand.

2. Another fascinating bit of prescience appears to have been displayed by Alfred Marshall in a celebrated article published in 1897 and entitled, 'The New Generation of Economists and the Old'. Here Marshall asserted that an important task of economists during the twentieth century would be to estimate and to measure or, in other words, to find empirical counterparts to the theoretical structure that had already been developed by the end of the nineteenth century. (Marshall probably did not anticipate how much theoretical macroeconomics would develop during the twentieth century.)

3. Suggestions for alternative models have come from other sources such as the school of rational expectations (e.g. R.E. Lucas, 1976, or Thomas J. Sargent, 1976) or the time-series, 'little theory' approach of Christopher A. Sims (1980).

4. Keynes's methods of attempting to corroborate his theoretical constructs (an informal examination of the data, grouping the years in pairs) seem rather casual, and it is no surprise to learn that Patinkin (1976) was unable to reproduce Keynes's estimate (between 2.5 and 3) for the multiplier for the US economy. (This might conceivably be the case because Patinkin not unreasonably considered only contiguous years, while Keynes may have carried out his estimation over two more widely separated years.) In any case, in that Keynes then inferred a value of the marginal propensity to consume parameter from the estimated multiplier, it seems likely that he carried out the first instance of reduced form estimation, as Patinkin notes.

5. Thus Keynes appears (in chapter 21) to have interpreted the marginal productivity condition of neo-classical economics (the equality, under pure competition, of the marginal physical product of labour to the ratio of the nominal wage rate to the price of final output) as a relationship for the determination of final goods prices, rather than as a labour demand relationship, at least under conditions of less than full utilization of the labourforce.

6. Stone traces Keynes's views on this subject to his own personality conflicts regarding a lack of success as a research mathematician. Patinkin sees these remarks as a ritualistic continuation of Marshall's attitudes, but also feels that Keynes's comparative advantage did not lie in this field. Presumably Keynes made his peace with mathematically oriented economic theory, as he seems to have acquiesced to Meade's (1936–7) and Hicks's (1937) representations, in fairly tight mathematical terms, of his basic system.

7. We may not note that, in his private correspondence, especially with R.F. Harrod and R.F. Kahn, Keynes showed himself to be even more sceptical than in the published review. See Moggridge (1973), pp. 285–306, for a substantiation of this point.

8. This point brings us back immediately to the rudimentary character of national income data in Britain and the USA during the 1930s, and hence this point would appear to have been particularly pertinent at the time of Keynes's review. Whether Keynes contributed to the improvement of this situation or whether, *au contraire*, he hindered some useful developments that were taking place in any case is a point of dispute between Stone (1980) and Patinkin (1976), following some correspondence with Colin Clark.

9. Keynes also appears not to have had a full appreciation of the technique of multiple regression as an artificial manner of holding other influences constant, as he asserts in his review that the technique requires the explanatory variables to be 'largely independent' statistically. On the other hand, an apologist for Keynes might interpret his remarks as anticipating the problem of (nearly perfect) multi-colinearity.

10. Opinions on Keynes's performance in this episode have certainly varied among commentators, over the years. Thus, thirty-five years ago, one of us (Klein, 1951) characterized Keynes's review of Tinbergen's work as 'one of his sorriest professional performances'; even with the passage of time, Klein sees no reason to revise this evaluation. (We recognize that some, including our commentator at this Conference, would consider this an extreme position.) On the other hand, Patinkin summarizes this same review and concludes that Keynes was more right than incorrect, as well as observing that he (Patinkin) finds it depressing to note how many of Keynes's criticisms are still relevant today. Another evaluation is that of Stone, who, while conceding the validity of some individual points, regards Keynes's review as 'a model of testiness and perverseness'; in particular, he argues that Keynes failed to realize that the new technique might have been exactly what might be very helpful 'to quantify the multiplier e.g., as in Clark's contemporaneous (1938) article and other parameters of the *General Theory*'. Finally, Johannes J. Klant, who is generally sympathetic to what he regards as Keynes's basic methodological position, concedes, 'Keynes displayed much ignorance and misunderstanding of what Tinbergen had done' (Klant, 1985, p. 91).

11. However, Tinbergen in his concluding remarks of *An Econometric Approach to Business Cycle Problems* (1937) clearly mentions testing various received theories as one of the advantages of such an approach.

12. Taken to its logical extreme, such a philosophical position would appear to imply that no macroeconomic policies (stabilization policies, in particular) are possible, because if the structure of the economy is so unstable, one can never be sure of what one is doing. In this regard, the proponents of this point of view would appear to join Robert Lucas (1976) and the rational expectations school, who argue that the parameters of the system are highly unstable, at least with a shift in the policy regime itself, thus rendering both economic policy and macroeconometric estimation extremely difficult, if not impossible.

13. Quoted by Stone (1980), p. 63, and by Patinkin (1976), p. 1092 (all but the final phrase, 'which would make me feel a bit of an imposter').

14. Stone (1980) concludes his review of the episode by noting that the renewal of the contact had convinced Keynes that Tinbergen's work should be given 'every scope and opportunity', and he (Stone) asserts, 'Nothing could show better the difference between Keynes' first impersonal impressions and his considered view based on personal experience' (p. 64). At the same time, we may note that Lawson (1985) has argued that Stone's analysis at most explains the *force* of Keynes's critique of Tinbergen, without 'explaining away' his well-founded (according to Lawson) logical objections.

15. If Keynes had lived to the ripe old age of his parents, it seems likely that his views would again have evolved further, under the combined influences of additional evidence and the further thinking of himself and others about these problems. What direction his further thoughts would have taken is, at this point, a matter of pure speculation.

At the convention, it was argued that it is not inconceivable that Keynes would have modernized his small models by use of the personal computer and that one could visualize a high-tech 'circus' about Keynes, with many current problems of policy being attacked by the intuition of this brilliant individual, aided by current technology. In this view, econometric estimation (but not testing) would have formed part of the picture. As noted in the text, Pesaran and Smith (1985) would appear to agree, noting that Keynes made use of numerically estimated models in his applied works, such as 'How to Pay for the War' and 'Can Lloyd George Do It?'.

16. In this context, it may be recalled that the Physiocrat, François Quesnay, developed in the 1750s an economic construct which he called the *tableau économique* and which some have interpreted as the first macroeconomic model. As the *tableau* is numerical (if not statistical), it is not difficult to see affinities with modern macroeconometric models or input–output tables.

References

Brown, A.J. (1939), 'Interest, prices and the demand schedule for idle money', *Oxford Economic Papers*, 2, May, 46–69.

Clark, C. (1938), 'Determination of the multiplier from national income statistics', *Economic Journal*, XLVIII(191), September, 435–448.

Hendry, D.F., (1980), 'Econometrics–alchemy or science', *Economica*, 47(4), November, 387–406.

Hicks, J.R., (1937), 'Mr Keynes and the "classics": a suggested interpretation', *Econometrica*, V(21), April, 147–159.

Keynes, J.M. (1936), *The General Theory of Employment, Interest and Money*, New York: Harcourt, Brace.

Keynes, J.M. (1939), 'Professor Tinbergen's method', *Economic Journal*, XLIX(195), September, 558–568.

Klant, J.J. (1985), 'The slippery transition', in T. Lawson and H. Pesaran (eds), *Keynes' Economics: Methodological Issues*, London and Sydney: Croom Helm, 80–98.

Klein, L.R. (1951), 'The life of John Maynard Keynes', *Journal of Political Economy*, LIX(5), October, 443–451.

Lawson, T. (1985), 'Keynes, prediction, and econometrics', in T. Lawson and H. Pesaran (eds), *Keynes' Economics: Methodological Issues*, London and Sydney: Croom Helm, 116–133.

Lucas, R.E., Jr (1976), 'Econometric policy evaluation: a critique', in K. Brunner and A.H. Meltzer (eds), *The Phillips Curve and Labor Markets*, Carnegie–Rochester Conference Series on Public Policy, Amsterdam: North-Holland, Vol. 1, 19–46; supplement to the *Journal of Monetary Economics*.

Marshall, A. (1897), 'The old generation of economists and the new', *Quarterly Journal of Economics*, 11, January, 115–135.

Meade, J.E. (1936–7), 'A simplified model of Mr Keynes' system', *Review of Economic Studies*, IV, 98–107.

Moggridge D.E. (ed.) (1973), *The Collected Writings of John Maynard Keynes. Vol. XIV, The General Theory and After, Part II: Defence and Development*, London: Macmillan.

Patinkin, D. (1976), 'Keynes and econometrics: on the interaction between the macroeconomic revolutions of the interwar period', *Econometrica*, 44(6), November, 1091–1123.

Pesaran, H. and Smith, R. (1985) 'Keynes on econometrics', in T. Lawson and H. Pesaran (eds), *Keynes' Economics: Methodological Issues*, London and Sydney: Croom Helm, 134–150.

Sargent, T.J. (1976), 'A classical macroeconomic model for the United States', *Journal of Political Economy*, 84(2), April, 207–237.

Sims, C. A. (1980), 'Macroeconomics and reality', *Econometrica*, 48(1), January, 1–48.

Stone, R. (1980), 'Keynes lecture in economics 1978', in *Proceedings of the British Academy*, London, Vol. LXIV, Oxford: Oxford University Press.

Tinbergen, J. (1968), *Business Cycles in the United States of America, 1919–1932*, Pt II of *Statistical Testing of Business Cycle Theories*, New York: Agathon Press; originally published in Geneva by the Economic Intelligence Service of the League of Nations, 1939.
Tinbergen, J. (1937), *An Econometric Approach to Business Cycle Problems*, Paris: Herman.

2 Keynes's vision and econometric analysis

Ingrid H. Rima

Keynes's contribution to the development of econometrics as an outgrowth of his formulation in the *General Theory* of concepts that have since become central to macroeconomic analysis has long been recognized (Leontief, 1948; Klein, 1954). Given the predilection of contemporary economists for positivist methods of inquiry which, among other things, consider empirical verification and prediction as essential hallmarks of science, econometric analysis is now firmly established as a sister discipline to economics. Yet Keynes himself had deep misgivings about the usefulness of the empiricism that had been developed in his day, in particular, as it related to Jan Tinbergen's efforts to test theories of the business cycle. Since these misgivings are often assessed as reflecting Keynes's own technical insufficiencies (Patinkin, 1976; Bodkin *et al.*, 1986), it is relevant to re-examine the bases for his reservations about the possibility for successful prediction in economics.

I

The question of prediction of economic outcomes moved to the forefront of economists' concerns during the post World War I era in connection with the possibility of forecasting business cycles. Early contributions by Ragnar Frisch in the 1920s undertook to formulate laws of economic behaviour mathematically from statistical data in order to establish economics as a predictive science. By this time, Keynes had already examined the relevance of mathematical discourse for addressing questions that arise in the 'moral sciences', among them economics and psychology. Long before his *Treatise on Money* and the later *General Theory*, Keynes had reached the conclusion that:

> where our experience is incomplete, we cannot hope to derive from it judgements of probability without the aid of intuition or of some further *a priori* principle. Experience, as opposed to intuition, cannot possibly afford us a criterion by which to judge whether on given evidence the probabilities of two propositions are or are not equal. (*CW*, VIII, p. 94)

This perspective later underlay his vision of the world and is evident in all his subsequent writings. Beginning with the *Treatise on Probability* (1921), he made the point that:

> We should be chary of applying to problems of psychological research the calculus of probabilities ... If therefore we endeavor to *calculate* the probability that some phenomenon is due to 'abnormal' causes, our mathematics will be apt to lead us into unjustifiable conclusions. (*ibid.*, pp. 334–9)

Thus Keynes had early taken the position that prediction of human behaviour and events cannot be successfully addressed by means of the principles of statistical probability. He made quite clear his view that the predictability puzzle is essentially a question of research methodology. This perspective bears directly on Keynes's subsequent evaluation of the difficulties inherent in the econometric method and his assessment of their usefulness as an adjunct to economic theory.

Among those who specifically undertook to address the problems inherent in making business cycle predictions there was, perhaps, no one closer to sharing Keynes's view than Oskar Morgenstern. His 1928 book, *Wertsschaftsprognose*, written as part of his business cycle research at the Vienna Institute, specifically addressed the problem posed by the interdependence of market participants for prediction of economic variables. He recognized that in economics one is concerned with 'live' variables rather than the 'dead' variables of nature (*ibid.*, 706). Prediction is possible only when 'dead' variables are involved; when 'live' variables are at issue, the matter is conceptually different, for these represent other 'wills' which may impact on another's behaviour and thereby influence predicted events. His now famous Holmes–Moriarty example (*ibid.*, p. 98) illustrated the untenability of the premiss that either man would out-think the other, making it clear that the problem posed when human beings interact is, necessarily, one of strategy. Morgenstern was, therefore, led to a particularly negative assessment of the possibilities for successful forecasting. He argued (1) that the use of economic theory and statistics for the purpose of forecasting is impossible 'in principle', and (2) that even if a technique for forecasting can be developed, it would not be applicable in actual situations, i.e. the forecast would itself alter the outcome.[1] His mathematical perception of the problem for prediction inherent in behavioural interdependencies persisted despite his awareness, as a participant of Menger's famed Vienna Circle, of John von Neuman's 1921 'Theory of Games' paper, which identified a solution in which both interacting parties have achieved mutually satisfactory maxima (or minima).[2] That von Neuman's approach might hold the key to solving the intellectual puzzle Morgenstern posed became apparent only later when it led to their collaboration in *The Theory of Games and Economic Behavior* (1944).

Besides Morgenstern, Keynes's early reservations about the relevance of mathematical probability to economic phenomena had a counterpart in the views of Frank Knight (1939) and Joseph Schumpeter (1938). Knight's opposition reflected both his philosophical aversion to quantification and empiricism in the social sciences, as well as its possible use as a basis for the formulation of policy. Schumpeter, on the other hand, entertained no philosophically based opposition to quantification, and he was quite willing to confront and evaluate theoretical hypotheses (specifically theories of the business cycle) with descriptive and historical tests. Should it be established that an historical variable displays a stochastic component, he would interpret that finding as having 'meaning' only if it is related to real economic processes. Statistical concepts and their associated techniques were considered as appropriate for use in testing procedures only if 'meaning', in the sense of distinct corresponding phenomena, can be established (1938, p. 1908).

II

Keynes's early assessment of the relevance of the laws of statistical probability to economics and the reservations entertained by Morgenstern and Knight concerning prediction and the quantification of economic variables stands in sharp contrast to that of those who, like Frisch, Tinbergen and Koopmans, pioneered in macroeconomic modelling. Tinbergen's pioneering work, sponsored by the League of Nations, to evaluate the various theories of the business cycle catalogued by Gustav Haberler in *Prosperity and Depression*, appears to have been the catalyst for bringing the puzzle of prediction to the forefront.[3]

Tinbergen's first volume, published in 1939 under the title *A Method and its Application to Investment Activity*, was a harbinger of future techniques in the development of econometrics in its formulation of a multiequation system defined by constant coefficients, lags, and 'shocks' that obey the laws of probability. While it was still only an unpublished draft, Tinbergen's 1939 volume was the subject of discussion at a 1938 Cambridge University Conference on business cycles. The League of Nations had also sent Keynes a proof copy, along with Tinbergen's earlier *Business Cycles in the United States of America*, with a request for a comment. In responding, Keynes immediately addressed[4]

> the central question of methodology – the logic of applying the method of multiple correlation to unanalyzed economic material, which we know to be non-homogeneous over time ... The volume which purports to be a note on method is, in fact, mainly occupied, just like the other volume, with

elaborate half-explained numerical examples, the method employed in which already begs the question. (*CW*, XIV, pp. 285–6)

In particular, Keynes complained that the coefficients Tinbergen arrived at are assumed constant for ten years or longer: 'Yet surely we know that they are not constant' (*loc. cit.*). This comment is followed by a critique of a specific example from Tinbergen's book, namely, the demand for investment in new rolling-stock.

Keynes also wrote to Richard Kahn on the subject of Tinbergen's book: 'I think it all hocus – *worse* than Haberler (*Prosperity and Depression*). But everyone else is greatly impressed, it seems, by such a mess of unintelligible figurings' (*ibid*, p. 289). Some weeks later, after a letter of attempted clarification to Keynes by Tinbergen himself, Harrod wrote Keynes:

that Tinbergen may be doing very valuable work in trying to model the rate of interest and the marginal efficiency of capital as joint determinants of investment ... if he can show over a wide range of countries and times that the influence of changes in the rate of interest is very small compared with the influence of changes in the marginal efficiency of capital – which is precisely what he does think he has shown – this without impugning the validity of the model, may affect our judgement with regard to various matters. (*ibid.*, p. 298)

Keynes's reply, echoing his earlier argument in the *Treatise on Probability*, observed in part that in economics 'to convert a model into a quantitative formula is to destroy its usefulness as an instrument of thought' (*ibid.*, p. 299). Harrod replied:

I think Tinbergen is well aware of the limited validity of the numerical coefficients he introduces into his equations. But if after working out his equations for a number of different countries and places, he finds that certain influences, which theory deems to be present, are consistently small compared with other influences – which must also of course be justified by theory – this must and ought to modify the emphasis we place in our general thinking on the problem. (*ibid.*, p. 301)

Keynes's subsequent letter to Harrod contained the following partial concession:

If Tinbergen is engaged in a large number of separate investigations aimed at checking and verifying the theory so as to discover the order of magnitude of various factors, I am entirely in favour of him. But I got the impression that, if this is his object, he is giving himself a great deal of unnecessary trouble in the form of the method adopted. His method seems to be to devise a formula based on one or a very small number of instances capable of being applied to subsequent cases. He could arrive at his results with immensely less labour if he were simply examining statistically particularly cases, regarding them as particular cases, and no more. However, I may be wrong. I have not studied his work as carefully as you have. (*ibid.*, p. 302)

Keynes apparently did study Tinbergen's work further and published a quite critical review in the September 1939 issue of the *Economic Journal*. His most fundamental technical point was the possibility that, in consequence of structural changes, data might not be drawn from a single universe. His other specific criticisms were that Tinbergen's model was vulnerable to multi-colinearity, errors in measurement, omitted variables, and a bias inherent in single-equation estimations of a system of simultaneous equations. Keynes further complained of a mis-specification that derives from estimating only a linear version of the model, although Tinbergen did use non-linear equations in writing out the theories to be tested. In concluding his review, Keynes remarked 'that Tinbergen's brand of statistical alchemy is ripe to become a branch of science, I am not yet persuaded. But Newton, Boyle and Locke all played with alchemy. So let him continue'.

Whether or not Keynes envisioned the possibility that valid econometric techniques for testing economic theories would be devised at some future time is, of course, beyond speculation, but a possible parallel to Keynes's 1946 paper, 'Newton the Man', is perhaps worth noting. Based on his reading of Newtonian primary sources, Keynes concluded that while alchemy was not scientific, it could make valuable contributions to the development of science. It is possible he conceded that for analogous reasons, Tinbergen might succeed in establishing econometric testing as scientific.[5]

Keynes's reservations notwithstanding, Tinbergen's pioneering books about the statistical implementation of mathematically formulated theories anticipated the objective shortly to be expressed by mathematical economists to achieve a 'genuinely predictive' theory (Neuman and Morgenstern, 1944, p. 8) This goal became particularly apparent in the work of Tinbergen's student, Tjalling Koopmans, whose 1937 volume placed him at the forefront of work aimed at the development of a probabilistic model that uses the technique of maximum likelihood to address error in regression models. Trygve Haavelmo further surmised that it may be possible to make an empirically significant statement about the probability that a random variable will affect an outcome (1944). He argued that by adopting probability theory, economists can provide themselves with a basis for testing hypotheses. Haavelmo's views that a theoretical model 'will have an economic meaning only when associated with a design of an actual experiment that describes and indicates how to measure a system of "true" variables (or objects)

$x_1, x_2, \ldots, x_n$ that are to be identified with the corresponding variables in theory ...' (*ibid.*, p. 8).

Except in special cases, the probability reformulation of statistical analysis requires that all the structural relationships of a theoretical model be dealt with simultaneously. A change in any one of, say, a dozen structural relationships requires an entirely new set of statistical estimates of all coefficients in all equations. The Walras–Pareto conception of mutual interdependence is therefore implicit in the probability approach, rendering it in essence the statistical counterpart of the Walras–Pareto system of simultaneous equations. Thus the probability revolution provided an essential tool for the development of macroeconomic models that reflects a clear line of descent from the work of Frisch and Tinbergen and the general equilibrium and game theoretical work of von Neuman.

III

The ascendancy of econometrics as the economists' major research tool has made it clear that Keynes's reservations about the usefulness of the general equilibrium approach and his critique of the truth-seeking claims of econometrics has not persuaded very many in the economics profession.[6] On the contrary, the probability approach to problem solution now dominates the research work of the economics profession. This is, perhaps, nowhere in clearer evidence than in the prestigious Cowles Commission, in whose own history all of the philosophical and methodological controversies that relate to economic research have been played out.

Alfred Cowles financed the research institution bearing his name in 1932, after the stock-market crash of 1929 and the depression that followed called attention to the information gap as it relates to stock prices. Shortly afterwards, the Cowles Commission became associated with the Econometric Society organized two years earlier by a small group of academics, among them Irving Fisher who was the Society's first president, Ragnar Frisch of the University of Oslo and Charles Roos, then research director of the National Recovery Administration of the US government. Roos became the first director of research for the Cowles Commission and, simultaneously, professor of econometrics at Colorado College. Summer conferences held at Colorado Springs, which attracted a virtual Who's Who among statisticians, mathematicians and economists oriented towards mathematical and statistical approaches, were among the highlights of the Commission's activities. Trygve Haavelmo from the University of Oslo, and Abraham Wald, were among the participants at the summer conferences during the years

1937–9. The international character of these meetings and the quality of their research work suggests that at least part of the flavour of Karl Menger's famous Vienna Colloquium was transferred to America, where it also established a base for the 'University in Exile' as refugee scholars fled the Nazis (Szilard, 1969, pp. 94–145).

After Cowles moved his business headquarters to Chicago in 1939, the Commission sought a new affiliation, ultimately with the University of Chicago where, under the direction of Jacob Marshak, the general equilibrium approach to problem perception and the probability approach to problem solution came to dominate the research work of the Commission (Christ, 1952, pp. 30–1).

The orientation of Cowles Commission associates to the multi-equation probability methodology for doing macroeconomic research proved highly controversial and pitted them against other quantitative researchers at Chicago and the National Bureau. It also provoked a more philosophically grounded disagreement with other Chicagoans, in particular, Frank Knight. The controversy with the National Bureau over method was provoked by the empirical work of Arthur Burns and Wesley Mitchell in their 1946 book, *Measuring Business Cycles*, which became the prototype for the Bureau's research programme to collect statistical data and develop statistical techniques. This work was profoundly influenced by Mitchell's institutionalist perspective, which looked to empirical research to provide the basis for economic theory. This approach led Tjalling Koopmans, writing under the provocative title 'Measurement without Theory' (1947), to argue that without resort to theory, Burns and Mitchell cannot know what variables to study and that, further, in the absence of theory, relevant policy conclusions cannot be drawn.

Without defending the particular methodological procedure of the National Bureau, Rutledge Vining (1949) suggested that the critical point of the methodological controversy between them related less to the 'existence or absence of a hypothetical framework as upon the nature of the entity the behavior of which is to be accounted for' (*ibid.*, p. 79) Implicitly, Koopmans's argument was predicated on the formal economic theory of aggregating dual maximizing decisions, which Vining (and other institutionalists) rejected. Vining viewed this 'Walrasian conception ... [as] ... a pretty skinny fellow of untested capacity on which to load the burden of a general theory accounting for the events in space and time.' Economic research, in Vinings view, is still at the 'Kepler stage' of seeking hypotheses and is not yet ready for the 'Newton stage' of testing and application that follows from the methodology that Koopmans proposed.

The second area of controversy in which the Cowles Commission found itself embroiled was more philosophically oriented and closer to home. Frank Knight, as has already been noted, was philosophically opposed to the premiss that prediction of human behaviour and events is possible; he was also opposed to empiricism in the social sciences, economics included, at least partly because of his fear that it might serve as the basis for policy (Reder, 1982, p. 6). The work of Oskar Lange (1944) and its related policy recommendations called forth the ire of the 'Knight group' with Milton Friedman taking up the cudgels of counter-argument (Friedman, 1946). Friedman's paper approximately coincided with Lange's 1945 departure for his native Poland to assume a political post.

Lange's departure by no means ended the controversies between Cowles's associates and other Chicagoans. Indeed the rift appears to have widened after 1947 with the publication of Laurence Klein's 'The Use of Econometric Models as a Guide to Economic Policy'. This marked a shift in emphasis by the Commission from illustration and exposition of principles to constructing models relating to current decision-making by government. Leaving aside speculation about the relative importance of these aspects of controversy, which is pointless for an outsider, their outcome was that the Cowles Commission relocated from the University of Chicago to Yale in 1953.

While the Cowles Commission research methodology was soundly rejected by their Economics Department colleagues at Chicago, its reception elsewhere was generally positive. The 'method of simultaneous equations' was hailed by R.G.D. Allen potentially as having 'great value in dynamic economics' in the *Review of the International Statistical Institute*. It is relevant to recall that Allen was J.R. Hicks's co-author in a paper that anticipated the approach of *Value and Capital*. Allen's positive assessment no doubt contributed to the rapidity with which the research programme of the Cowles Commission established the essential role of the general equilibrium CUM probability methodology for doing macroeconomic research. The heuristic of the profession has become that theoretical models, such as those of Keynes and Hicks, acquire meaning only in terms of a properly specified stochastic model from which a set of values can be identified.

With the removal of the practical limitation of manipulating large numbers of equations by even early model computers, econometric research has become, for many, the *sine qua non* of economic science. This development is clearly inconsistent with Keynes's reservations about the usefulness of statistical probability to explain economic outcomes that come into being under uncertainty. The vision of the real world to which Keynes first gave expression in *A Treatise on Probability* and which provided the epistemic foundation for *The General Theory of Employment, Money and Interest* is a perspective which is *conceptually* incompatible with the mid-century transformation of economics that has accompanied the formalist revolution. This transformation has become institutionally embodied in the Econometrics Society and the Cowles Commission and is an expression of the contemporary view that the hallmark of science is its ability to predict social as well as natural phenomena. The triumph of the neo-Walrasian synthesis that had its origin when Hicks recast Keynes's system into a Walrasian general equilibrium format is less attributable to its theoretical superiority than it is to the intellectual appeal of the empirical results that the multi-equation probability method, coupled with the technology of the computer, has made possible.

Notes

1. It is also relevant that Arthur Marget, who reviewed Morgenstern's *Wirtschaftsprognose*, noted that 'the formal technique of probability analysis can only rarely, if ever, be applied to economic data with any hope of obtaining reasonably significant results' (Marget, 1929, p. 315). Presumably he would make the same comment in relation to the probabilistic approach that later became associated with the Cowles Commission's econometric technique.
2. In view of E. Roy Weintraub's comprehensive exploration of the modern development of general equilibrium analysis (1983), it is sufficient here only to note the aforementioned facts which are germane to the argument about to be developed.
3. It is relevant to note that there were earlier efforts of statistical testing of cycles, specifically Ralph G. Hawtrey, 'The monetary theory of the trade cycle and its statistical test', *Quarterly Journal of Economics* (1926–7); M.A. Copeland, 'Money, trade and prices – a test of causal primacy', *Quarterly Journal of Economics* (1928–9); and R. Glenday, 'Business forecasting: a quantitative investigation of the influence of money on trade development', *Journal of the Royal Statistical Society* (1932) with discussion by Hawtrey and others.
4. In a letter to Roy Harrod, 23 August 1938.
5. This possible parallel was called to my attention by Robert Dimand.
6. Some degree of appreciation of the rapidly developing field of macroeconomic modelling shortly before the publication of the *General Theory* can be gleaned from a perusal of vol. III of *Econometrica* (1935) which included three papers from the Leiden meeting of the Econometric Society in October 1933: Tinbergen's survey 'Suggestions on quantitative business cycle theory', Ragnar Frisch and Haraold Holme on 'The characteristic solutions of a mixed difference and differential equation occurring in economic dynamics' and Michal Kalecki's 'A macrodynamic theory of business cycles'. Also relevant for establishing this rapidly emerging area are: Charles F. Roos's 'A mathematical theory of price and production fluctuations and economic crises', *Journal of Political Economy* (1930), his *Dynamic Economics*, Cowles Monograph No. 1, Bloomington, Ind.: Indiana Principia Press, 1934; and E. Theiss, 'A quantitative theory of industrial fluctuations caused by the capitalistic technique of production', *Journal of Political Economy* (1933).

References

Anderson, R.L. (1945), 'Review of T. Haavelmo: the probability approach in economics', *Journal of the American Statistical Association*, 40, 393–394.

Arrow, K.J. and Debreu, G. (1954), 'Existence of an equilibrium for a competitive economy', *Econometrica*, 22, July, 265–290.

Arrow, K.J. and Hurwicz, L, (1958), 'On the stability of the competitive economy', *Econometrica*, 26, October, 522–552.

Baumol, W. J. and Goldfeld, S. M. (eds) (1968), *Precursors in Mathematical Economics*, Reprints of Scarce Works on Political Economy series No. 19, London: London School of Economics.

Bennion, E.G. (1952), 'The Cowles Commission's simultaneous equation approach: a simplified explanation', *Review of Economics and Statistics*, 49–56.

Bodkin, R., Klein L.R. and Marwah, K. (1986), 'Keynes and the origins of macroeconometric modelling, *Conference on Keynes and Public Policy after Fifty Years*, Glendon College, York University.

Burns, A. and Mitchell, W. (1946), *Measuring Business Cycles*, New York: National Bureau of Economic Research.

Christ, C.F. (1952), 'History of the Cowles Commission 1932–1952', in *Economic Theory and Measurement*, Chicago: Cowles Commission, 3–67.

Friedman, M. (1946), 'Lange on price flexibility and employment: a methodological criticism', *American Economic Review*, 36, September, 613–631.

Haavelmo, T. (1943), 'The statistical implications of a system of simultaneous equations', *Econometrica*, 11, 1–12.

Haavelmo, T. (1944), 'The probability approach in econometrics', supplement to *Econometrica*, 12.

Hicks, J.R. (1937), 'Mr Keynes and the "classics": a suggested interpretation', *Econometrica*, 5, 147–159.

Hicks, J.R. (1974), *The Crisis in Keynesian Economics*, Oxford: Blackwell.

Hicks, J.R. (1983), 'A sceptical follower,' *The Economist*, 18 June, 17–19.

Hildreth, C. (1986), 'The Cowles Commission in Chicago 1939–1955'. Vienna, Springer-Verlag.

Keynes, J.M. (1971–   ), *Collected Writings*, D.E. Moggridge (ed.), London: Macmillan.

Klein, L.R. (1947), 'The use of econometric models as a guide to economic policy', *Econometrica*, 15, April, 111–151.

Klein, L.R. (1954), 'The empirical foundations of Keynesian economics', in K. Kurihara (ed.), *Post Keynesian Economics*, New Brunswick, NJ: Rutgers University Press.

Koopmans, T.C. (1937), *Linear Regression Analysis of Economic Time Series*, Haarlem: Netherlands Economic Institute.

Koopmans, T.C. (1947), 'Measurement without theory', *REStat*. 29, 161–172; reprinted in *Readings in Business Cycle Theory*, AEA, Blakiston, 1949.

Lange, O., (1944), *Price Flexibility and Employment*, Cowles Commission Monograph No. 8, Bloomington, Indiana: Principia Press.

Leontief, W. (1948), 'Econometrics', in H.S. Ellis (ed.), *A Survey of Contemporary Economics*, Philadelphia, Penn., and Toronto: Blakiston for the American Economic Association.

Marget, (1929), 'Morgenstern on the methodology of economic forecasting', *Journal of Political Economy*, 37, 312–339.

Morgan, M.S. (1984), 'The probablistic revolution: Haavelmo's contribution to econometrics', unpublished ms.

Morgenstern, O. (1928), *Wirtshaftsprognose: Eine Untersuchung Ihrer Voraussetzungen und MöRichkeiten*, Vienna: Springer.

Morgenstern, O. (1941), 'Professor Hicks on value and capital', *Journal of Political Economy*, 49.

Morgenstern, O. (1976), 'Collaborating with von Neuman', *Journal of Economic Literature*, 14, 805–816.

von Neuman, J. and O. Morgenstern (1944), *Theory of Games and Economic Behavior*, Princeton, NJ. Princeton University Press.

Patinkin, D. (1976), 'Keynes and econometrics'. *Econometrica*, 44, 1091–1123.

Reder, M.W. (1982), 'Chicago Economics: Performance and Change', *Journal of Economic Literature*, XX, March, pp 1–38.

Samuelson, P.A. (1947), *Foundations of Economic Analysis*, Cambridge, Mass.: Harvard University Press.

Schumpeter, J.A. (1936), 'Review of the *General Theory*', *Journal of the American Statistical Association*, 31, 791–795.

Szilard, L. (1969), 'Reminiscences', in D. Fleming and B. Barlyn (eds), *The Intellectual Migration*, Cambridge, Mass.: Harvard University Press.

Tinbergen, J. (1939), *Statistical Testing of Business-Cycle Theories. Vol. II, Business Cycles in the United States of America, 1919–1932*, Geneva: League of Nations.

Vining, R. (1949), 'Koopmans on the choice of variables to be studied and of methods of measurement'. *Review of Economic Statistics*, 31, 77–86; reply by Koopmans, pp. 86–91; rejoinder by Vining, pp. 91–94.

Weintraub, E.R. (1983), 'On the existence of a competitive equilibrium: 1930–1954', *Journal of Economic Literature*, 21, 1–39.

3 The Keynes–Tinbergen exchange in retrospect

Robin Rowley

Almost a half-century has passed since Keynes was asked to review a book prepared by Tinbergen for the League of Nations. Keynes saw 'a mass of unintelligible figurings' with 'not the slightest explanation or justification of the underlying logic' (according to his letter to Kahn of 23 August 1938). He found the book 'grievously disappointing' and his adverse review of 'Professor Tinbergen's Method', which appeared in the *Economic Journal* (1939), clearly reflects both this disappointment and his doubts concerning the application of multiple-correlation techniques to complex economic problems. Tinbergen (1940a, 1940b) responded to this criticism with a further clarification of his approach and more illustrations of its use in business cycle research, but left many of Keynes's objections unanswered. Letters from the two principals and from Harrod, which partially clarify Keynes's position in this exchange, are now available following their reprinting by Moggridge (1973), so that some of the ambiguities and poorly expressed portions of Keynes's review can be put aside and its primary arguments reassessed in terms of a more recent econometric perspective.

Interest in Keynes's discussion of econometric methodology, as represented in this exchange with Tinbergen, has recently been revived by Hendry (1980), Klant (1985), Lawson (1985), Patinkin (1976, 1984), Pesaran and Smith (1985), Stone (1978) and Bodkin *et al.* (1986), partly as a constituent element in a new appreciation of the history of econometric thought and practice and partly due to emerging challenges to the orthodox (or procrustean) form of econometrics in the Cowles Commission tradition. The Keynes–Tinbergen exchange initially generated further responses in support of multiple correlation or regression models and extending them to systems of equations with economy-wide coverage. Examples include Koopmans (1941) and Haavelmo (1943, 1944). These responses containing discussions of logical issues that affect econometrics quickly lost attention as the methodology developed at the Cowles Commission during the 1940s came to dominate empirical research. Leamer (1985), with sufficient justification, felt it appropriate to describe the subsequent period of neglect in the following terms: 'The slippery issues of causal inference have been kept in the econometric closet for over thirty years since Marschak, Koopmans and Simon wrote about them. Those who rumaged in the closet in the intervening years no doubt quickly concluded that these were problems better left alone lest they devour our energies with little to show for the effort.' Recent attempts to redefine exogeneity, to develop tests of causality, to question structural autonomy and to acknowledge the sequential nature of modelling provide ample grounds for looking once more at the specific complaints by Keynes. For the comments that follow, Bodkin *et al.* (1986) provided the immediate stimulus, but the choice of themes explored by Jain (1985) and Rowley and Jain (1984) indicate some prior consideration of related matters.

For Keynes, the central question of methodology was the 'logic of applying the method of multiple correlation to unanalysed economic material, which we know to be non-homogeneous through time' (according to his letter to Tyler of 23 August 1938). However, his contribution to econometrics has generally been placed elsewhere with a much stronger stress given to aspects of his *General Theory*. For example, the *Handbook of Econometrics* edited by Griliches and Intriligator (1983, 1984) contains only one reference to Keynes: 'Macroeconometric modelling also began in the 1930s by Tinbergen and was given additional impetus by the development of National Income Accounts in the United States and other countries and by Keynes' theoretical work.' It contains no assessment of his views on econometric methodology. Bodkin *et al.* (1986) also point to the impact of the *General Theory*. They argue that (1) it 'is no exaggeration to say that originally macroeconometric models were designed to implement the Keynesian system', that (2) it 'is reasonable to argue that the most important single antecedent for the construction of macroeconometric models' is Keynes's *General Theory* and that (3) parts of this book 'contain concepts that are easily put into theoretical formulations susceptible to econometric testing and estimation without much difficulty'. In response, it might be pointed out: (1) that the business cycle macrodynamics of Frisch, Tinbergen and others in the 1930s must be assigned to the history of macroeconometrics unless this term is reserved for post-1940 developments; (2) changes in computational software and statistical frameworks were also major antecedents for the emergence of fitted, economy-wide econometric models; and (3) the integration of Keynes's theoretical constructs into quantitative models has proved so difficult that many economists have difficulty in locating these constructs directly in large econometric models, while other economists seem to deny the possibility of expressing Keynes's theory in this particular way. Certainly the features of all macroeconometric models are quite inconsistent with Keynes's own treatment of probability and with the methodological views expressed by him in the exchange with Tinbergen.

Turning to the specific criticisms by Keynes, Bodkin *et al*, argue that these are 'in general, reasonably taken', while other criticisms 'seem reasonable in themselves and appear to have stood the test of time'. In similar vein, Patinkin (1982, 1984) points out such criticisms could not be dismissed 'for some of them became basic concerns of the econometric literature'. He excludes the misplaced criticism by Keynes of non-cyclical linear specifications and confesses to 'find it somewhat depressing to see how many of them are, in practice, still of relevance today'. These comments are surprising in view of the contents of most econometric textbooks. A quick review of eight prominent textbooks by Dhrymes (1970), Goldberger (1964), Johnston (1963, 1972), Judge *et al*. (1980) Kmenta (1971), Maddala (1977), Malinvaud (1970), and Theil (1971) reveals that none of them mentions the dispute between Keynes and Tinbergen and none cites the basic references in the *Economic Journal*. Given this background, it seems appropriate to take a contrary view; namely, that Keynes's criticisms have been diluted, forgotten or mis-stated rather than absorbed into the prevalent orthodoxy.

Bodkin *et al*. (1986) suggest that Keynes's criticisms 'could be interpreted as' pointing to single-equation bias, omitted-variable bias, problems of measurement errors in explanatory variables, functional mis-specification due to a preoccupation with linearity and (especially) to structural change, while Patinkin also re-interprets some of these criticisms as involving specification bias and simultaneous-equations bias. These newer terms are indeed 'incorporated into econometrics textbooks today' but the re-interpretation introduces a fundamental change in focus. It converts the focus of concern from structural autonomy, non-homogeneity and specification to estimation by stressing bias. Recall that bias is the existence of some difference between the expected value of an estimator and the population parameter, or structural constant, being estimated. Did Keynes accept the validity in complex economic situations of such notions as expectation in the sense of the centre of a completely specified probability density function or of other parameters that characterize this function? Did Keynes accept the severe constraints on non-homogeneous behaviour that are necessary for ergodicity, so that time-averages over available data could be assumed to converge to corresponding population elements? What would Keynes have said concerning the edifice of asymptotic distribution theory that supports much macroeconometric modelling in the Cowles

Commission tradition and contains such crucial features as asymptotic bias and consistency in the statistical sense?

When Keynes discusses structural change or instability, he has in mind erratic phenomena that are markedly different from those typically invoked when we use Chow tests, Goldfeld–Quandt procedures, recursive-residual checks or models with switching regimes. Moreover, his concern (like that of Koopmans with identification) affects specification and precedes estimation rather than following it as part of post-estimation diagnostic checks. From the beginning, Keynes reacts adversely to the structural stability implicit in much of Tinbergen's modelling. This is revealed in his letter to Tyler of 23 August 1938. 'The coefficients arrived at are apparently assumed to be constant for 10 years or for a longer period. Yet, surely we know that they are not constant. There is no reason at all why they should not be different every year.' Earlier he points out to Harrod (in a letter of 16 July 1938) that since economics deals with motives, expectations and psychological uncertainties, one 'has to be constantly on guard against treating the material as constant and homogeneous' in contrast with situations occurring in the natural sciences. Finally, in the published review itself, he expresses himself unequivocally by asserting the 'main prima facie objection to the application of the method of multiple correlation to complex economic problems lies in the apparent lack of any adequate degree of uniformity in the environment'.

Such comments are reinforced when Keynes considers the 'inductive transition' from a narrow focus on statistical description to prediction. In his letter to Tyler, he raises the issue of extrapolating from a situation in which a researcher has a free hand to choose coefficients and time-lag and, hence, can 'always cook a formula to fit moderately well a limited range of past facts' but has little likelihood of a good post-sample approximation. He also points to the problems of (1) relying on data that are available rather than on data that are appropriate, (2) dealing with non-numerical influences that are not constant in their impact and (3) assessing potential differences in model fits due to the flexibility of choices available to researchers. All of these features might be linked to within-sample instabilities or predictive inadequacies.

In communicating with Tinbergen, Keynes appears to recommend split-sample methods and pseudo-replication to check for instability: 'The first step ... is to break up the period under examination into a series of sub-periods, with a view to discovering whether the results of applying our method to the various sub-periods taken separately are reasonably uniform. If they are, then we have some ground for projecting our results into the future' (Keynes's review):

Suppose you have statistics covering a period of 20 years, what is required, it seems to me, is to divide these into convenient sections, say, of 5 years each, and calculate a proper equation for each period separately, and then consider what concordance appears between the different results. Until this has been done, a formula applying to the whole of the 20 years can have very little significance. (Keynes, letter to Tinbergen, 20 September 1938)

Such advice is surprisingly modern. It could be seen as involving the repeated use of Chow tests but is, perhaps, more appropriately viewed as an aspect of interior data analysis based on exploratory econometric methods rather than on the orthodox confirmatory ones. Thus it appears closer to the techniques described by Belsley *et al.* (1980) and Cook and Weisberg (1982) than to the techniques found in the econometric textbooks listed earlier.

Keynes's review also reveals his concern for the interpretation of statistical tests. With respect to the feasibility of such tests supporting the rejection of economic theories, he points to the conditional softness of testing procedures. Thus, at best, 'only those theories can be shown to be incorrect which, in the view of the economist who advances them, accept as applicable the various conditions' that are essential for the validity of statistical testing procedures. Much of Keynes's review is an attempt to clarify these conditions, including homogeneity and stability, and to assess their potential acceptability in the economic context. He insists Tinbergen's account is incomplete, for he 'leaves unanswered many questions which the economist is bound to ask before he can feel comfortable as to the conditions which the economic material has to satisfy, if the proposed method is to be properly applicable'. Clearly he failed to foresee how economists would ignore the conditional nature of statistical inference for many years and yet remain comfortable. Keynes's non-technical list of auxiliary conditions is supplemented in Tinbergen's reply by the explicit recognition of three conditions that are necessary (but not sufficient) for unbiased estimation. These are the need for relevant explanatory variables to be included in the statistical framework, the need for omitted variables to be such that equation errors are uncorrelated with the variables included explicitly and the need for the mathematical form of the relationship among variables to be given.

A modern restatement of Keynes's stress on conditions for modelling and inference is provided by Smith:

[An] econometric model provides a mapping from specifications into conclusions about preferences, technology, and institutions. Insofar as the conclusions are sensitive to the specifications, we are left with scientific propositions that are open-ended with respect to the environment, institutions, and agent behavior. (Smith, 1982)

Against this background, Smith provides an awkward scenario that would have confirmed Keynes's scepticism to the extent that it represents common practice among economists:

> Based on introspection, some casual observations of some process, and a contextual interpretation of the self-interest postulate, a model is specified and then 'tested' by estimation using the only body of field data that exists. The results turn out to be ambiguous or call for 'improvements' . . . and now one is tempted to modify the model in ways suggested by these results to improve the fit with 'reasonable expectations'. (*ibid.*)

Both Keynes and Tinbergen identified the sequential character of testing that is noticeably absent from econometric textbooks until Judge *et al.* (1980), although the attendant problem of pre-test bias was recognized by Bancroft in the 1940s and later associated with conditional regression.

The impact of auxiliary conditions on the interpretation of testing is only considered by Bodkin *et al.* (1986) when they comment on discussions by Pesaran and Smith (1985) and link them with a post-Keynesian critique that is said to hold 'no coherent model, macroeconometric or otherwise, can capture the essential message of Keynes [due to] the important role of uncertainty, the uniqueness of particular historical episodes' and some aspects of indeterminacy. It is not difficult to locate such factors in Keynes's own criticisms of econometrics but this account by Bodkin *et al.* fails to give adequate emphasis to auxiliary hypotheses, which cannot be avoided in testing. Perhaps Bodkin *et al.* have become complacent, too comfortable with the neglect of conditional qualifications in macroeconometric modelling, especially in the estimation and testing of large, economy-wide macroeconomic models where pragmaticism and 'tender loving care' adjustments are common features. They may also have been affected by the assimilation of Cowles Commission methodology that began shortly after the Keynes–Tinbergen exchange was published. The contrast between the postulates of this methodology and the alternative perspective associated with Keynes is dramatic. Haavelmo (1943, 1944) provides a valuable illustration for explicating differences here.

In response to Keynes' criticisms of Tinbergen's approach, Haavelmo (1943) makes two initial claims. He suggests that 'there is no harm in considering economic variables as stochastical variables having certain distribution properties' and, further, that 'only through the introduction of such notions are we able to formulate hypotheses that have a meaning in relation to facts'. These suggestions are markedly at odds with Keynes's perspective and somewhat more restrictive than the views expressed by Tinbergen. They lead to the identification of testing with the Neyman–Pearson framework of drawing samples from a complete probability distribution instead of the informal notions of Keynes and Tinbergen. Haavelmo's view of testable hypotheses is straightforward:

> The observable variables involved have a joint probability law which belongs to a specified class of probability laws. If the hypothesis is true, we can make certain probability statements about the type of samples . . . it will produce. (*ibid.*)

Keynes's concern with the existence of any complete probability distribution for economic phenomena is clearly replaced by a presumption of existence. Moreover, the tester is assumed to have a specific class of distributions in mind for the observable variables. This is a substantial requirement. It extends the potential impact of auxiliary conditions on research, raises the difficulty of specifying distributions consistent with non-homogeneity and other features of economic behaviour and introduces a procedure affected by the possibility of incorrect choices (now entrenched in the concepts of significance levels, p-values and power). Such new elements reinforce the implicit criterion contained in Keynes's letter to Tyler:

> Would someone else . . . faced with the same problem and using the same method and the same statistics, but without having seen these calculations, necessarily bring out the same result? . . . [How] far are the results mechanically and uniquely obtainable from the data, and how far do they depend on the way the cook chooses to go to work?

In exploring this radical approach to hypotheses and testing, Haavelmo (1944) provides the definitive basis for much of the subsequent macroeconometric methodology associated with the Cowles Commission. He asserts that the problems of estimation in relation to economic equation systems 'all come down to one and the same thing, namely, to study the properties of the joint probability distribution of the random (observable) variables in a stochastic equation system', so that it is 'clear that the joint probability law of all the observable random variables in an economic system is the only general basis for estimating the unknown parameters of the system'. In his review, Keynes mistakenly suggests that specification must be comprehensive in a particular sense: 'Am I right in thinking that the method of multiple correlation analysis essentially depends on the economist having furnished, not merely a list of the significant causes, which is correct as far as it goes, but a complete list?' A similar question is contained in his letter to Tyler and adequately answered by Tinbergen in his reply to the effect that omitted variables are collectively treated as equation errors. Haavelmo's framework also contains a comprehensiveness issue, for it requires the stochastic inter-relationships among explanatory variables and these errors to be specified for the whole system prior to estimation. Thus, for example, the familiar transformation from the structural form of a simultaneous equations model (SEM) to its reduced form requires the prior partition of explanatory variables into endogenous and predetermined classes according to their hypothetical correlations with equation errors. Further, identification within the SEM involves the concept of a system being complete in a statistical sense (due to Koopmans), which again presumes this partition of variables. Even in the estimation of single equations within a system, advocacy of 2SLS, LIML and instrumental-variable estimators is associated with the classification of variables. Keynes's confusion with the listing of variables to include in a model is supplemented by the hazards of specifying stochastic properties for all of these variables.

Keynes indicates Tinbergen's book 'has been a nightmare to live with' (in his review) and describes the archetypal feature of an econometrician as 'much more interested in getting on with the job than in spending time in deciding the job is worth getting on with!' He would have been appalled by the subsequent form taken by macroeconometrics. In particular, he would have dismissed the excessive reliability on probability distributions, stationarity, homogeneity and the Neyman–Pearson testing framework. He would also have been distressed by the neglect of logical issues until the rational expectations viewpoint provoked attempts to defend or refine the Cowles Commission orthodoxy of econometric methodology. He would probably have recognized the partial retraction of Haavelmo (1958), scorned the comment by Bodkin *et al.* (1986) that it 'can be asserted without too much fear of controversy today that intuitive estimates . . . are even more likely to be misleading than the econometric estimates' and found some small comfort in the recent re-birth of scepticism. For the rest of us, there remains regret that we have waited too long for econometric methodology to come of age and address its logical bases.

References

Belsley, D.A., Kuh, E. and Welsch, R.E. (1980), *Regression Diagnostics*, New York: Wiley.

Bodkin, R.G., Klein, L.R. and Marwah, K. (1986), 'Keynes and the origins of macroeconometric modelling', *Conference on Keynes and Public Policy after Fifty Years*, Glendon College, York University, Toronto.

Cook, R.D. and Weisberg, S. (1982), *Residuals and Influence in Regression*, London: Chapman and Hall.

Dryhmes, P.J. (1970), *Econometrics*, New York: Harper and Row.

Goldberger, A.S. (1964), *Econometric Theory*, New York: Wiley.

Haavelmo, T. (1943), 'Statistical testing of business-cycle theories', *Review of Economics and Statistics*, 25, 13–18.

Haavelmo, T. (1944), *The Probability Approach in Econometrics*, supplement to *Econometrica*, 12.

Haavelmo, T. (1958), 'The role of the econometrician in the advancement of economic theory', *Econometrica*, 26(3), 351–357.

Hendry, D.F. (1980), 'Econometrics: alchemy or science?', *Economica*, 47, 387–406.

Jain, R. (1985), 'Econometric fluctuations, structure, and measurement', PhD dissertation, McGill University.

Johnston, J. (1972), *Econometric Methods*, 2nd Edn, New York: McGraw Hill, (1st Edition 1963).

Judge, G.C., Griffith, W.E., Hill, R.C., and Lee, T.C. (1980), *The Theory and Practice of Econometrics*, New York: Wiley.

Keynes, J.M. (1939), 'Professor Tinbergen's method', *Economic Journal*, 49, 558–568.

Klant, J.J. (1985), 'The slippery transition', in T. Lawson and H. Pesaran (eds), *Keynes's Economics: Methodological Issues*, Armonk, NY: M.E. Sharpe, 80–98.

Kmenta, J. (1971), *Elements of Econometrics*, New York: Macmillan.

Koopmans, T. (1941), 'The logic of econometric business-cycle research', *Journal of Political Economy*, 49(2), 157–181.

Lawson, T. (1985), 'Keynes, prediction and econometrics', in T. Lawson and H. Pesaran (eds), *Keynes' Economics: Methodological Issues*, Armonk, NY: M.E. Sharpe, 116–133.

Lawson, T. and Pesaran, H. *Keynes's Economics: Methodological Issues*, Armonk, N.Y.: M.E. Sharpe.

Leamer, E.E. (1985), 'Vector autoregressions for causal inference?', in K. Brunner and A.H. Meltzer (eds), *Understanding Monetary Regimes*, Amsterdam: North Holland, 255–304.

Maddala, G.S. (1977), *Econometrics*, New York: McGraw Hill.

Malinvand, E. (1970), *Statistical Methods of Econometrics* 2nd Edn, Amsterdam: North Holland.

Moggridge, D.E. (ed.) (1973), *The Collected Writings of John Maynard Keynes. Vol. XIV, The General Theory and After, Part II: Defence and Development*, London: MacMillan, 285–320.

Patinkin, D. (1976), 'Keynes and econometrics: on the interaction between the macro-economic revolutions of the interwar period', *Econometrica*, 14, 1091–1123.

Patinkin, D. (1982), *Anticipations of the General Theory? And Other Essays on Keynes*, Chicago: University of Chicago Press.

Patinkin, D. (1984), 'Keynes and economics today', *American Economic Review*, 74, 97–102.

Pesaran, H., and Smith, R. (1985), 'Keynes on econometrics', in T. Lawson and H. Pesaran, *Keynes's Economics: Methodological Issues*, Armonk, NY: M.E. Sharpe, 134–150.

Rowley, J.C.R. and Jain, R. 'The demise of structural estimation?', *Proceedings of Business and Economic Statistics Section, American Statistical Association*, Washington: ASA.

Smith, V.L. (1982), 'Microeconomic systems as an experimental science', *American Economic Review*, 72(5), 923–955.

Stone, R. (1978), 'Keynes, political arithmetic and econometrics', *Proceedings of the British Academy*, 64, 55–92.

Theil, H. (1971), *Principles of Econometrics*, New York: Wiley.

Tinbergen, J. (1940a), 'On a method of statistical business-cycle research. A reply', *Economic Journal*, 50, 141–154 (with further 'comment' by Keynes, pp. 154–156).

Tinbergen, J. (1940b), 'Econometric business cycle research', *Review of Economic Studies*, 7, 73–90.

PART II

THE THEORY
OF INVESTMENT

4 Keynes's view of investment

Clarence L. Barber

The key element in Keynes's theory of effective demand is the level of capital spending relative to the rate of savings. As Keynes saw it,

> there has been a chronic tendency throughout human history for the propensity to save to be stronger than the inducement to invest. The weakness of the inducement to invest has been at all times the key to the economic problem ... The desire of the individual to augment his personal wealth by abstaining from consumption has usually been stronger than the inducement of the entrepreneur to augment the national wealth by employing labour on the construction of durable assets. (Keynes 1936, pp. 347–8)

This view made a lot of sense at the time the *General Theory* was published. As I will argue later, it still makes a lot of sense today.

Keynes made savings primarily a function of income. Investment spending he explained by his concept of the marginal efficiency of capital relative to the rate of interest. Here he placed particular emphasis on the returns expected over the life of each capital asset. It was Keynes's view that there was little knowledge on which to base an accurate estimate of the returns that could be expected on a capital investment of a longer-term nature. As he saw it,

> the outstanding fact is the extreme precariousness of the basis of knowledge on which our estimates of prospective yield have to be made ... If we speak frankly, we have to admit that our basis of knowledge for estimating the yield ten years hence of a railway, a copper mine, a textile factory, the goodwill of a patent medicine, an Atlantic liner, a building in the City of London amounts to little and sometimes to nothing; or even five years hence. (*ibid.*, pp. 149–50)

As a result, the schedule of the marginal efficiency of capital can be subject to violent shifts over the course of the cycle. Thus he argued that:

> it is an essential characteristic of the boom that investments which will in fact yield, say, 2 per cent in conditions of full employment are made in expectation of a yield of, say, 6 per cent, and are valued accordingly. When the disillusion comes, this expectation is replaced by a contrary 'error of pessimism'. (*ibid.*, pp. 321–2)

These fluctuations, he argued, were 'too great to be offset by any practicable changes in the rate of interest' (*ibid.*, p. 164).

Keynes also held that if we had to depend on a sober calculation of expected returns for an adequate volume of capital spending, there would be a lot less capital investment than actually occurs. The difference he attributed to something he called 'animal spirits – a spontaneous urge to action rather than inaction' (*ibid.* p. 161). In concluding his assessment of the basis of capital spending, Keynes stated: 'I expect to see the State, which is in a position to calculate the marginal efficiency of capital goods on long views and on the basis of the general social advantage, taking an ever greater responsibility for directly organizing investment' (*ibid.*, p. 164). Or again, in his concluding chapter he states, 'I conceive therefore, that a somewhat comprehensive socialisation of investment will prove the only means of securing an approximation to full employment' (*ibid.*, p. 378).

Keynes also believed that it would be 'comparatively easy to make capital goods so abundant that the marginal efficiency of capital is zero' (*ibid.*, p. 221). Again, in his concluding chapter he states: 'I feel sure that the demand for capital is strictly limited in the sense that it would not be difficult to increase the stock of capital up to a point where its marginal efficiency had fallen to a very low figure' (*ibid.*, p. 375). In view of the enormous volume of capital spending that has taken place over the past few decades, such a view coming from a person with Keynes's practical knowledge and experience is, at first sight, puzzling. The explanation must be, I believe, that Keynes shared the widespread view of the 1930s that the developed world was moving rapidly towards a stationary or declining population. Referring to the 1930s, the demographer, D.V. Glass (1973), observed:

> For many industrial countries that period saw the lowest birth rates and level of fertility since the initiation of the secular decline in family size – a decline which began in the nineteenth century ... In much of the Western World there was a feeling of impending depopulation, a feeling added to by the publication of population projections, many of which assumed a further fall in fertility. (Glass, 1973, pp. 72–3)

I have found one sentence in the *General Theory* that supports this view. Near the end of the first chapter on the 'Propensity to Consume' the following rhetorical statement appears: 'What will you do, it is asked, when you have built all the houses and roads and town halls and electric grids and water supplies and so forth which the *stationary population* of the future can be expected to require?' (Keynes, 1936, p. 106; italics added). However, the relationship between population size or rate of growth and the capital stock or rate of investment is never developed in the *General Theory*.

Nevertheless, shortly after the publication of the *General Theory*, in February 1937, Keynes (1973) gave the Galton Lecture to the Eugenics Society. It was entitled, 'Some Economic Consequences of a Declining Population'. It is a remarkable although much neglected piece of analysis. In it, Keynes sets forth some of the ideas which Alvin Hansen later developed into the theory of secular stagnation. One can see in it too some of the ideas Harrod (1939) would later develop in his 'Essay in Dynamic Theory'.[1]

In the introductory remarks to this lecture, Keynes argues: 'We know much more securely than we know almost any other social or economic factor relating to the future that, in the place of the steady and indeed steeply rising level of population which we have experienced for a great number of decades, we shall be faced in a very short time with a stationary or a declining level' (1973, p. 125). He then goes on to estimate the relative importance of population growth as a factor sustaining the demand for capital in the UK over the fifty-year period from 1860 to 1913. His rough conclusion is that population growth accounted for just over 40 per cent of the total increase in the stock of capital, a rise in the standard of life for 50 per cent and a lengthening of the period of production for just under 10 per cent. He then argues that, if there had been a stationary population over this same period, the demand for new capital would have been only a little over one-half of its actual level. He concludes:

> It follows, therefore, that to ensure equilibrium conditions of prosperity over a period of years it will be essential, *either* that we alter our institutions and the distribution of wealth in a way which causes a smaller proportion of income to be saved, *or* that we reduce the rate of interest sufficiently to make profitable very large changes in technique or in the direction of consumption which involve a much larger use of capital in proportion to output. Or, of course, as would be wisest, we could pursue both policies to a certain extent. (*ibid.*, p. 131)

Thus, Keynes's argument in the *General Theory* that it would be fairly easy to increase the stock of capital to the point where the return to new investment at the margin was close to zero or even negative, and his emphasis on a future need for the 'socialization of investment', suggest that he was implicitly assuming an economy which was rapidly moving towards a stationary population, and as well an economy in which the rate of productivity growth averaged only about 1 per cent per annum.[2]

Much to everyone's surprise World War II was followed by a baby-

boom which quickly dispelled any thoughts that a stationary population was imminent. Further, within a few years nearly all developed
countries began to record very high rates of productivity growth. For the
Organization for Economic Cooperation and Development (OECD)
output per capita increased at an average rate of more than 3 per cent
over the twenty-five-year period from 1948 to 1973. Keynes had believed
that it was rarely possible for what he called the 'standard of life' to
increase at more than 1 per cent per year. This combination of revived
fertility rates and rapid productivity growth produced an output growth
rate in the OECD of 5 per cent. Rapid growth in output produced, in
turn, a high level of capital spending. Throughout the 1960s and into the
1970s investment for the OECD was growing at an annual rate of about
6 per cent.

A variety of factors contributed to this remarkable record of growth.
A steady reduction in tariffs and other trade barriers and the creation
of customs unions and free trade areas facilitated the rapid growth in
productivity, as did the international transfer of new technology. An
easing of immigration barriers facilitated the movement of labour to
more economic locations. Exceptionally low real interest rates throughout the period facilitated the financing of capital spending. And monetary and fiscal measures inspired by Keynes's *General Theory* kept
economic output moving upward at what must have been close to its
potential.

Nevertheless, it is useful to recall, as Andrea Boltho (1982) has
recently emphasized, that in the early postwar years there was a good
deal of pessimism and a fear that the world could lapse into another
major depression. It was only gradually that the developed world
acquired the kind of economic momentum which saw output in the
OECD as a whole rising by 5 per cent, year in and year out. Once
this pattern of growth had continued for a number of years, it must
have inspired a good deal of confidence among businessmen reflected
in their willingness to make major long-term investment expenditures.
Thus, for a time, the uncertainty about future prospects which Keynes
emphasized so strongly was dispelled.

This halcyon period came to an end with the rude shocks of OPEC's
fourfold increase in the price of crude oil late in 1973, preceded by the
commodity price explosion which began in the summer of 1972. Since
then we have had stagflation, high rates of inflation and real growth at
only about half its pre-1973 rate. The outlook for long-term investment
was further dimmed by the interest rate crunch of the early 1980s and
the even slower growth that followed it. While inflation rates have come

down sharply, the world shows few signs of resuming a more satisfactory rate of growth.

How should these recent events be viewed from the perspective of
the analysis advanced by Keynes in the *General Theory*? I would like to
argue that there have been at least three significant changes since 1936
that substantially affect the outlook for a resumption of a better rate
of economic growth and the higher rate of investment that would
accompany it. First, there has been a major growth in all countries in the
size of government. As a result, while the built-in stabilizing effects of
government transfers and taxes slow the decline in the economy during
periods of recession, they also slow the advance when an expansion
recurs. In effect, the interaction of the multiplier and acceleration is
much weaker than it was prior to the 1930s. Secondly, the major reduction in tariff and other trade barriers has made all countries more
dependent on external markets. As a result, individual countries now
find themselves in less control of their own destiny. Only the very largest
countries feel able to take the steps needed to revive their economies.
Thirdly, the legacy of a decade of higher inflation rates coupled with
a widespread acceptance of at least some of the analysis advanced by
monetarists and by the rational expectations school has left us with
higher real interest rates and an unwillingness of monetary authorities to
make a vigorous use of monetary policy.

Thus, the developed world is back in the situation which Keynes
argued was its norm, where the propensity to save is much stronger than
the inducement to invest. Perhaps the best evidence for this is the
widespread existence of government deficits. In a closed system, such as
the world economy as a whole, an overall government deficit position implies an equivalent private sector surplus, where such a surplus
is defined as the excess of private sector saving over private sector
investment. It is perhaps no accident that one of the few countries that
has managed to reduce its unemployment level to that existing in
1980–1, the USA, is a country with one of the lowest private sector
savings rates.

What, then, are the prospects for the revival of a strong and sustained
growth in capital spending? In a majority of developed countries birth
rates have now fallen to, or below, the replacement level. Consequently,
within a comparatively few years the population of labourforce age
in these countries will begin to grow much more slowly. On the other
hand, there are many unemployed or underemployed people in the
developing countries who would be happy to move to developed countries. And in many developed countries female participation rates

are still rising. Thus the potential for labourforce growth is still high. In addition, productivity growth rates have fallen sharply from their pre-1973 levels and show little signs of revival. Moreover, future economic growth rates as projected by major forecasting organizations are for levels little more than half of those that prevailed for two decades or more prior to 1973. All this, taken together with the three major changes I have outlined above, suggest that it will not be easy to restore the growth pattern of the 1950s and 1960s. Thus the outlook is very much for the kind of world Keynes considered the norm, one in which the propensity to save is much stronger than the inducement to invest and one in which longer-term investment projects are hedged with a high level of risk and uncertainty. In my view, the essential corpus of the *General Theory* is as valid today as it was when first published.

Notes

1. Using notation similar to that used by Harrod, the formulation used by Keynes can be expressed as follows:

$$s = K/Y (n + n')$$

   where s, the percentage of income saved, Keynes places at from 0.08 to 0.15 and the capital output ratio (K/Y) he estimates at 4.0. If n, the rate of population growth falls to zero and n', the rate of productivity growth, is normally about 0.01, Keynes estimates that an additional demand for capital equal to 2–4 per cent of income will be required to absorb the amount the economy wishes to save.
2. Keynes gives no source for his estimate that the standard of life in the period from 1860 to 1913 only rose about 1 per cent per year. However, more recent data confirm the validity of this estimate. A. Maddison in his *Economic Growth in the West* (1964), provides data on the growth of output per man in the UK over the period from 1870 to 1913 that show a growth rate of 1.1 per cent.

References

Boltho, A. (1982), 'Growth', in A. Boltho (ed.), *The European Economy: Growth and Crisis*, Oxford: Oxford University Press.

Glass, D.V. (1973), 'Population growth in developed countries', in H.B. Parry (ed.), *Population and its Problems: A Plain Man's Guide*, Oxford: Clarendon Press.

Harrod, R.F. (1937), 'An essay in dynamic theory', *Economic Journal*, 49, April, 14–33.

Keynes J.M. (1936), *The General Theory of Employment Interest and Money*, New York: Harcourt, Brace.

Keynes J.M. (1973), *Collected Writings. Vol. XIV, The General Theory and After*, pt II, London: Macmillan.

Maddison, A. (1964), *Economic Growth in the West*, London: Allen and Unwin.

5 The q-ratio and replacement investment: an extension of Keynesian theory

Michael Perelman

Introduction

Although investment is critical in Keynes's theory, he generally ignored replacement investment, even though it constitutes more than half of gross investment. Worse yet, Keynes's discussion of replacement investment was usually untouched by his monetary theory of production. He often fell into a crude, deterministic theory of replacement cycles, driven by the speed with which capital wore out. None the less, despite important shortcomings in his presentation, Keynes occasionally came close to an important theory of replacement investment, especially in the *Treatise*.

In a monetary economy the replacement rate for existing plant and equipment is not a constant fraction of gross investment, as Keynes implicitly assumed. Economic conditions can and do modify expectations and thereby affect the willingness of business to commit itself to longer-lived investment goods. This subject has only been lightly touched on by modern macroeconomics, and then usually only with respect to tax laws.

Keynes's treatment of replacement investment may have been related to his impression that most fixed capital would not fall victim to moral depreciation because it was associated with a low variable relative to sunk cost. He estimated: 'Much the greater part – probably not less than three-quarters of the Fixed Capital of the modern world consists of Land, Buildings, Roads and Railways' (Keynes, 1930, p. 88; see also p. 326). Keynes's interest in practical, short-run policy considerations may explain his neglect of the supply-side impacts of investment. Unlike Keynes, who rarely went beyond the influence of investment on demand, I am concerned with the influence of replacement investment on the long-run structure of the production system.

Although the level of gross investment is a major determinant of the near-term level of economic activity in the short run, the mix of replacement and net investment does not affect economic performance. By failing to take notice of the long-term effect of replacement investment, those who followed Keynes were unprepared to recognize how their policies influenced the pattern of replacement investment.

Normal backwardation and the market for capital services
Let me begin by outlining a few basic principles of replacement investment. First, investment in fixed capital goods involves a commitment to an uncertain future. The longer-lived a capital good is, the more risky the investment will be.

Secondly, purchasing capital goods is akin to participating in a future market for capital services (Terborgh, 1949, p. 29). The longer-lived a capital good is, the less liquid it will be, because more funds are tied up in the provision for future capital services. In contrast, short-lived capital goods depreciate relatively quickly, thereby providing a greater flow of capital services per dollar invested. Moreover, because short-lived capital returns its value rapidly, it is more marketable, or, if you like, more liquid. Consequently, a firm's willingness to pay for a supply of capital services from a capital good will be lower, the longer that it must wait to profit from the services that the capital good is expected to supply.

Conventional capital theory focuses on the first moment of the discounted expected value of the services that a good provides. With a null rate of discount, a capital good that depreciates like a one-hoss shay will bear a price proportional to its expected service life. When the second moment of the expected value of capital services is taken into account, the relative value of older capital goods will be higher than the conventional calculation because of their greater liquidity. The more uncertain economic conditions are, the larger their liquidity premia will be.

This premium for short-lived capital is comparable to Keynes's liquidity premium. Consider two identical capital goods that differ only in their durability. For simplicity, let one be expected to provide one year of service and the other, two. Assume that the cost of each good is proportional to its respective expected years of service life and that the expected annual revenues from each is constant. The purchasers of the more durable good commit money for two years of capital services, while the others roll their investments over at the end of the year.

If the economy moves according to a random walk, then rational, risk-averse investors will prefer the one-year option since its variance will be smaller. If during the first year, they realize that their expectations were wrong, they can partially rectify their error next year, when new, more appropriate capital goods can be purchased.

In the spot market for capital services, the value of a piece of equipment in its last period of use minus salvage costs, exceeds the amount firms had been willing to commit themselves in the past to pay for the use of equivalent capital services today. In other words, normal backwardation occurs. Thus a leasing company, much like the speculators in commodities, can profit from normal backwardation by bearing the risk of holding long-lived capital goods.

Breaking new ground

Keynes provided the beginnings of a framework for the analysis of replacement investment. In his fundamental equations of the *Treatise*, Keynes demonstrated how the price levels of consumer goods and capital goods could move independently of each other. In interpreting these equations he was often careless in distinguishing between real and financial investment, especially in the form of equities. He generally assumed that the respective price levels for used capital goods, new capital goods and equities all coincided.

Keynes's inattention to the possibility of varying relative prices of real and financial assets is most surprising, considering his interest in a monetary theory of production. Kahn correctly singled out the assumption of the equality of real and financial assets in the *Treatise* as evidence of confusion on Keynes's part (Kahn, 1978, p. 549).

Perhaps Keynes neglected this cause of changing relative prices of new and used capital goods because it would detract from his message that sticky money wages are a major cause of changing relative prices (see Keynes, 1930, p. 83). None the less, the possibility of different price levels for real and financial assets was important for Keynes. For example, he noted that during the speculative boom of the 1920s the price of equities rose without a corresponding increase in the price of new capital goods (Keynes, 1930; 5, p. 122). Since Keynes usually assumed that prices of new and used capital goods moved together, he implicitly recognized that equity prices need not correspond to capital goods prices. In his words:

> Nor does the price of existing securities depend at all closely over short periods either on the cost of production or on the price of new fixed capital. For existing securities largely consist of properties which cannot be quickly reproduced, of natural resources which cannot be reproduced at all, and of the capitalised value of future income anticipated from the possession of quasi-monopolies of peculiar advantages of one kind or another. The investment boom in the United States in 1929 was a good example of an enormous rise in the price of securities as a whole which was not accompanied by any rise at all in the price of the current output of fixed capital. (*ibid.*, p. 222)

Although Keynes often got mired down in confusion about different price levels, he offered the beginnings of a remarkably robust theory of replacement investment. Consider the following citation:

> The stimulus to new investment ... (frequently comes) about through a lower bank rate first of all affecting the financial, as distinguished from the industrial, situation, and so sending up the price level of *existing* investments ... In so far as these investments are capable of reproduction, the prices of *new* capital goods (in particular) will then rise in sympathy. (*ibid.*, p. 189)

Actually the reverse causality is more important. An increasing demand for new investment will cause the price of existing capital goods to move at much greater rate than the price of new capital goods. First, the supply of used capital goods is fixed, except for the ageing of the most recently purchased capital goods. Used capital good prices will have to absorb all demand shocks since quantity adjustments are virtually ruled out. In addition, reproduction costs set the value of new capital goods. Although shifting degrees of uncertainty may have a minimal influence on reproduction costs, they can influence prices of used capital goods considerably. Consequently, the values of used capital goods are unstable relative to the values of new capital goods.

Keynes was close to the mark when Robertson directly challenged his idea that changing asset values could affect the level of economic activity. Robertson took the position that price increases for new capital goods represent a transfer rather than an expansion of income. For Robertson, one person's gain is another's loss. Keynes disagreed, observing, 'It was vital to D.H.R.'s argument that the buyers of non-liquid assets should be compelled to buy *newly produced* non-liquid assets' (Keynes to Sraffa, 15 May 1931; in *CW*, XIII, p. 210).

Keynes recognized the importance of distinguishing between new and existing capital goods in his system with words that clearly point in the right direction: 'There is in any given state of bearishness, a *curve of preference* ... *relating the price of new investment goods to that of total capital assets*; and it is reasonable to assume that the two move in the same direction though not at an equal pace' (Keynes to Robertson, 5 May 1931; in *CW*, XIII, p. 229n.; see also 1936, appendix, ch. 6).

The conclusion to be drawn from Keynes's insight about the possibly differing price paths of new and used capital goods is obvious. Once business is recognized as choosing among a variety of investment options, including the prolonged operation of existing capital goods, everything should fall into place. Used capital goods allow for relatively more hoarding since a part of their value is already depreciated away. Consequently, an increase in bearishness should affect the price of used capital goods more than new ones.

Later, Keynes cast additional light on the probable reason for changes in the price ratios for new and used capital goods. For example, in discussing the nature of the determination of the interest rate, he wrote:

> And the current rate of interest depends, as we have seen, not on the strength of the desire to hold wealth, but on the strengths of the desires to hold it in liquid and in illiquid forms respectively, coupled with the amount of the supply of wealth in one form relatively to the supply of it in the other. (Keynes, 1936, p. 213)

Keynes's subject, the effect of the type of wealth desired on the interest rate, obviously can be inverted. The interest rate, or more precisely liquidity preference, certainly has some effect on the *type* of wealth desired, not just whether or not wealth is held as money. Keeping in mind that used capital goods generally represent a less expensive form of acquiring a productive capacity, they should become more attractive when the desire for liquidity intensifies.

In the *Treatise*, Keynes never pushed this part of his theory to the fore. He abandoned it altogether in the *General Theory*. Perhaps he was treading too close to Austrian capital theory. None the less, I concur with Hicks's evaluation of this effort:

> Here at last we have something which to a value theorist looks sensible and interesting! It seems to me that this ... theory of Mr Keynes really contains the most important part of his theoretical contribution ... that it is from this point that we ought to start in constructing the theory of money. (Hicks, 1935, p. 64)

Keynes's analysis of investors' bearishness in the *Treatise* brought him exceedingly close to his later liquidity preference theory of investment. Within this framework the shadow price of investment goods includes a correction for the perceived riskiness of investment in general. In defending his theory, Keynes wrote:

> My central thesis regarding the determination of the price of non-liquid assets is that ... the price of non-liquid assets is a function of the quantity of inactive deposits in conjunction with the degree of propensity to hoard. (Keynes, 1931 [1973], p. 222)

Keynes's theory of the relationship between bearishness and real asset prices should have been recognized as the centrepiece of his investment theory. Instead it was lost in the mechanisms of the IS/LM and the Marginal Efficiency of Capital (MEI). Unfortunately, Keynes failed to develop this theory to its fullest. He was partly to blame by confounding existing capital goods with equities. When he attempted to correct this error, both Sraffa and Kahn were unable to appreciate the importance of what he had begun to do (see Kahn, 5 April 1931a; Kahn to Keynes, 17 April 1931; Sraffa, 9 May 1931). Years later, Kahn himself confessed that upon rereading his letters to Keynes, he saw that they were 'confused' on this subject (Kahn, 1978, p. 549). If the likes of Kahn and Sraffa could not follow Keynes's analysis, who could? No wonder he despaired of making himself clear to the general public!

Keynes and the q-theory of investment

How does replacement investment fit into the q-theory? Consider the normal continuum of liquidity premia for different investments. They should be high for equities, which are readily marketable; less so for capital goods that are largely depreciated away; and low for new long-lived capital goods.

The typical reading of the q-ratio associates a high q with a willingness to invest. I suggest the opposite may be true. A high degree of uncertainty makes people seek more liquid investments. Stocks become attractive relative to real investment. Only because stock prices become so elevated that investors are crowded out of equities do firms resort to substantial real investment, other things being equal.

Conversely, when investors shy away from liquidity, stock prices suffer relative to real capital prices. Recall how perplexingly weak US equity prices were during the inflation of the 1970s. Even more dramatically, equity prices rose at an astonishingly mild rate during the German hyperinflation (Bresciani-Turoni, 1937).

I propose to break down the q-theory into the product of two components: first, the ratio of used to new capital goods; and secondly, the ratio of equity prices to the value of used capital goods. Both ratios might be unstable. In addition, they need not move in tandem; however, notice that the numerator represents a more liquid investment than does the denominator for both ratios. Thus rising bearishness should increase both ratios.

Although aggregate investment may be closely associated with the q-ratio, replacement investment need not be. The same conditions that create high q-values also raise the relative price of used capital goods. Given this price ratio, firms may be reluctant to replace existing, highly valued capital goods. Thus policies that lead to a high q-ratio generally cause capital widening without much replacement investment.

Firms choose investments with a rapid payback. What could return its cost more quickly than a simple repair or gerryrigging a machine? Such investments typically provide a higher rate of return than replacing obsolete plant and equipment wholesale. Notice the irony here: the more that firms with a high liquidity preference are unwilling to commit themselves to long-lived capital investments, the longer-lived existing plant and equipment becomes. Thus the capital stock ages despite substantial investment.

Here this chapter becomes more interpretive. Historically US firms scrapped capital far more readily than their European counterparts. In the postwar period US firms seemed to have become reluctant to scrap plant and equipment. The US capital stock apparently aged substantially during much of the postwar period, especially in the late 1960s and throughout the 1970s. As the US capital stock deteriorated, US industry became less and less able to compete in world markets.

By the time that firms came to recognize that pressure from imported competition threatened scrapping and even complete plant closures, modernization was long overdue. In contrast, Japanese firms seem to be more willing to replace whole factories because of their lower target payback period.

Consider this situation in terms of the ratio of the price of used to new capital goods. Some combination of uncertainty, expansionary conditions, lack of competition and stable relative prices, as well as a high expected rate of return, can maintain a high ratio. One factor seems to far outweigh all others, namely, the need to modernize because of strong wage demands.

I interpret the historical tendency towards rapid replacement of capital in the USA largely as the result of high wage pressures. From 1939 to 1947 average hourly wages of industrial workers increased by 95 per cent, compared to only 39 per cent for the prices of machine tools; from 1965 to 1977 the average prices of metalworking tools rose by almost exactly the same amount as wages. During the latter part of that period the ratio became even more unfavourable to labour. Between 1971 and 1978 wages increased 72 per cent, and prices of machine tools 85 per cent. In fact each year after 1975 the index of capital costs rose faster than the index of unit labour costs.

Although aggregate wages have risen somewhat, hourly wages have barely kept up with inflation. In fact correcting for inflation, overtime and the changing relative size of different industries, hourly compensation in manufacturing has fallen by more than 6.4 per cent since 1972. As the pressures of high labour costs subsided, scrapping obsolete plant and equipment became less profitable.

For example, from 1950 to 1965 business expanded the capital stock by only two percentage points more than the growth in total hours of labour. After 1965, the capital stock growth rate exceeded the rate of growth in hours by only 1 per cent. Because low wages offer especially strong benefits to those who employ low-wage workers most intensively, this sort of firm has accounted for a high percentage of the recent new jobs created in the USA, especially in service industries that are immune from foreign competition. In conclusion, I propose that Keynes had laid the groundwork for an appropriate analysis of the contemporary conditions just described.

References

Bresciani-Turoni, C. (1937), *The Economics of Inflation: A Study of Currency Depreciation in Post-War Germany*, tr. by Millicent E. Sayers, London: Allen and Unwin.

Hicks, J.R. (1935). 'A suggestion for simplifying the theory of money.' *Economica* No. 5, 5 February, pp 1–19.

Kahn, R. (1973), 'The price level of investment goods, 5 April 1931, a note to Keynes', in D.E. Moggridge (ed.) *The Collected Writings of John Maynard Keynes. Vol, XIII, The General Theory and After: A Supplement, Part I: Preparation*, London: Macmillan, 203–206.

Kahn R.F. (1978), 'Some aspects of the development of Keynes's thought', *Journal of Economic Literature*, 16(2), June, 545–560.

Keynes, J.M. (1936), *The General Theory of Employment, Interest and Money*, New York: Macmillan.

Keynes, J.M. (1971), *A Treatise on Money* (1930), Vols V and VI, *The Collected Writings of John Maynard Keynes*, London: Macmillan.

Keynes, J.M. (1973), *The Collected Writings of John Maynard Keynes: Vol. XIII: The General Theory and After: A Supplement, Part I: Preparation* London: Macmillan.

Sraffa, P. (1973), 'Note, 9 May 1931', in D.E. Moggridge (ed.), *The Collected Writings of John Maynard Keynes. Vol. XIII, The General Theory and After: A Supplement, Part I: Preparation*, London: Macmillan, 207–209.

Terborgh, G. (1949), *Dynamic Equipment Policy*, New York: McGraw-Hill.

6 Keynesian microeconomics and the microeconomics of Keynes in public sector investment decisions

Alan Abouchar

Introduction

Most discussion about the contributions of Keynes concentrates on his macroeconomics. When commentators do concern themselves with his microeconomics, it is typically in terms of psychological proclivities and propensities of entrepreneurs and consumers. But there is another extremely important applied microeconomics area which has been influenced by the legacy of Keynes. This is the area of public sector project decision-making, and here the influence has been unfortunate due to widespread confusion and self-serving interpretation of what Keynes said. However, I am convinced that Keynes would have had too much good sense to subscribe to these erroneous views and, moreover, did have insight into the theory of price formation which, were it implemented, would spare us many of the excesses that public sector investment policy and project decisions are heir to. I am convinced, in short, that it *is* worth distinguishing between the microeconomics of Keynes and Keynesian microeconomics.

This perversion of the Keynesian idea has its roots primarily in the divorce or, at least, the increasing separation between microeconomics and macroeconomics and in the intensifying specialization which is the bane of our profession. In the macro branch people concern themselves with macro magnitudes and variables, and in the public finance branch (expenditure department) with some aspects of microeconomic optimization, while the revenue department is more concerned with issues of income distribution. Meanwhile, pursuing the conventional microeconomics of the firm and consumer behaviour leads all too often to fanciful criteria for project selection on both the cost and the benefit sides, the usual result being to exaggerate the benefits of a project with consequent higher (but quite unjustified) public expenditure which is thought to be quite in harmony with what is presumed to be the key Keynesian principle, that more rather than less public sector spending is desirable in and of itself.

Although we will be concerned principally with the way in which the misinterpretation of Keynes's microeconomics affects public sector investment decisions, it will also be apparent that it has influence on the analysis of private sector response to public sector influences. Three problems may be examined: (1) the tendency to identify public expenditures (and revenue, which is potential expenditure) with macroeconomic stimuli exclusively rather than as *prices* (in part) for activities which are provided by the public sector; (2) the modern treatment of costs in microeconomic theory, which neglects or pays only short shrift to interest as a cost (a treatment which logically precludes *any* macroeconomic policy which may seek to influence businessmen through interest rate policy), and also omits one very important cost component from its definition of either marginal cost or variable cost; and (3) the tendency to regard labour input as employment creation. In all areas closer attention to Keynesian principles as expounded in the *General Theory* would lead to greater efficiency in resource use.

Public sector expenditure as cyclical policy
The great concern with macroeconomic models has created a tendency to think about public expenditures as an homogeneous mass, analysing impacts on national income and/or employment. This hides the pricing aspect that *should*, but all too often *does not*, characterize a large part of public sector revenue. This may be most typical in the highway sector, where there has been little attempt in the past to introduce rational highway user charges.

Now it should be possible – and it would be desirable – to think about efficient resource allocation for activities which are performed in the public sector in terms similar to those used to think about efficiency of activities performed privately, that is, think of them in terms other than labels such as 'public goods', since this expression has come to be rather generally and indiscriminately applied to public expenditures of whatever kind, rather than those activities having certain special characteristics only, and tracing its lineage as it does to some of the giants of our profession, has acquired a kind of sanctity which only the young or the reckless would dare to impugn. The fact is that the public sector *may* engage in activities today for reasons as varied as historical accident or administrative convenience combined with lower cost (e.g. provision of fire fighting whose relatively inexpensive cost may be lumped together with other payments, including income distribution transfers such as school taxes, and collected through property taxes), and we should not assume that the mere performance of an activity in the public sector obviates the propriety of recovering from consumers of the service the total cost of providing it.

A refreshing characteristic of the first year or two of the Reagan administration was the attempt to price a wide range of public sector activities closer to cost than has been presumed to be appropriate in the last few decades. We might observe that such attempts need not conflict in any way with income distribution goals or, indeed, with stabilization goals, to use Musgrave's three-way classification for economic public activities. But politicians, as well, unfortunately, as their economic advisers, frequently neglect this obvious fact. One recent manifestation of this was the 'nickel tax' for motor vehicle fuels in the USA which was imposed in late 1982 in response to the tidal federal deficits – imposed strictly as a revenue-raising and deficit-reducing measure. Now it is the nature of highway technology that highway damage is imposed in proportion to the fourth power of the axle weight, as was discovered at Ottawa, Illinois (in a test whose significance for Canada extends beyond the mere coincidence of place-name), and reported on in AASHO (1962). The consequences of this relationship, when allowing for tandem axles under the trailer, are that a standard 80,000-lb rig does 10,000 times as much damage as a mid-sized car! Therefore, this 5 cent tax per gallon represents a most inefficient policy since the price to use the highway not only is not brought *closer* to cost, but actually moves *further* away from cost, encouraging as it does, even more intensive use of heavy vehicles to reap their *private* scale economies at exponentially greater imposed social costs. Moreover, as long as user charges are not rationalized, deficits accruing on account of maintenance needs will rise in the future, although there may be some short-term gains in federal revenue.

One need not go south of the border to observe this phenomenon. The failure to consider money flows as prices paid for services is widespread in Canada as well. One may recall a rhetorical question of the Bovey Commission on government finance: 'Do you want more higher education or fewer potholes?' But anyone concerned with optimal resource use must ask why the revenue flows arising in fuel taxes should be construed as in any way comparable to expenditures on education, which is presumably an income-distribution activity. (School access-related roads, of course, should also be construed as an income-distribution activity, at least in part.)

The modern theory of public finance often takes pride in eschewing the earmarking of taxes. But to proceed thus in much of the transport sector is to forget that these revenues, in part, represent payment for road use. (Not entirely, of course, it continues to be appropriate to levy sales taxes comparable to those on other consumer goods.) Recognizing this would prompt us to make the obvious next step, which is to ask the question whether the prices now being charged through the taxes on fuels do form part of an optimal pricing structure, which would have to rely on other instruments as well, including licence fees, tolls and 'third structure taxes' (such as payments for monthly reported AASHO-weighted mileage produced) and this would, in turn, force us to confront the challenge of defining a meaningful concept of cost and determining cost relationships.

The whole energy sector provides other current Canadian examples of confounding prices and taxes. Thus, when Ottawa contemplated the removal of federal royalties on crude extraction, the imposition of which certainly made good sense from a resource-scarcity and rent point of view when first imposed, speculation arose about the probable future evolution of fuel taxes imposed at the retail level, again behaving as though all taxes and prices (including rents) in this sector were of the same essence!

I have spoken of the need for correct cost-based pricing in transportation, a notion sure to be greeted with scepticism by those nurtured on public goods, high collection costs, externality arguments, decreasing cost assumptions, second-best theory, Ramsey pricing, sunk costs and other apologies for evading the challenge of relating prices – and through them the selection of investments – to costs in this important sector. This deficiency is particularly striking where heavy trucks are concerned. Thus, according to a recent survey of thirteen individual state pricing policies, the price–cost ratio for large combination rigs varied from 0.44 (Georgia) to 0.97 (Maine) with a median ratio of 0.58 (summarized in Sinha *et al.*, 1984, p. 46). Since the individual studies employed different definitions of cost and price, they are not directly comparable, but the overall impression can hardly be challenged. On the basis of my own work, I believe that, if anything, these estimates paint too bright a picture, partly, but not only, because many of them classify as automobile highway user charges the fuel taxes which are generated within cities, which really have nothing to do with the inter-city network. This treatment then reduces the portion of the system common costs that must be laid at the door of the heavy vehicle users.

Attuned as we are to equating marginals, we should of course ask what is the basis for making such comparisons. What cost concept is being employed here? And what is marginal cost? The notion of short- or long-run marginal cost of highway transportation is decidedly difficult to cope with even at this stage of abstraction, and if it is difficult to formulate, it must be even more difficult to measure. But surely any sensible concept must include the consumption caused by individual vehicles of at least that part of the fixed capital stock which is to be replaced when worn, which is to say, most of the road network in areas which are not dying. Interestingly, however, economists commenting on transportation – the highway sector especially – appear to have concentrated exclusively on congestion cost when attempting to define marginal cost, disregarding entirely the initial construction and maintenance costs. I suggest that a much more meaningful concept would consist of three elements: the damage imposed on the network, including the network to be built in future; the once-for-all costs of enlarging it in future, what I have called 'isochronic' (i.e. those elements, such as grade reduction or tunnel blasting, which will not wear out either with time or use per unit time); and annual common costs, such as slope tending or snow removal, discriminatorily allocated and recovered, roughly according to something like Ramsey pricing.

Are we getting too deeply immersed in microeconomics for a Conference like this? Let us look at Keynes's relevance for microeconomic cost theory and the compatibility of modern microeconomics with the Keynesian analytic context.

Microeconomic cost theory

To jog us back to the object of our celebration, let me start by quoting Keynes himself apropos of the modern cost analysis. In his appendix on user cost following chapter 6 of the *General Theory*, Keynes writes as follows:

> Now in the modern theory of value it has often been a usual practice to *equate short-period supply price* to the *marginal factor cost* alone. It is obvious, however, that this is only legitimate if *marginal user cost* is zero. (Keynes, 1936, p. 67; emphasis added)

Or to translate it into more recent terminology, while not breaking faith with the original:

> Now in the modern theory of value it has often been a usual practice to *define short-run marginal cost* as *incrementally engaged factor* alone, i.e. *new current expenditures*. It is obvious, however, that this is only legitimate if capital consumption with respect to output is zero.

The situation is like that today, only more so, with a great diversity of formulations of variable cost. This is evident in a wide range of statistical cost studies of railroad cost behaviour. The elements included under the variable cost rubric vary as widely as all expenditures beyond the initial acquisition of capital inputs (which would include fixed annual administration expenses but would exclude capital consumption) to the rate of change of total, fully distributed cost (i.e. evidently including capital assigned to the period as well as administrative and overhead items which are fixed for individual firms), with respect to output. Clearly it matters very much what approach is pursued in transportation networks or among regulatory agencies.

Incidentally, a greater appreciation of the benefits of studying history would serve us well in this regard. If modern economists were more inclined in this direction, the lessons to be learned from a tome such as Edwin Pratt's 1912 *History of Inland Transportation and Communication in England* would be that (1) people have long been aware that roads wear out with respect to various dimensions of use and tried to discover and price these relationships, and (2) the main reason for taking to heart Dupuit's (1952) advice about forgoing a toll-collection mechanism in certain cases was not that zero-pricing would avoid the heavy resource costs involved in implementing the collection, but rather that the turnpike system had succumbed to monopoly abuse over the decades, which is a totally different matter. Moreover, given that the bridge to which Dupuit paid greatest attention was a footbridge, it made perfectly good sense to have it paid for by the local community as a whole, rather than by individual users, since no pedestrian would impose more than a virtually infinitesimal cost on the bridge, obviating the need to put a collection mechanism in place to ensure that marginals would be equated. And a footbridge would not be part of an inter-city network which *would* have to be priced for carriages and would present problems of demand revelation for common costs and pricing over a wide geographic area.

Yet another parting of the ways between modern microeconomics and Keynes's legacy is the failure of the former to provide a framework within which to analyse the impact of one of Keynes's major contributions, the recognition of the central role played by the rate of interest. The fact is that interest is rarely introduced into the firm's cost structure in microeconomics textbooks, although it may constitute a very important cost component, whether on an initial borrowing or for day-to-day operations such as loans against current invoices. It would be interesting to speculate on the extent to which Keynes himself may have fostered a second-class status for interest through his analysis which, after integrating money together with real economic forces and flows into a total scheme, argued that the rate of interest was a powerless instrument for influencing business behaviour *at that time*. The amazing thing is that our micro textbooks can persist in their neglect of the interest rate after the North American experience of 1979–81! The third problem stimulated by neglect or misinterpretation of Keynes is the tendency to equate labour input and employment creation.

Labour input vs employment creation

The pricing policy that I have often advocated (in e.g. *Pricing Highways*) would recover from users all public sector costs involved in expanding, maintaining and operating the highway network and related services. It is recognized that imperfections might arise in payments by users both between and within traffic classes. But the result in the use of the existing capital resource, as well as the guidance to expansion and investment, would be much superior to present practices which rely heavily on empire-building and catering to special interest groups, often certified by inflated cost–benefit studies employing fanciful criteria, including measurement of consumer surplus trapezoids under putative demand curves without netting out forgone surplus under *replaced* demand curves, a practice that Dupuit (1952) himself warned against. Another speaker at this Conference suggested that a classic might be defined as a work that no one ever reads. As evidenced by people's failure to recognize this admonition of Dupuit's (p. 54), as well as his advocacy (p. 40) of positive pricing to cover an annual interest payment or maintenance cost (which by its nature is time variable and common rather than output variable owing to the special nature of his footbridge), Dupuit's contribution to the theory of marginal cost pricing would seem to qualify as a classic!

Many writers have advocated the use of national income or some related criterion for public sector project decisions, and the widespread use of national income in macroeconomic analysis has provided a spur to such microeconomic use. But let us recall for a moment what Keynes did and what he did not argue in the *General Theory*. He did not argue for pervasive public sector activity, and he did not advocate indiscriminate counting of bodies engaged in some activity to determine its value from the social point of view. Rather his great contribution was to integrate monetary theory into a meaningful overall economic analysis and show why monetary policy would have no impact in the peculiar conditions of the Great Depression of the 1930s and fiscal policy must instead be invoked. At its most extreme, even digging holes and refilling them would be helpful – this would induce wage payments and, thereby, consumer spending with its multiplier effect. However, it has been generally viewed as more appropriate to work within the national income framework since doing so enables us to commensurate bodies employed with other transactions in the economy, in the form of a single criterion expressed in terms of macroeconomic change rather than multiple objectives expressed in physical terms. In this case, to increase government-sponsored employment, even on digging holes, would increase government expenditures, and since the service involved is one which no one in his right mind would be prepared to pay for, the effect on national income would be to increase 'G' on the expenditure side of the accounts to the full extent of the government expenditure on hole-digging. Then, since besides providing a stimulus for the multiplier, it would improve income distribution by giving something to those who would have zero income otherwise, such an increase in national income was considered good, and national income seemed to work as a welfare measure.

But something happened on the way from the Central Statistics Office, which prepares the national income accounts, to Legislation Hall, where project and policy decisions are enacted, and too often those at the Project Planning Department become innocent or witting accomplices when they allow politicians to speak of the 'job creation' which would follow the undertaking of some project or other, and provide them pretty computerized coloured reports to buttress their claims. What they mean, at best, is that so many employees will be *engaged* in the task. But they too frequently forget to net out those who might have been engaged in something else anyway! This means that in situations which are already near full employment the labour input to a project should be regarded as a cost (with equally offsetting benefit) while in areas of labour surplus, whether due to cyclical or secular factors, the labour expense may appropriately be adjudged a benefit.

The ultimate irony and inconsistency occurs when a proposal treats the engagement of labour on the investment as a gain and, in discounting net benefit streams, treats the maintenance labour as a cost. In road projects this prejudices the selection in favour of capital-intensive projects, with a high maintenance equipment import component and relatively little domestic labour. (This conclusion is correct wherever the road expenses involved in 'G' are not recovered from users, which is to say, most places.) However, instead of going to the root of the problem, which is bad bookkeeping, to keep better track of what resources are being used – and where – too many economists' energies are directed instead to more esoteric pursuits such as calculation of optimal shadow prices for labour and foreign exchange. These latter problems are difficult enough, but they could be reduced by thinking more clearly in the first place: there would be less argument about the acceptability of the market wage as correct statement of the value of a labour input if the worker's employment were treated in such labour-surplus areas as a benefit rather than a cost.

Conclusion

In this chapter we have examined the frequently neglected micro-economic aspect of the impact of the macroeconomic analysis that was conditioned and given impetus by Keynes. The impact has generally been perverse, but this *in spite of* rather than *because of* the underlying analysis of the *General Theory*. It may be traced to the distortion – and neglect – by politicians, statesmen and, sorrowfully, many economists as well, of the Keynesian ideas which remain essentially correct: that in cyclical or secular unemployment, fiscal policy may be required to raise employment, but that at the same time capital consumption must be regarded as true incremental cost, a recognition which would have special relevance to many of the activities performed for reasons other than stabilization in the public sector.

References

AASH(T)O (American Association of State Highway (and Transportation) Officials) (1962), *The AASHO Road Test, Proceedings of a Conference Held May 16–18, 1962, St Louis, Mo.*, Washington, DC: National Academy of Sciences/National Research Council.

Abouchar, A. (1984), *Project Decision Making in the Public Sector*, Lexington, Mass.: Heath-Lexington.

Abouchar, A. (1985), *Pricing Highways*, White Paper for US Department of Transportation.

Dupuit, J. (1952), 'On the measurement of the utility of public works', *International Economic Papers*; originally published in *Annales des Ponts et Chaussées*, 1844.

Keynes, J.M. (1936), *The General Theory of Employment, Interest, and Money*, New York: Harcourt, Brace.

Pratt, E.A. (1912), *A History of Inland Transportation and Communication in England*, London: Kegan Paul, Trench, Trubner.

Sinha, K.C. and associates (1984), *Indiana Highway Cost Allocation Study: Final Report*, Purdue University School of Civil Engineering.

PART III

ASPECTS OF THE
LABOUR MARKET

7   Wage flexibility and employment

Peter Howitt[1]

Introduction

One of the central messages of Keynes's *General Theory* was that unemployment was not attributable to wage inflexibility. Although he believed that wages were not in fact very flexible, he also argued that if they were more flexible, matters would be even worse. Greater wage flexibility would be detrimental to social justice, would lead to greater labour unrest and would destabilize the value of money. More to the point, it would probably also make unemployment even worse because wage reductions would cause the level of aggregate demand to fall.

Keynes pointed to several channels through which a wage reduction might reduce aggregate demand. The one he seemed to rely on most was an expectation effect: 'If . . . the reduction leads to the expectation, or even to the serious possibility, of a further wage-reduction in prospect . . . it will diminish the marginal efficiency of capital and will lead to the postponement both of investment and of consumption' (Keynes, 1936, p. 263). He pointed out that if wages were suddenly to fall so low that they were believed to have 'touched bottom', then the expectation of wage inflation would stimulate aggregate demand. But he argued that this was 'scarcely practical', and that:

> it would be much better that wages should be rigidly fixed and deemed incapable of material changes, than that depressions should be accompanied by a gradual downward tendency of money-wages, a further moderate wage reduction being expected to signalize each increase of, say, 1 per cent in the amount of unemployment. (*ibid.*, p. 265)

Another channel was the distribution effect of a wage reduction, between wage-earners and 'other factors entering into marginal prime cost whose remuneration has not been reduced' (*ibid.*, p. 262). This effect, he argued, would probably diminish the propensity to consume. Still another channel was the increase in the real burden of nominal debts. This would transfer income 'from entrepreneurs to rentiers' (Keynes's archetypal debtors and creditors), which he believed was more likely to lower than to raise the propensity to consume. It would also depress entrepreneurial confidence, with adverse effects on investment. And if the reduction was large enough, it would even lead many entrepreneurs to the point of insolvency, 'with severely adverse effects on investment' (*ibid.*, p. 264).

There are two separate propositions involved in Keynes's argument, although he was not careful to distinguish between them. The first is that the impact effect of a given wage reduction is to reduce employment. The second is that an increase in the degree of flexibility of wages will make employment more variable – that depressions will be deepened or prolonged by the expectation that they will cause wage deflation. The distinction between these two propositions corresponds to the now familiar rational expectations distinction between the effects of a one-time policy action and the effects of a policy regime.

Despite the enormous influence that Keynes has had (and continues to have) on the development of macroeconomics, his ideas concerning wage flexibility have never 'caught on'. Modern Keynesian economics has been built on the assumption of sticky wages (and possibly prices). Most Keynesian models would exhibit no involuntary unemployment without this assumption. Several authors have noted that the impact effect of wage reductions might be perverse, but that possibility has played no part in the development of mainstream Keynesian models. Likewise, the idea that the variability of output is positively related to the degree of flexibility of wages seems hardly to have been examined in recent years.[2] Instead it is commonplace to assert that wage and employment variability are substitutes.

The purpose of this chapter is to re-examine Keynes's two propositions using a simple rational expectations macro model. The assumption of rational expectations is useful for distinguishing clearly between Keynes's two propositions. It is also appropriate for analysing the second proposition, since it deals not with a once-over unique historical event, but with a recurrent systematic pattern of wage behaviour that people can reasonably be supposed to anticipate.

The model distinguishes between two sorts of wage flexibility: sensitivity to employment, and speed of adjustment. Sensitivity is represented by the effect of a given increase in employment on a target wage. The change in the money wage each period is a fraction of the gap that existed last period between the target wage and the actual wage. That fraction represents the speed of adjustment.

The model also includes two kinds of random shock that affect employment: shocks to aggregate demand, and wage shocks. Demand shocks are included for obvious reasons; wage shocks are included in order to make the experiment of a once-over reduction in wages logically admissible in a rational expectations model.[3]

Keynes's second proposition also has a temporal dimension to it that his analysis does not address. Specifically, if we interpret the variability of employment as the variance of a rational forecast of employment, it matters how far ahead that forecast is made. In the following analysis, I consider two forecast horizons: one period and infinity. Thus I consider the effects of varying wage flexibility on both the one-period-ahead conditional variance of employment and on the unconditional stationary variance of employment.

This re-examination confirms that Keynes's first proposition is correct under the conditions that he postulated – a large real-debt effect or a large real-wage effect. It also tends to confirm the short-run version of his second proposition. Specifically the one-period-ahead variance of employment is an increasing function of the sensitivity of wages to employment; it is also an increasing function of the speed of adjustment of wages if either demand shocks account for a large enough fraction of the variability of output or Keynes's first proposition is invalid.

The main reason for the confirmation of Keynes's second proposition is the expectation effect that he stressed in his own analysis. Through this effect wage adjustment generates a multiplier process. An increase in aggregate demand causes a rise in employment, and hence a rise in this period's target wage. This will cause a rise in wages next period. The anticipation of this rise in wages induces a secondary rise in aggregate demand this period. The greater the sensitivity of wages to employment, or the greater the speed of adjustment, the greater is the anticipated rise in wages and hence the greater the multiplier effect.

The analysis is less clear-cut concerning the long-run version of Keynes's second proposition, because raising the flexibility of wages can cause shocks to be dampened more quickly, which tends to reduce the stationary variance of employment. However, the model does imply that an increased sensitivity of wages will raise the stationary variance of employment in the case where Keynes's first proposition is correct. It also implies that an increase in wage flexibility by either interpretation will raise the stationary variance in the special case where the only channel through which wages affect employment is the expectation effect.

The results depend heavily on the assumption that the effect on wages of an increase in employment works with a one-period delay. Without this delay, the multiplier process resulting from Keynes's expectation effect would not arise, because an increase in demand would have an immediate effect on wages, which would start to go away in the following period. Thus it would give rise to the expectation of deflation – not inflation – an expectation that would dampen the impact on employment rather than amplify it. The sensitivity of the main result of the paper to this timing assumption illustrates the importance of the considerations stressed by Keynes. If wages were to 'touch bottom' in response to a fall in demand, the expectation of the subsequent rise would stabilize employment. The model presented below rules out such a response by assumption. This is consistent with Keynes's view that the case is 'scarcely practical', but it is none the less an arbitrary timing assumption in the context of the formal model.

The model

The model employs the following notation:

n_t = log of employment;
p_t = log of price level;
w_t = log of money wage rate;
ε_{dt} = demand shock;
ε_{wt} = wage shock.

The shocks are independent white-noise processes with variances σ_d^2 and σ_w^2 respectively. The variables are related by the following three equations:

$$n_t = e(E_t p_{t+1} - p_t) + dp_t + r(w_t - p_t) + \varepsilon_{dt} \tag{1}$$
$$w_t = a(fn_{t-1} + p_{t-1}) + (1 - a)w_{t-1} + \varepsilon_{wt} \tag{2}$$
$$p_t = mw_t \tag{3}$$

All constants are suppressed, and E_t denotes the rational expectation conditional on an information set I_t that includes all parameters and current dated variables.

Equation (1) can be derived as the reduced form of an IS/LM system in which the distribution of wealth between debtors and creditors, and the distribution of income between workers and others are included as arguments in the IS curve, and where Mundell's (1963) analysis of real and nominal interest rates is included.

The parameter e in equation (1) represents Keynes's expectation effect, and is positive. A rise in expected inflation increases demand and hence employment. The parameter d is the effect on employment of an increase in demand caused by a rise in the price level. If Keynes's real-debt effect is large enough, d will be positive; but if the Keynes or Pigou effect is large enough, it will be negative. The parameter r embodies the income distribution effect of a change in real wages, and is positive.

Equation (2) represents the assumed outcome of the wage bargain. It states that wages adjust with a lag to a target wage. The target wage adjusts one-for-one to changes in the cost of living. The speed of adjustment is measured by the parameter, a, which lies between 0 and 1. The sensitivity of wages to employment is measured by the parameter, f, which is positive.

Equation (3) is a log-linear approximation to a simple mark-up of price over a weighted average of short- and long-run cost, under an assumption of constant returns. Thus the parameter, m, lies between 0 and 1.

Employment and wages
It is straightforward to verify that the unique solution to equations (1)–(3) is given by the two equations:

$$w_t = \lambda w_{t-1} + (af/(1 - afme))\varepsilon_{d,t-1} + \varepsilon_{wt} \tag{4}$$
$$n_t = \phi w_t + (1/(1 - afme))\varepsilon_{dt} \tag{5}$$

where:

$$\lambda \equiv \{af[(d - e)m + r(1 - m)] + am + 1 - a\}/(1 - afme) \tag{6}$$
$$\phi \equiv [(d - ae(1 - m))m + r(1 - m)]/(1 - afme) \tag{7}$$

Therefore, the impact effect on employment of a demand shock is:

$$\partial n_t/\partial \varepsilon_{dt} = 1/(1 - afme) \tag{8}$$

Assume that:

$$afme < 1 \tag{9}$$

Then equation (8) can be interpreted as a multiplier formula. When a demand shock causes a one-unit direct effect on employment, this causes the target wage to rise by f, causing the rational expectation that wages next period will rise by af, and that prices will therefore rise by afm. This expectation has a secondary effect of making employment this period rise by afme through the expectation effect, causing another increase in the target wage, and so forth. The limit of this process is equation (8). The greater is the sensitivity of wages f or the speed of adjustment a, the larger is this multiplier.

Next, note that the impact effect on employment of an exogenous change in wages is:

$$\partial n_t/\partial \varepsilon_{wt} = \phi \tag{10}$$

Keynes's first proposition is that ϕ is positive. It follows from equations (7) and (9) that this will be the case whenever the real-debt effect d and/or the real-wage effect r are positive and large enough relative to the expectation effect, e, and/or the speed of adjustment, a.

The expectation effect, e, works against Keynes's first proposition because in this model an exogenous increase in wages always reduces the rate at which wages are expected to rise next period. Thus a negative ε_{wt} works like the case discussed by Keynes of wages being thought to have 'touched bottom'.

To analyse Keynes's second proposition consider the one-period-ahead conditional variance:

$$\text{var}(n_t|I_{t-1}) = (1/(1 - \text{afme}))^2 \, \sigma_d^2 + \phi^2 \sigma_w^2 \tag{11}$$

Note that an increase in either the sensitivity, f, or the speed of adjustment, a, of wages will increase the part of this conditional variance attributable to demand shocks $(1/(1 - \text{afme})^2)\sigma_d^2$ by increasing the size of the expectation multiplier. By equation (7) an increase in sensitivity will also increase the part attributable to wage shocks because the coefficient ϕ can be expressed as the product of a direct effect, $(d - ae(1 - m))m + r(1 - m)$, and the expectation multiplier, and an increase in f increases the multiplier. An increase in the speed of adjustment, a, has an ambiguous effect on the conditional variance attributable to wage shocks because it reduces the direct effect but increases the multiplier. Note, however, that under 'classical' conditions, i.e. assuming that $\phi < 0$, this effect $(\partial\phi^2/\partial a)$ is unambiguously positive.

Thus the short-run version of Keynes's second proposition is borne out by the model, with one exception. Specifically the proposition is invalid only if demand shocks account for a small enough proportion of the variability of output, flexibility is interpreted as speed of adjustment and Keynes's first proposition $(\phi > 0)$ is valid.

The model is less clear-cut concerning the long-run version of Keynes's second proposition. This is because an increase in the speed of adjustment, a, while it may increase the impact effect on employment of a demand or wage shock, may increase the speed with which that effect is dampened by the system. The more rapid dampening tends to offset the larger impact with an ambiguous overall effect on the unconditional stationary variance of employment. The effect of an increase in sensitivity f is similarly ambiguous.

More specifically, the dampening factor of the system is the eigenvalue λ given by equation (6); the dynamic response of employment to a wage or demand shock is:

$$\partial n_{t+i}/\partial \varepsilon_{wt} = \phi\lambda^i; \qquad\qquad i = 0, 1, \ldots$$
$$\partial n_t/\partial \varepsilon_{dt} = 1/(1 - \text{afme})$$
$$\partial n_{t+i}/\partial \varepsilon_{dt} = \lambda^{i-1}\text{af}\phi/(1 - \text{afme}) \qquad i = 1, 2, \ldots$$

Assume that the system is stable:

$$\lambda^2 < 1$$

Then the unconditional variance of employment is:

$$\text{var}(n_t) = (1 + a^2 f^2 \phi^2/(1 - \lambda^2))(1/(1 - \text{afme}))^2 \sigma_d^2 \\ + (\phi^2/(1 - \lambda^2))\sigma_w^2 \tag{12}$$

which could be increasing or decreasing in a or f because λ^2 could be increasing or decreasing in a or f.

There is, however, one important case in which the unconditional variance (12) is increased by an increase in sensitivity f. This is the case in which Keynes's first proposition is valid; i.e. where $\phi > 0$. Under this assumption the dampening factor λ is positive because from equations (6) and (7):

$$\lambda = \text{af}\phi + \text{am} + 1 - a \tag{13}$$

Since $\phi > 0$, it follows from equation (7) that $\partial\phi/\partial f > 0$; it follows from this and equation (13) that $\partial\lambda/\partial f > 0$. Therefore, equation (12) implies that $\text{var}(n_t)$ is increasing in f.

The economic interpretation of this result is as follows. If wage increases raise employment ($\phi > 0$), then the employment effect of a wage shock will remain positive into the future because high employment this period will raise wages next period, which will feed back positively on employment next period. An increase in sensitivity f makes the future employment effect stronger by raising the effect on next period's wage. Likewise, the employment effect of a demand shock will remain positive, to an extent that varies positively with f because the induced high wages next period will keep employment high. Thus, in this case, raising the sensitivity of wages to employment will not only raise the impact effect on employment of either shock, but will also reduce the speed with which that effect is dampened.

Finally, there is a special case in which the unconditional variance of employment is an increasing function of the degree of wage flexibility under either interpretation of flexibility. That is the case in which the real-debt effect just cancels the Pigou and Keynes effects, and the real-wage effect is absent; that is, d = r = 0. To show this, according to equation (12), it suffices to show that the expression $\phi^2/(1 - \lambda^2)$ is increasing in a and f. In this case, the expression equals $(\text{mae}(1 - m))^2/ [(1 - \text{afme})^2 - (1 - \text{afme} - a(1 - m))^2] = m^2 ae^2(1 - m)/[2(1 - \text{afme}) - a(1 - m)]$, which is strictly positive, and increasing in a and f as required.

Notes

1. David Laidler provided helpful comments on an early draft that was presented to the Eastern Economics Association meetings in Philadelphia in April 1986. Except for minor changes, this chapter is identical to the one appearing in the 1986 Proceedings of the EEA.
2. Before the *General Theory*, Keynes's first proposition was a central aspect of Fisher's (1933) theory of depressions. Fisher's analysis has recently been revived by Tobin (1980). Keynes's first proposition was also invoked by Patinkin (1951, p. 271–7), who emphasized the possibly perverse effects of wage/price reductions working through expectations, and through increased bankruptcy induced by greater real debt. None of these authors, however, articulated Keynes's second proposition. In particular, the idea stressed by Patinkin, and analysed more formally by Tobin (1975), that a full employment equilibrium might be dynamically unstable does not imply that greater wage flexibility would increase the likelihood of dynamic instability. In fact it would decrease that likelihood in Tobin's model.
   More recently, deLong and Summers (1986) have presented an analysis of Keynes's second proposition. Their paper, which was cast in terms of Taylor's (1980) overlapping-wage model does not include the possibility of Keynes's first proposition because it excludes the real-debt effect and the real-wage effect. It deals exclusively with the unconditional stationary variance of output, and it employs numerical simulations rather than the theoretical demonstrations of the present chapter. Caskey and Fazzari (1985) develop a model with a real-debt effect. They carry out simulations to show results like those of deLong and Summers. They also show analytically that (a) the immediate output loss following a monetary contraction, and (b) the likelihood of asymptotic instability, are both increased by greater wage flexibility.
3. Shocks to the price equation could be added with little effect on the main results. The presence of the expected inflation term in equation (1) does not yield indeterminacy because the lagged adjustment of wages and the rigid link between wages and prices prevent expectations formed at t from having any effect on w_t or p_t, and hence preclude any bubble-paths, stable or otherwise. To verify that equations (4) and (5) do indeed constitute a unique solution it suffices to derive them from equations (1)–(3). To do this use equation (3) to eliminate p_t, p_{t-1} and $E_t p_{t+1}$ from equations (1) and (2). Use the modified equation (2) to derive: $E_{t-1} w_t = w_t - \varepsilon_{wt}$. Use this to eliminate $E_{t-1} w_t$ from the back-dated version of the modified equation (1), and use the resulting equation to eliminate n_{t-1} from the modified equation (2), thus yielding equation (4). Thus use equation (4) to eliminate $E_t w_{t+1}$ from the modified equation (1), yielding equation (5).

References

Caskey, J. and Fazzari, S. (1985), 'Monetary contractions with nominal debt commitments: is wage flexibility stabilizing?', unpublished paper, Washington University.

Fisher, I. (1933), 'The debt–deflation theory of Great Depressions', *Econometrica*, October, 337–357.

Keynes, J.M. (1936), *The General Theory of Employment, Interest, and Money*, London: Macmillan.

deLong, J.B. and Summers, L.H. (1986), 'Is increased price flexibility stabilizing?', unpublished paper, Harvard University.

Mundell, R. (1963), 'Inflation and real interest', *Journal of Political Economy*, June, 280–283.

Patinkin, D. (1951), 'Price flexibility and full employment', in F.A. Lutz and L.W. Mints (eds), *Readings in Monetary Theory*. Homewood, Ill: Irwin, pp. 252–83.

Taylor, J.B. (1980), 'Aggregate dynamics and staggered contracts', *Journal of Political Economy*, February, 1–23.

Tobin, J. (1975), 'Keynesian models of recession and depression', *American Economic Review Proceedings*, May, 195–202.

Tobin, J. (1980), *Asset Accumulation and Economic Activity*, Chicago: University of Chicago Press.

8 The aggregate supply function and the share economy: some early drafts of the *General Theory*

A. Asimakopulos[1]

Introduction

Keynes's General Theory[2] has two main strands. It explains why (1) given the level of investment and money wage rates, an economy in any short period can be in stable equilibrium (a position of rest) at less than full employment, and (2) it points to investment as the factor that makes output and employment 'so liable to fluctuation' since it is so much 'influenced by our views of the future about which we know so little' (Keynes, 1937, p. 121). In order to arrive at the first proposition, Keynes developed aggregate demand and supply functions or curves, whose intersection determines the short-period equilibrium position for the economy, a position that could also be marked by the existence of involuntary unemployment. An examination of the early drafts of the *General Theory* shows the difficulty Keynes experienced in trying to develop these aggregate functions. He was not totally successful in this endeavour since the definition of the aggregate demand function in the *General Theory* is inconsistent with the micro foundations of his theory.

The early drafts also show that Keynes's attempt to explain why equilibrium would be possible with involuntary unemployment, that is, without the satisfaction of what he termed the 'second postulate of classical theory', emphasized the nature of the economy in the world around him as opposed to that assumed by classical theory. One of the terms he used to describe the economy implicitly assumed by the classical theory is a 'co-operative economy', and many of its features have reappeared in Weitzman's (1984) 'share economy'. By contrast, Keynes believed that the world around him could be more accurately described by the term 'entrepreneur economy'. Keynes's policy proposals were aimed at making an entrepreneur economy function more satisfactorily, rather than changing the basic nature of the economy, a task of a different order of magnitude.

The transition from the *Treatise* to the *General Theory*

In his *Treatise on Money*, Keynes was, as he stated in a lengthy response to comments on the *Treatise* made by Hawtrey,[3] 'primarily concerned with what governs *prices*' (Keynes, 1973a, p. 145; emphasis in original). This does not mean that output was assumed to be constant, since there is in the *Treatise* an examination of the credit cycle where changes in output are taking place, but that Keynes is 'not dealing with the complete set of causes which determine volume of output' (*ibid.*, pp. 145–6).[4] He realized that a consideration of the latter in the *Treatise*,

> would have led me an endlessly long journey into the theory of short-period supply and a long way from monetary theory ... As it is I have gone no further than that anticipated windfall loss or profit affects the output of entrepreneurs and their offers to the factors of production; but I have left on one side the question *how much* output is affected and also whether output can be affected in any other way. (*ibid.*, p. 146; emphasis in original)

Economic conditions in the world around him led Keynes to undertake this 'long journey' that eventually led to the *General Theory*.

Keynes realized that a substantial revision of standard theory – which he called 'classical' theory – was required in order to explain the persistence of high levels of unemployment: 'The existence of chronic unemployment is, in itself, a proof that the classical theory is insufficiently general in its postulates' (Keynes, 1979, p. 102). What he was looking for was a theory that explains the determination of aggregate output and employment as the result of the interplay of aggregate demand and supply functions, at levels that are consistent with the existence of unemployment. This search occupied several years. What is, in retrospect, a conceptually fairly straightforward extension of Marshallian industry short-period supply curves into an aggregate supply curve for the economy was complicated by Keynes's initial attempts to relate output to profit rather than to price.

Keynes's contribution to the Harris Foundation lecture series in Chicago, in June 1931, gives a hint of unemployment equilibrium due to a low level of profits related to a low level of investment (cf. Moggridge, 1973):

> Now there is a reason for expecting an equilibrium point of decline to be reached. A given deficiency of investment causes a given decline of profit. A given decline of profit causes a given decline of output. Unless there is a constantly increasing deficiency of investment, there is eventually reached, therefore, a sufficiently low level of output which represents a kind of spurious equilibrium. (Keynes, 1973a, pp. 355–6)

But this passage, as Patinkin (1982, pp. 24–5) has pointed out, is part of a discussion of cyclical movements that explain why a temporary trough will be reached rather than an explanation of continuing involuntary unemployment. An early version of his aggregate supply function was also presented at a seminar at these meetings in Keynes's discussion of a paper presented by H. Schultz and C. Goodrich. The setting for this function is 'the short period . . . when there is not time for obsolescence, and in which very little new plant is being set up . . . We might call the difference between their gross receipts and their prime costs their prime profit' (*ibid.*, p. 368). Keynes then continues:

> Now let us consider the totality of industries. You have over a short period something of the nature of a supply curve which tells you that for a given level of prime profit there will be a given level of output, that if you have a certain amount of prime profit, that would be sufficient to bring a certain quantity of potential output over the prime cost level. Every increase in aggregate prime profit will enable somebody to expand, because he will just get over the prime cost point, and every diminution will knock someone out, so if you have a supply curve which is valid over the short period only, so that for every quantity of aggregate prime profit you have a given quantity of output, you could only increase employment and output by increasing prime profit. (*loc. cit.*)

This early formulation of the aggregate supply function can be brought into equivalence with the final version in the *General Theory*. If in the latter it is implicitly assumed that short-period expectations of prices and proceeds are equal to their realized values, then with user costs being deducted each expectation of proceeds, given the short-period cost curves, corresponds to an expectation (realization) of prime profit. The concluding part of Keynes's 1931 statement can thus be rephrased: 'so that for every quantity of proceeds you have a given quantity of output, you could only increase employment and output by increasing proceeds.' But Keynes apparently did not, at this time, see this possible logical equivalence between price, proceeds and profit because, in a 12 May 1932 letter to Joan Robinson, he concluded that: 'even when one is dealing with separate industries, or separate groups of industries, my supply curve is one which relates output and profit, not one which relates output and price' (*ibid.*, p. 380).

Keynes gave a reason why the first version of his aggregate supply function related output to profit and not to price in a 1932 draft of the *General Theory*:

> In the foregoing we have assumed that the supply schedules of assets and consumables are dependent on the *prices* of the articles produced. This would be reasonable for a single industry where it can be assumed that the

price of the product does not sensibly react on the cost of production. But it is not reasonable for industry as a whole, in the case of which it is more nearly accurate to think of the supply schedule as relating output to *profit*. (*ibid.*, p. 403; emphasis in original)

The move to an aggregate supply function that relates output to aggregate supply price (proceeds) required that the latter be purged of changes in the prices of material inputs, and this was subsequently accomplished with the elaboration of the concept of user costs. The proceeds used to define the aggregate supply function were *net* of user costs.

In the 1933 drafts of the *General Theory* the independent variable in the aggregate supply function shifted from being the prospective prime profit or quasi-rent (see e.g. Keynes, 1979, pp. 65, 76) to being the prospective selling price (*ibid.*, p. 98). Each firm is seen as calculating 'the prospective selling price of its output and its variable cost in respect of output on various possible scales of production ... Output is then pushed to the point at which the prospective selling price no longer exceeds the marginal variable cost (*loc. cit.*). This formulation makes clear that output and employment decisions are made by individual entrepreneurs in perfectly competitive markets on the basis of their short-period expectations of prices and their marginal costs. Keynes affirmed this micro foundation for his aggregate supply function when he responded to a query by Robertson who had just read the first proof of the *General Theory* that it 'is simply the age-old supply function' (Keynes, 1973a, p. 513).

The aggregate supply function is thus not a function on which decisions are based. It is simply a conceptual device used to illustrate the effect on aggregate employment of different values for the entrepreneurial expectations of prices, when money wage rates are given, in a particular short-period situation. Its derivation from the industry supply curves requires that: (1) expected prices for individual products be transformed into expected receipts when the profit-maximizing output is produced (and sold); and (2) user costs be deducted from these receipts to arrive at 'proceeds', and that these proceeds be then combined according to some weighting scheme (see Asimakopulos, 1982). Thus, even though Keynes's final definition of this function, 'the aggregate supply price of the output of a given amount of employment is the expectation of proceeds which will just make it worth the while of the entrepreneurs to give that employment' (Keynes, 1936, p. 24), refers to the 'expectation of proceeds', the relevant expectations do not occur at this level of aggregation.

Keynes's 30 August 1936 letter to Harrod (Keynes, 1973b, p. 85) shows how important it was for his transition from the *Treatise* to the *General Theory* to develop the idea of a demand schedule for output as a whole. This schedule was based on a given level of investment and assumed that the marginal propensity to consume was less than one. It could be used to show, given the money wage rate, the proceeds (defined as in the aggregate supply function) obtained by entrepreneurs, as a function of the level of employment in the economy. Keynes, however, did not present it this way in the *General Theory*, but in an 'expectational' form that was not consistent with the micro foundations of his theory (see Parrinello, 1980; Casarosa, 1981; Asimakopulos, 1982). It is defined as 'let D be the proceeds which entrepreneurs expect to receive from the employment of N men' (Keynes, 1936, p. 25). The volume of employment is, however, not an independent variable for these competitive firms, it is a function of expected prices. What is in keeping with the assumptions of this theory is an *ex post* relationship for the economy between employment as the independent variable, and realized proceeds – a relationship that may reflect the desired relationship between consumption and income as well as the achievement of the planned level of investment. Keynes's carelessness in defining the aggregate demand function in the *General Theory* thus does not affect the conclusions of his theory since the *ex post* function can be used in conjunction with the aggregate supply function to determine a stable position of short-period equilibrium for the economy.[5]

The nature of the economy and the possibility of involuntary unemployment

The equilibrium level of employment determined by the intersection of the aggregate demand and supply functions may be insufficient to prevent the emergence of involuntary unemployment. This level of employment could be less than the labour workers would want to supply at the prevailing real-wage rates. This possibility is one of the features of Keynes's General Theory because only money wage, and not real-wage, rates are set in labour markets. The latter are determined, given the money wage rates, along with employment, by effective demand in product markets.[6] In early drafts of the *General Theory*, Keynes was trying to explain why involuntary unemployment could persist in the real world while such a phenomenon had no place in classical theory. It was in this context that he made a distinction between an 'entrepreneur economy', which corresponded to the world around him, and a 'cooperative economy' that produced results that accorded with classical theory.

In a draft chapter belonging to a December 1933 table of contents,

Keynes defined a co-operative economy as one in which 'the factors of production are rewarded by dividing up in agreed proportions that actual output of their cooperative efforts' (Keynes, 1979, p. 77). For this economy,

> there is no obstacle in the way of the employment of an additional unit of labour if this unit will add to the social product output expected to have an exchange value ... which is sufficient to balance the disutility of the additional employment. Thus the second postulate of the classical theory (i.e. the utility of the wage when a given volume of labour is employed is equal to the marginal disutility of that amount of unemployment) is satisfied (*ibid.*, p. 78)

In the perfectly competitive economies implicitly assumed by Keynes the size and number of cooperative production units would be determined by the net marginal product of labour and the marginal disutility of labour. If the marginal product of labour was greater than its marginal disutility, then more labour would be employed in existing production units and/or new units would be established until equality was obtained. In such an economy total output and employment, as well as the real-wage rate, would be determined in the labour market. There is thus no place in such an economy for independent aggregate demand and supply functions whose point of intersection indicates the level of effective demand, and which determines the equilibrium level of employment. All the employment, and thus output decisions, taken on the basis of conditions in the labour market are then automatically validated in product markets by the payment of output shares to the factors of production.

Keynes surmised that these special labour market conditions would also be fulfilled in an economy 'where the starting up of productive processes largely depends on a class of entrepreneurs who hire the factors of production for money and look to their recoupment from selling the output for money' (*ibid.*, p. 77), as long as total expenditure is sufficient to purchase, at expected prices, whatever total output is produced. He calls this second type of economy,' a *neutral entrepreneur economy*, or a *neutral economy* for short' (*ibid.*, p. 78; emphasis in original). Although it is possible to define an aggregate supply function for this 'neutral economy', there is no independent aggregate demand function since it coincides with the aggregate supply function throughout its length. Keynes wrote that classical theory 'as exemplified in the tradition from Ricardo to Marshall and Professor Pigou, appears to me to presume that the conditions for a Neutral Economy are substantially fulfilled in general' (*ibid.*, p. 79). There is no explicit reference to a neutral economy in the *General Theory*, but its consequences are attributed to classical theory: 'The classical theory assumes, in other words, that the aggregate demand price (or proceeds) always accommodates itself to the aggregate supply price' (Keynes, 1936, p. 26).

In contrast to the cooperative and neutral economies, there is what 'we will call a *money-wage* or *entrepreneur economy*' (1979, p. 78; emphasis in original). Here production and employment decisions depend on the expectations of money proceeds relative to variable costs, and 'it is in an entrepreneur economy that we actually live today' (*loc. cit.*). It was this economy that provided the setting for the General Theory, and it is here that there is scope for the independent aggregate demand and supply functions discussed in the preceding section, and for the existence of involuntary unemployment.

The share economy

Weitzman's recent book, *The Share Economy* (1984), which advocates a basic change in the method of wage payment in order to overcome stagflation, has important features of Keynes's cooperative economy. The effect of the policy recommendation is to have output and employment determined in labour markets. There is no reference to Keynes's comparison of the cooperative and money wage (entrepreneur) economies, but Weitzman is in effect making the same comparison and advocating a change in the basic nature of the economy from the latter to the former: 'The nature of the required wage reform is not terribly complicated. Essentially the issue is to turn a wage system ... into a share system' (*ibid.*, p. 4).

Weitzman departs from Keynes in assuming that firms sell in monopolistically competitive markets, but he mistakenly indentifies profit maximization for his giant firms with short-period profit maximization. In these markets firms set prices on the basis of their costs at some standard rate of utilization of capacity. The mark-up on unit costs reflects the relations with competing firms, the barriers to entry into these markets and the firms' assessments of the medium- to longer-term effects on profits and growth of different values for mark-ups. Weitzman's statement that giant firms (he uses General Motors as an example) set their 'output level at the point where marginal revenue equals marginal cost is a fundamental principle (it may even be *the* fundamental principle) of microeconomics' (*ibid.*, p. 18; emphasis in original) is false.[7] The outputs of these firms are determined by the market demands for their products at the prices (determined by the complex factors noted above) they set. The equality of marginal revenue and marginal cost is only consistent with profit maximization in its true meaning – i.e. profit maximization over time – in perfectly competitive markets where a firm cannot affect the market conditions it faces in the future by altering its current output and price. For Weitzman's giant firms, the statement that 'the major economic decisions of the firm are derived from the profit-maximizing rule marginal revenue equals marginal cost' (*ibid.*, p. 22) confuses maximization of profit in the short period, given demand and cost curves, with profit maximization *per se*. For these large firms that are price-makers, rather than price-takers, there are no supply curves – there are only price lines that show the prices at which they are prepared to sell, with actual sales (and output) determined by demand for their product.

Instead of the aggregate supply function that can be constructed for Keynes's competitive economy, there is in an oligopolistic economy what can be called an 'aggregate proceeds' curve that is built up from the price lines. It would show the total proceeds (net of user cost) that *would* result if the output, corresponding to the employment shown, could be sold at the prices set by the firms.[8] (The distribution of total employment amongst different firms could be conceptually handled as in Keynes's competitive case.) This aggregate proceeds function would be distinct from the aggregated demand function that shows, in its *ex post* form, the proceeds that *do* result from different levels of employment, given the assumptions about money wage rates and prices that underlie the corresponding aggregate proceeds curve. The intersection of these two curves, the point of effective demand, would show the short-period equilibrium level of employment. All of Keynes's conclusions about the possibility of involuntary unemployment hold in this case.

Weitzman advocates a radical change in the system of labour compensation that would transform a money wage economy into a share economy. This change would result in employment consequences similar to those in Keynes's cooperative economy. Output, employment and the real-wage rate would be determined in the labour market, and there would not be any independent aggregate demand and supply functions. In his proposed arrangement a firm's workers are paid some agreed share of the firm's total revenue. (This share is fixed over some time period.) Wage compensation per hour would be equal to the product of the firm's total revenue and the agreed wage share, divided by total hours of (some standard unit of) labour worked. With this scheme, it is in the firm's interest to increase employment as much as possible because, even though marginal revenue product may be declining, an increase in employment always makes a positive contribution to a firm's gross profits. The firm's revenue goes up by the marginal revenue product of labour, but its total wage payment only increases by the agreed wage share of this amount. Marginal revenue product thus always exceeds marginal factor cost, and 'there always exists a significant number of unfilled job vacancies' (*ibid.*, p. 4).[9] With this arrangement, there is no effective market constraint on a firm's output, there can only be a labour constraint. The level of employment is determined by the workers' willingness to work, given the conditions established by labour productivity and the agreed wage share.

Conclusion

Keynes's search for an explanation of the factors affecting the aggregate level of output and employment led to the development of aggregate demand and supply functions. They were used to demonstrate that an economy, whose essential features resembled those of the world around him, could get stuck in a position of involuntary unemployment. His policy recommendations took as given the basic nature of the economy around him and were concerned with measures that could shift the aggregate demand function in order to achieve a higher level of employment.

Weitzman's work, on the other hand, advocates a radical change in the nature of the economy in order to deal with the problem of unemployment, a problem that he feels cannot be handled, because of upward pressures on money wage rates, by Keynesian policies. His statement that 'the required wage reform is not terribly complicated' (Weitzman, 1984, p. 4) glosses over the fundamental restructuring of the economy being proposed. It is interesting to note that Weitzman's share economy has important similarities to Keynes's cooperative economy, whose sketch he presented in early drafts of the *General Theory*, in trying to explain why, unlike his entrepreneur economy, there is no involuntary unemployment in classical theory. In both the cooperative and share economies, total output and employment are determined in the labour markets, and there is no role for independent aggregate demand and supply functions.

Notes

1. This paper was written while I was on a sabbatical leave that was financed, in part, by the Social Sciences and Humanities Research Council.
2. The following convention is used in this paper: 'the General Theory, when not emphasized, refers to the theory developed in *The General Theory on Employment, Interest and Money*; and when it is emphasized, it refers to the book.
3. The date on Keynes's covering letter is 30 November 1930.
4. Kahn has noted that members of the 'circus' criticized Keynes's reference to profits as a 'widow's cruse' whose expenditure on consumption goods never depletes the wealth of entrepreneurs on the ground 'that Keynes was here implicitly assuming a fixed output of consumption-goods' (Kahn, 1984, p. 107). This criticism now appears to him to be unjustified: 'I do not see how we members of the Circus could have attributed to Keynes the assumption of inelastic supply' (*ibid.*, p. 108).

5. In the first three proofs of the *General Theory* the aggregate demand function (which was there called 'the state of effective demand') was defined in a manner consistent with Keynes's microfoundations: 'by *the state of effective demand* I mean the schedule relating the sum (D), for which the current output resulting from the employment of any given number of men can be sold, to the number of men employed (N)' (Keynes, 1973b, p. 370; emphasis in the original). A few pages later, however, he mistakenly turns this into an expectational function when he refers to 'the expected sales proceeds (D) of the output from employing N men' (*ibid.*, p. 375).

6. There is in the *General Theory* an inverse relation between the level of employment and the real-wage rate because of Keynes's assumption of competitive conditions in product markets and diminishing returns in the short period (Keynes, 1936, p. 17). This relation should not be confused with a demand curve for labour. In Keynes's system both employment and real-wage rates are functions of the level of effective demand. This point was emphasized in a 1933 draft chapter: 'we may well discover empirically a correlation between employment and real wages. But this will occur, not because the one causes the other, but because they are both consequences of the same cause' (Keynes, 1979, p. 100).

7. Weitzman (1984), on p. 35, notes, correctly: 'that producers *set* prices in systematic relation to costs', but his 'rule' for the setting of this price ignores important features of the real world.

8. For an alternative approach to the derivation of the aggregate supply function when firms are not perfectly competitive, see Tarshis (1979).

9. One of the effects of Weitzman's share economy would be to have part of the payment to additional workers borne by the firm's current group of workers. This is implicit in the relationship between marginal and average revenue products. With the firm operating in the range where the former is smaller than the latter, additional employment lowers average revenue product and thus the payment to each worker. Although the firm pays this same amount to the newly hired employee, the additional cost to the firm is this amount *less* the decrease in payments to its initial group of employees.

References

Asimakopulos, A. (1982), 'Keynes' theory of effective demand revisited', *Australian Economic Papers*, 21, 18–36.

Casarosa, L. (1981), 'The microfoundations of Keynes's aggregate supply and aggregate demand analysis', *Economic Journal*, 91, 188–193.

Kahn, R.F. (1984), *The Making of Keynes' General Theory*, Cambridge: Cambridge University Press.

Keynes, J.M. (1936), *The General Theory of Employment, Interest and Money*, London: Macmillan.

Keynes, J.M. (1937), 'The general theory of employment', *Quarterly Journal of Economics*, 51, 209–223; reprinted in Keynes, 1973b, pp. 109–23, all page references are to the latter.

Keynes, J.M. (1973a), *The General Theory and After. Part I, Preparation*, ed. D.E. Moggridge, Vol. XIII, *Collected Writings*, London: Macmillan/Royal Economic Society.

Keynes, J.M. (1973b), *The General Theory and After. Part II, Defence and Development*, ed. D.E. Moggridge, Vol, XIV, *Collected Writings*, London: Macmillan/Royal Economic Society.

Keynes, J.M. (1979), *The General Theory and After: A Supplement*, ed. D.E. Moggridge, Vol, XXIV, *Collected Writings*, London: Macmillan/Royal Economic Society.

Moggridge, D.E. (1973), 'From the *Treatise* to *The General Theory*: an exercise in chronology', *History of Political Economy*, 5, 72–88.

Parrinello, S. (1980), 'The price level in Keynes' effective demand', *Journal of Post*

Keynesian Economics, 3, 63–78.

Patinkin, D. (1982), *Anticipations of the General Theory? And Other Essays on Keynes*, Chicago: University of Chicago Press.

Tarshis, L. (1979), 'The aggregate supply function in Keynes's *General Theory*', in M.J. Boskin (ed.), *Economics and Human Welfare: Essays in Honor of Tibor Scitovsky*, New York: Academic Press, 361–392.

Weitzman, M.L. (1984), *The Share Economy: Conquering Stagflation*, Cambridge, Mass.: Harvard University Press.

9 Weitzman's share economy and the aggregate supply function

Paul Davidson

Years ago, Dennis Robertson (1956, p. 81) uttered the following witticism about economic analysis: 'Now as I have often pointed out to my students, some of whom have been brought up in sporting circles, high-brow opinion is like a hunted hare: if you stand in the same place, or nearly the same place, it can be relied upon to come round to you in a circle.' Martin Weitzman's (1985) effort to demonstrate that (1) a money wage system is *the* cause of unemployment, and (2) a cooperative (share) economy presents no obstacle to full employment, is the latest example in this Robertsonian genre in several respects.

Weitzman, using a variant of the 'temporary equilibrium' system developed by Benassy (1982) and Grandmont (1983), 'proves' once again that in a fixed money wage system a short-run 'temporary competitive equilibrium' with less than full employment is possible. Of course, over forty years ago, in a less sophisticated analysis of equilibrium, Modigliani (1944) also 'proved' that unemployment was due to downward inflexible money wages. And again, even before Keynes's *General Theory*, it was well known to orthodox economists that unemployment occurred when money wages failed to decline in the face of unemployment. Thus, for at least the third time in a century, erudite opinion has 'demonstrated' that only labour's foolish reluctance to accept a flexible wage system causes it to be unemployed.

Weitzman's claim that his microeconomic model of monopolistic competition provides a 'natural underpinning for the standard aggregate demand specification' (1985, p. 937), however, seems to suggest that at least in this area he has provided a scholarly innovation. Apparently, Weitzman is unaware that in the *General Theory* Keynes assumed a given 'degree of competition' (1936, p. 245) (not necessarily pure competition) as part of his micro analytical foundations. Weintraub (1957, 1958) and later Davidson (1962) and Davidson and Smolensky (1964) have shown that this meant that Keynes's analytical Marshallian micro foundation framework assumed a constant degree of monopoly (as measured by Lerner's μ, 1935). Thus, in the section on the aggregate supply function, below, it is shown that Weitzman's micro underpinnings is a return to the Keynes–Weintraub aggregate supply analysis (even to the use of the symbol, μ, as a measure of the monopoly mark-up), despite Weitzman's disclaimer that he believes that the aggregate supply function is 'a dubious macroeconomic concept at best' (p. 940, n.6).

While Keynes combined this aggregate supply function with demand aspects which demonstrated that Say's law 'is not the true law relating the aggregate demand and supply functions' (Keynes, 1936, p. 26), Weitzman has grafted Keynes's aggregate supply analysis on to a neo-classical (really pre-Keynesian) demand micro foundation based on Say's law. That this latter hybrid analytical framework cannot be applicable as a description of real-world monetary economies is evidenced by the fact that important results implied in the Weitzman model are, as explained in the following section, contrary to the facts of history and experience.

These incongruities between the Weitzman model and the real-world experience is due to the use of some seemingly innocuous, but really very artificial, assumptions which make Weitzman's erudite framework inapplicable to real-world economic phenomena.

Weitzman's assumptions regarding perishability and demand
Weitzman's (1985) analysis is severely biased by his selection of suppositions which logically eliminate such real-world causes as variations in investment spending from affecting output levels, while requiring government policy to be the only destabilizing factor. These seemingly innocent assumptions include the following.

1.   *All products are 'highly perishable' (p. 938).* If this assumption is taken seriously, then there can be no capital goods industry, no capitalists, no existing stock of capital, no accumulation and, ultimately, no behavioural analysis of investment decision-making and spending.

This fundamental perishability assumption throws out with the bath water the Keynesian baby of variable investment expenditures as a possible source of employment instability in the private sector. Consequently, it is impossible to explain within the model the causes of employment instability as originating in the behavioural transactions of individual agents in the market-place in the absence of any government action. (Thus as Weitzman's table 1 (p. 942) implies, given the parameters of the system, *all* short-run changes in output and the price level are explained only by changes in autonomous government expenditures and/or government deficits!)

2.   *The households' utility function implies an intertemporal marginal*

propensity to consume of unity, i.e. in the long run Say's law holds,[1] even though households are assumed to have a parametrically determined (short-run) marginal propensity to consume out of current after-tax income of less than one. This Say's law household utility function, combined with the previous assumption of highly perishable goods, implies that the only possible barrier to full employment in the current period is a technological one of the time incompatibility between demand and supply. The demand for goods is more durable, extending over periods, while the supply of all goods are highly perishable and last only one (undefined) time period.

If Weitzman permitted firms to produce *non-perishable* working capital goods, then households' current demand for future goods – as proxied by households' real balances (p. 938) – would induce firms to start up the production of work-in-process inventories immediately in order to be prepared to provide the goods for the future.

In an Arrow–Debreu-type world of spot and forward markets (which is ultimately the foundation of Weitzman's 'temporary equilibrium' analysis), households would never hold any money. Instead households would maximize utility (Weitzman's equation (1)) by allocating their entire budget to either buying goods spot or ordering goods on forward contract. *Payment for all spot and forward transactions would be made*, as Debreu (1959, pp. 32, 100) has always insisted, *at the initial (current) period*. Firms would respond to all market orders by immediately hiring workers not only to produce goods for current consumption by households and government, but also to produce goods for future delivery under a technology which minimized the present value of the costs of production.

Consequently, if forward contracts and non-perishable inventories were permitted in the Weitzman model, there would not be any obstacles to full employment equilibrium – as this period's household's savings out of after-tax income would always equal this period's stock-building of work-in-process future consumer goods. It is only the assumptions of a highly perishable supply interacting with an intertemporal Say's law demand, so that today's supply does not create today's demand for current goods *and* current production of inventories, which permits Weitzman to have any possible barrier to full employment in his system.

In the real world where output and employment cycles are the greatest in the durable goods industries rather than in the nondurable sector, Weitzman's analysis of unemployment in a model where all goods are non-durables seems scarcely relevant!

3. *The government is the only autonomous spending sector* in the Weitzman model. All government deficits are financed by the govern-

ment printing money. The existing stock of money, therefore, is solely the result of past government deficits. Households are induced to hold more money any time the government decides to finance expenditures by printing money rather than via tax revenues (p. 939).

If, therefore, either government spending as a percentage of GNP is negligible, or if the government does not run a deficit (both of which are stylized facts describing the years just before the Great Depression), then there would be no money (or at least no changes in the money stock) in the system, and the level of aggregate demand would be basically unchanged. What, then, would have caused the Great Depression in the Weitzman model?

Furthermore, because the government is the only autonomous spender, it follows that households' savings are positively related to government deficits. Thus, if this model is a serious description of how the American economy currently operates, then we should have expected that in the years since 1980, with huge government deficits relative to both GNP and after-tax income, the US personal savings ratio should be at an all-time high.[2] In fact the personal savings ratio, in the last few years, has sunk to record lows as federal deficits grew to record highs. It would, therefore, appear that Weitzman's hypothetical world is quite remote from the facts of experience.

Moreover, if the government were continuously to run a current period balanced budget (as required in 1991 by the Gramm–Rudman legislation), then, as n.2 demonstrates, household savings out of after-tax income would be zero. Surely no one expects a permanent zero personal savings rate after 1990!

4.   *Households hold money balances only for one reason, i.e. to buy future consumer goods (p. 938).* Even though Weitzman mentions the existence of an uncertain future (p. 938, n.4) and the unpredictability of changes in variables (p. 943), his model contains no concept of households holding money for the liquidity purposes associated with the precautionary motive. The speculative (but not the precautionary) motive is eliminated by the assumption that no durables exist (besides money) which can be resold in organized spot markets – hence there is no future spot price to speculate on. But as Keynes cogently argued:

> in the absence of an organised market, liquidity preference due to the precautionary motive would be greatly increased; whereas the existence of an organised market gives an opportunity for wide fluctuations in liquidity preference due to the speculative motive. (Keynes, 1936, p. 170)

In the real world the demand for inactive precautionary (and speculative) money balances is due to human recognition that future economic outcomes cannot be predicted by the statistical analysis of existing data, i.e. economic processes are non-ergodic (Davidson, 1982–3). Weitzman's (1985) elimination (by assumption) of the possibility of speculation will merely increase household demand for money for precautionary purposes, if, in his model, there is an 'uncertain future' (p. 938) 'and at any time or place . . . variables are changing too rapidly and unpredictably' (p. 943).

In a non-ergodic economic system sensible economic agents hold money – not simply for the purchase of goods either currently or in the future. Money is also held for the purposes of precautionary *liquidity*, i.e. to meet either existing and/or potential future *money contractual obligations* when uncertain and statistically unpredictable future events can cause unforeseeable variations in cash flows and/or future spot purchase opportunities (Davidson, 1982–3).

Moreover, sensible agents will enter into money contracts which make them legally responsible for organizing long-lived complex and interdependent production (and durable consumption) activities, only because they are assured that no matter how wrong future events may go, their liabilities are limited by their nominal contracts. Hence as long as they possess money, or liquid assets readily resaleable for money at an expected spot price in the future, agents 'know' they will have the funds necessary to meet these commitments as they come due. In a non-ergodic world the institution of money contracts has evolved to permit sensible economic agents to limit, in advance, their potential losses when they undertake activities the outcomes of which will only become known in the non-predictable future (Davidson and Davidson, 1984).

In an uncertain world where money contractual obligations span a significant period of calendar time, utility functions of all *sensible economic agents* must contain three arguments (rather than only two as proposed by Weitzman: (a) current goods, (b) future goods and (c) money (and/or liquid assets readily resaleable for money on organized spot markets) to meet unforeseen and statistically unpredictable events (Davidson, 1983).

If (i) money and liquid assets have the *non-producibility properties (for the private sector)* assumed by Weitzman (1985, p. 938), *and* (ii) if money and other liquid assets are *non-substitutable with producible goods* (a condition which violates Weitzman's household utility function specification but is consistent with Keynes's (1936, chapter 17) specification of the essential properties of money), then *a three-argument household utility function* involving current goods, future goods and liquid assets (including money) *will provide the necessary and sufficient conditions to make Say's law inapplicable in both the short run and the long run* (see Davidson, 1984).

In this case, money is never neutral. Its very existence can form a barrier to full employment. For example, an increased demand for liquid money balances due to increased fears about an uncertain future can cause an increase in Keynesian unemployment (cf. Keynes, 1936, chapter 17; Davidson, 1972, 1978). Moreover, as Keynes readily demonstrated (1936, chapter 18) in such a monetary system, even if money wages were flexible, unemployment can be an equilibrium outcome in both the short and long run.

Is technology independent of the compensation system?

Because of Weitzman's (1985) assumptions of highly perishable goods and a ubiquitous technology where labour is the only fixed *and* variable input, no investment behaviour specification is possible to explain the labour intensity of the production process used by all firms. Instead a constant marginal productivity of the variable labour input is assumed,[3] in the short as well as the long run (p. 940). The same productivity of labour is also assumed in a wage system as in a profit-sharing system (p. 944).

Is this *unvarying productivity of labour assumption*, independent of the labour compensation scheme, justifiable? If the gains of conversion from a wage system to a share economy involves only the real benefits of an end to unemployment and inflation and no real costs of productivity declines, as Weitzman claims (pp. 949–51), why has the historical development of industry tended to 'convert' the other way?

Weitzman's share economy is merely an extension of the ancient agricultural system of agreeing to share sales revenue from future farm production known as 'share-cropping'. The share-cropping system disappeared when it could not compete with the money wage compensation system used by all modern large-scale agriculture firms. Share-cropping did not provide the capitalist–landowner incentives to apply labour-saving, cost-efficient technology, while it simultaneously tended to reduce the real income of share-cropping labourers to a bare subsistence. These facts suggest that the same technology (and productivity) will not occur in a share system as in a wage system.

The reason is obvious. In the simple model of firms converting over from a wage system to a pure share system, where workers agree to accept a fixed proportion of total revenue independent of the existing hired labourforce, there will be no incentive for managers of the firms to economize on labour use. The marginal cost of additional workers, for any given sales level, is zero.

If firms had any capital stock before they converted from a money wage system (with its incentives to seek out reduction in unit labour costs, given any demand specification) to a profit-sharing system, there would be no incentive in the share economy for rent-seeking managers to replace equipment as it wears out. Hiring more workers to replace the worn-out equipment to produce the same output would not cost the firm anything, while the cost of replacing the equipment would. Ultimately, for example, we would see an automobile industry where workers hand-carried car-frames down the assembly-line, thereby increasing the rate of return on the declining capital base.

Consequently, if the marginal productivity of labour is a function of the capital–labour ratio, any conversion from an existing wage system to a pure profit-sharing system would encourage the adoption of a more labour-using technology and, as a result, lead to a decline in the real productivity of labour. Firms would have the incentive to maximize their pure monopoly rents by eliminating all capital costs and instituting a complete labour-using technology (such as the one underlying Weitzman's equation (3)).

The aggregate supply function

Keynes wrote the *General Theory* in order to show that Say's law, where (aggregate) supply created its own (aggregate) demand, was not a 'true law' (Keynes, 1936, p. 26) applicable to a monetary, production economy. *In a Say's law world, the aggregate demand function would be coincident with the aggregate supply function*, so that 'effective demand, instead of having a unique equilibrium value, is an infinite range of values all equally admissible; and the amount of employment is indeterminate except in so far as the marginal disutility of labour sets an upper limit' (*loc. cit.*). In other words, under Say's law the economy is, at any employment level determined by firms' hiring decisions, in neutral equilibrium. Actual demand is constrained by actual income and employment; but there is no barrier to the economy obtaining a full employment output level (Davidson, 1984, pp. 563–5).

Keynes's revolutionary analysis stemmed from his belief that, in a monetary, entrepreneurial economy, *the aggregate demand function differed from, and was not coincident with, the aggregate supply function*. Weitzman, on the other hand, as we have shown, assumes an intertemporal Say's law, and hence his system will always be in neutral equilibrium, while his implicit supply and explicit demand function must be intertemporally coincident.

Weitzman's doubt about the concept of an aggregate supply function (1985, p. 940, n.6) is somewhat surprising since we demonstrate below that his equations (30), (42) and (43) imply a Keynesian aggregate supply function deeply imbedded in his framework.

Keynes's aggregate supply function is readily derived from ordinary Marshallian firm-supply functions (1936, pp. 44–5). Hence, Keynes argued that the properties of the aggregate supply function 'involved few considerations which are not already familiar', while 'it was the part played by the aggregate demand function which has been overlooked' (*ibid.*, p. 89). Accordingly, though Keynes briefly described the aggregate supply function (*ibid.* pp. 25, 44–5) and its inverse, the employment function (*ibid.*, pp. 89, 280–1), aggregate supply was treated perfunctorily, while the bulk of the *General Theory* was devoted to developing the characteristics of aggregate demand. (This may explain why many neo-classical synthesis Keynesians never explicity developed the aggregate supply aspects of their model.)

It was left to Weintraub (1957, 1958) to elucidate Keynes's aggregate supply function, which relates the aggregate number of workers (N) that profit-maximizing entrepreneurs would want to hire for each possible level of expected sales proceeds (Z), given the money wage rate (w), technology and the degree of competition or monopoly (μ) (cf. Keynes, 1936, p. 245). If firms are fully integrated, aggregate sales proceeds equals GNP.

Following Keynes's argument (*ibid.*, p. 41) that money values and quantities of employment are the only two 'fundamental units of quantity' to be used when dealing with aggregates, the aggregate supply proceeds should be specified either in money terms (Z) or in Keynes's wage unit terms (Z_w) which is money sales proceeds divided by the money wage rate. Hence the aggregate supply function is specified as:

$$Z = f_1(N) \tag{1}$$

or

$$Z_w = f_2(N) \tag{2}$$

The Marshallian supply curve[4] for a single firm (s_f) indicates alternative price (p_f) vs quantity (q_f) profit-maximizing combinations based on the degree of monopoly facing the firm (μ) and its marginal production costs (mc):

$$s_f = f_3(\mu, mc_f) \tag{3}$$

μ depends on the market demand conditions facing the firm. Each profit-maximizing firm's mark-up over marginal costs is related to Lerner's (1934) measure of the degree of monopoly power ($\mu = 1/E$), where E is the price elasticity of demand facing the firm for any given level of effective demand; (cf. Weitzman's (1985) equation (42) ($\mu = E/(E - 1)$)).

In the simplest case, as aggregate demand changes, the firm faces a shifting isoelastic demand curve (cf. *ibid.*, p. 942), so that employment and output varies without any change in the mark-up over marginal costs.[5]

The firm's marginal cost (mc_f), assuming labour is the only variable input in the production process, equals the money wage (w) divided by marginal labour productivity (γ), where the latter is a function of employment (and the laws of returns involved in the technology of the firm). Accordingly, Weitzman's equation (43) is equivalent to equation (3), above.

Although output across firms in the same industry may be homogeneous and therefore can be aggregated to obtain the industry supply schedule in terms of prices (p) and quantities (q), this homogeneity of output assumption cannot be accepted as the basis for summing across industries or across firms in monopolistic competition to obtain the aggregate supply function (Keynes, 1936, chapter 4). Accordingly, each firm's Marshallian supply function must be transformed into Keynes's (*ibid.*, p. 44) micro-firm supply function which relates each firm's expected sales proceeds in money terms ($z_f = p_f \times q_f$) with the firm's employment hirings (n_f).

With given returns, the money-wage and the degree of monopoly, every point on a Marshallian supply function is associated with a unique profit-maximizing price quantity combination whose multiple equals total expected sales proceeds, and since every firm's output level can be associated with a firm's unique hiring level, i.e. $q_f = f(n_f)$, then every point of equation (3) (Weitzman's equation (43)) of the S-curve in p vs q space can be transformed to a point on a Z-curve in pq vs n space to obtain:

$$z_f = f(n_f) \tag{4}$$

Keynes's firm supply functions can then be aggregated in terms of homogeneous money and employment units together to obtain the aggregate supply function relating aggregate money sales proceeds (Z) and the aggregate quantity of employment units (N) as specified in equation (1).[6]

Weitzman, by assuming a specified law of production returns, degree of monopoly and money wage system, has in effect utilized a Keynes–Weintraub aggregate supply function in his system, in spite of his disclaimer. Unfortunately, his demand assumptions constrain his aggregate demand curve to be intertemporally coincident with aggregate supply, while Keynes permitted a more general, non-coincident demand relationship.

Wage system vs share system or entrepreneurial economy vs cooperative economy

Weitzman attempts to draw real-world policy implications from his logically very restrictive and contrived Say's law temporary equilibrium model rather than attempting to follow the more general aggregate supply–demand analysis laid out by Keynes.

Just as Weitzman, in his limited framework, compared a money wage economy with a share economy, Keynes, in his more general theory, juxtaposed an entrepreneurial economy with a cooperative economy. In an entrepreneurial economy fixed money commitments (contracts) and especially money wage contracts are used to organize production processes and hence money is never neutral. A cooperative economy, on the other hand, is a system where the 'factors of production are rewarded by dividing up in agreed proportions the actual output of their cooperative efforts' (Keynes, 1979, p. 77). In the cooperative system (Weitzman's pure share system), Keynes noted, Say's law was applicable and money was neutral (*ibid.*, pp. 77–8). But in the non-ergodic monetary world we lived in, which Keynes labelled an entrepreneurial system, the conditions of a pure share economy are 'not satisfied in practice; with the result that there is a difference of the most fundamental importance between a cooperative economy and the type of entrepreneurial economy we actually live in' (*ibid.*, p. 79).[7]

Weitzman, who has previously (1982, p. 794) argued that Say's law is a 'first principle' upon which to build a consistent micro foundation of macroeconomics, cannot accept that we live in an non-ergodic entrepreneurial economy where liquidity and money contractual institutions are important and therefore Say's law is inapplicable. Instead Weitzman, like Ricardo before him, 'offers us the extreme intellectual achievement of adopting a hypothetical world remote from experience and then living in it consistently' (Keynes, 1936, p. 192). Keynes, on the other hand, thought it more useful to build a hypothetical world which had the characteristics of the world we lived in and offer us proposals for improving the operation of that world rather than *assuming* the easy transmutation of existing human economic systems.

Notes

1. What Weitzman does not seem to recognize is that Say's law does not assure full employment as an equilibrium outcome. It only asserts that at any level of employment the economy is in neutral equilibrium and hence there is no obstacle to full employment (Keynes, 1936, p. 26). If, in a Say's law world, firms hire less than capacity employment, then the supply produced will create exactly its own demand (and no more!), and equilibrium production will be at less than capacity. If firms then, for any reason, increase their labour hirings to full employment, then the additional

supply produced creates additional demand, so that all the additional output will be sold. (For a further discussion, see the section on the aggregate supply function, below.)

2. Aggregate nominal income is:

$$PY = PC + PA \tag{1a}$$

where Y is real aggregate output, C is real consumption, A is real government expenditures and P is the price level. Tax revenue (T) is:

$$T = s\,PY \tag{2a}$$

where 'the government collects the fraction s of each household's current income as taxes' (Weitzman, 1985, p. 939), so that aggregate after-tax disposable income (PY_d) is:

$$PY_d = (1 - s)\,PY \tag{3a}$$

Government expenditure is equal to tax revenues plus new money (M) created to finance the deficit (D), where M = D, so that:

$$PA = s\,PY + M = sPY + D \tag{4a}$$

If the government budget is balanced, then:

$$PA = s\,PY \tag{5a}$$

Substituting equation (5a) into (1a) and rearranging terms shows that if the government runs a balanced budget, the ratio of personal savings to after-tax income is zero as aggregate consumption on current output just equal households' aggregate disposable income; i.e.;

$$PC = (1 - s)\,PY \tag{6a}$$

If, on the other hand, the government runs a deficit, then substituting equation (4a) into (1a) and rearranging terms shows that therefore the personal savings ratio is equal to D/PY_d, so that the larger the deficit, *ceteris paribus*, the greater the personal savings ratio.

3. Although earlier, Weitzman (1982) had claimed that the existence of increasing returns was the foundation of all unemployment theory, his current analysis does not rely on increasing returns to demonstrate unemployment. In his recent model discussed herein, unemployment would occur due to the perishability of supply and the intertemporal stretch of demand whether there was increasing, decreasing or constant returns to labour, while the price of each firm (equation (43)) as well as the price level either decreases or increases, or remains constant (via equation (43)) as employment varies under the different laws of returns.

4. For purposes of simplicity and ease of comparability with the ordinary Marshallian firm supply function, only the form of equation (1) will be developed in the following discussion. Equational form (2) of the aggregate supply function can then be derived merely by dividing all money sums expressed in equation (1) by the existing money wage rate.

5. For example, in the purely competitive case, it is always assumed that changes in aggregate demand do not affect the elasticity of the demand curve facing each firm. In more complex cases the degree of monopoly may vary as aggregate demand changes and the firm's demand curve shifts, i.e. $\mu = f(N)$, as, for example, suggested by Harrod (1936).

6. Provided one reasonably assumes that corresponding to any given point of aggregate supply there is a unique distribution of proceeds and employment between the different firms in the economy (Keynes, 1936, p. 282). Weitzman's assumption that the government and all households have the same trade-off among goods and all firms have the same production function assures this unique distribution of proceeds and employment.

7. Small closed homogeneous communities, such as a kibbutz or a monastery, may be able to hammer out a social order based on a sharing concept. Weitzman postulates a homogeneous community of interests with the *same* utility function for all households (p. 939). For large economic systems with production and consumption processes involving interdependencies and feedback among a large number of heterogeneous and different interest (i.e. differing utility functions) subsectors, the institution of money contracts appears to be the best civilized system yet devised by humans over centuries to encourage the undertaking and carrying out to completion of these complex economic processes.

References

Benassy, J.P. (1982), *The Economics of Market Disequilibrium*, New York: Academic Press.

Davidson, P. (1962), 'More on the aggregate supply function', *Economic Journal*, June, 72, pp. 452–57.

Davidson, P. (1972), 'A Keynesian view of Friedman's theoretical framework for monetary analysis', *Journal of Political Economy*, September–October, 80, 5, pp. 864–82.

Davidson, P. (1978), *Money and the Real World*, 2nd edn, London: Macmillan.

Davidson, P. (1982–3), 'Rational expectations: a fallacious foundation for studying crucial decision-making processes', *Journal of Post Keynesian Economics*, Winter V, 2, pp 182–98.

Davidson, P. (1983), 'The marginal product curve is not the demand curve for labor', *Journal of Post Keynesian Economics*, Fall VI, 1, pp 105–17.

Davidson, P. (1984), 'Reviving Keynes's revolution', *Journal of Post Keynesian Economics*, Summer VI, 4, pp. 561–75

Davidson, P. and Davidson, G.S. (1984), 'Financial markets and Williamson's theory of governance', *Quarterly Review of Economics and Business*, Spring.

Davidson, P. and Smolensky, E. (1964), *Aggregate Supply and Demand Analysis*, New York: Harper and Row.

Debreu, G. (1959), *Theory of Value*, New York: Wiley.

Grandmont, J-M., (1983) *Money and Value: A Reconsideration of Classical and Neo-Classical Monetary Theories*, Cambridge: Cambridge University Press.

Harrod, R.F. (1936), *The Trade Cycle*, Macmillan: London.

Keynes, J.M. (1936), *The General Theory of Employment, Interest and Money*, New York: Harcourt, Brace.

Keynes, J.M. (1979), *The Collected Writings of John Maynard Keynes*, Vol. XXIX, ed. D.E. Moggridge, London; Macmillan.

Lerner, A.P. (1934), 'The concept of monopoly and the measurement of monopoly power', *Review of Economic Studies*, I, pp. 157–75.

Modigliani, F. (1944), 'Liquidity preference and the theory of the interest rate', *Econometrica*, 12 January, 45–88.

Robertson, D.H. (1956), *Economic Commentaries*, London: Macmillan.

Weintraub, S. (1957), 'The micro-foundations of aggregate demand and supply', *Economic Journal*, September 67, pp 455–70

Weintraub, S. (1958), *An Approach to the Theory of Income Distribution*. Philadelphia: Chilton.

Weitzman, ML. (1982), 'Increasing returns and the foundation of unemployment theory', *Economic Journal*, 92, December, pp 787–804.

Weitzman, M.L. (1985), 'The simple macroeconomics of profit sharing', *American Economic Review*, December 75, 5, pp 937–53.

10 Hicks's wage-theorem and Keynes's *General Theory*

Christopher Marme and Paul Wells

Sir John Hicks's imaginatively written *The Crisis in Keynesian Economics* is both an interpretation and an extension of several of the *General Theory's* more fundamental theoretical constructs. As readers of his work have come to expect, Hicks packed this slender volume with shrewd insights, valuable observations and abundant good theory. In all, the *Crisis* adds much to our understanding of the *General Theory* and, more important, to the functioning of modern capitalist economies. Nevertheless, in sharp contrast to the overall excellence of this work, Hicks has, in one instance, seriously misinterpreted the *General Theory*.

The error of interpretation we believe Hicks committed has to do with a piece of analysis which he calls the 'wage-theorem' (Hicks, 1974, pp. 59–60), a theorem which states that when money wages change, they, and prices too, all change by equal percentage amounts. Hicks credits this theorem to Keynes, and claims that it is central to the theoretical structure of the *General Theory* and that it adequately describes the wage–price behaviour of the *General Theory*. Because Hicks's wage-theorem rendition of Keynes's work produced a number of highly surprising conclusions – conclusions which turn the *General Theory* into a book we do not recognize – this chapter will examine Hicks's wage-theorem analysis in detail.

Hicks's argument in brief

Hicks's wage-theorem interpretation opens with this key observation:

> One of the things in the *General Theory* which caused most trouble to its first readers ... was the [Keynes's] habit of working in what were called 'wage-units'. Income in wage-units; even money supply in wage-units; they seemed at first very awkward concepts. They depended (we learned at last) upon a principle, very important to Keynes, which I shall call the *wage-theorem*. (Hicks, 1974, p. 59)

The theorem in question is:

> When there is a general (proportional) rise in money wages ... the *normal* effect is that all prices rise in the same proportion – provided that the money

supply is increased in the same proportion (whence the rate of interest will be unchanged). (*ibid.*, pp. 59–60)

Hicks continued with the statement that: 'The wage-theorem could not be understood until one had grasped the rest of [Keynes's] theory; yet the rest of the theory . . . could not be understood without the wage-theorem' (*ibid.*, p. 60). To break what he called 'this circle', a circle of his own making, Hicks surmised that Keynes developed the rest of his theory (the multiplier, liquidity preference, and so forth), 'on the assumption of *fixed* money wages. Then with that behind one, it was fairly easy [for Keynes] to go on to the wage-theorem'.

The theorem, he noted, implies that wage and price fluctuations will have no real effect on the economy. With wages, prices and the money supply all changing by equal percentage amounts, relative prices, real income and the distribution of real income will remain unchanged come inflation or deflation. Having woven the wage-theorem into the fabric of Keynes's work, Hicks could then conclude that: 'the view which emerges from the *General Theory* . . . is nothing less than the view that inflation does not matter', and in slight retreat he added,

> I do not suppose that Keynes held, at all consistently, to this radical view . . .
> The extreme position which he takes, by implication, in the *General Theory*,
> is surely to be explained by the circumstances of its time. (*ibid.*, p. 61)

In sum, Hicks has argued that the validity of Keynes's wage-unit deflator depends upon the wage-theorem, a principle which he believes to be very important to Keynes; that the wage-theorem is central to the theoretical structure of the *General Theory*; that Keynes thought the wage-theorem usually held true, and so held the radical view that inflation did not matter; and that a good part of the *General Theory* was written simply to provide a foundation for the wage-theorem.

We shall now render a point-by-point comparison of Hicks's wage-theorem interpretation of the *General Theory* with that which Keynes wrote in the *General Theory*.

The *General Theory* according to Keynes

Keynes's wage-units and Hicks's wage-theorem
We begin with an examination of Hicks's initial statement that the validity of Keynes's wage-unit deflators depends upon the wage-theorem. To do this we shall carefully define Keynes's wage-unit and wage-unit measures and then examine Hicks's assertion in light of Keynes's own analysis.

Keynes defined an hour's employment of ordinary labour to be his *labour-unit.* The money wage paid the labour-unit is the *wage-unit* (*CW*, VII, pp. 41–5).[1] If ordinary labour earned $3 an hour, $3 is the wage-unit. If carpenters receive $6 and machinists $12 per hour, they would be rated at two and four labour-units respectively. Keynes then defined the quantity of employment measured in wage-units, N_w, to equal (E/w), where 'E is the wages (and salaries) bill, [and] w the wage-unit' (*ibid.*, p. 41). Thus N_w measures the number of hours of ordinary labour services which the wages and salary bill could purchase. Similarly, the money supply in terms of wage-units states the number of hours of ordinary labour which the current stock money could command. This same interpretation also applies to Keynes's wage-unit measures of income, Y_w, consumer spending, C_w, and investment spending, I_w.

To illustrate Keynes's troublesome wage-unit measures suppose just one worker from each of the three skills mentioned above were employed; each for just one hour per day. Employment in terms of wage-units, N_w, would then be seven, the number of hours of ordinary labour which the $21 wages and salaries bill could command. If the wage-unit were to increase and expenditures on wages and salaries, E, rose by the same percentage amount as the wage-unit, N_w would remain unchanged at seven. However, if the percentage change in E exceeded (fell short of) the change in the wage-unit, N_w would rise (fall), even though the same three workers are still the only workers employed. It follows that the stability of Keynes's wage-unit measure of employment requires only that E rise (or fall) in proportion to the wage-unit. The stability of this measure *does not* require that all money wages rise (or fall) by equal percentage amounts. In addition, since this measure is defined independently of product prices, its stability does not depend upon any particular price response to an increase in the wage-unit. In short, the validity of Keynes's wage-unit measure of employment, N_w, does not depend upon either the wage-half or the price-half of Hicks's wage-theorem.

Keynes's expectation was that money wages would generally (but not always) rise in proportion (*ibid.*, pp. 42–3, 302–4). If expenditures on wages and salaries did rise more or less in proportion to the wage-unit, then his wage-unit measure of employment would serve 'as an adequate working index of changes in real income' (*ibid.*, p. 114). In the event that the relation between E and w were seriously disturbed, Keynes would deal with this difficulty 'by supposing a rapid liability to change in the supply of labor and the shape of the aggregate supply function' (*ibid.*, p. 43).

The stability of Keynes's wage-unit measures which involve product prices (such as income, consumer spending, investment spending, etc.)

also do not depend upon the wage-theorem. To illustrate assume as before a given level of employment (our same three workers each of whom is employed for just one hour a day at $3, $6 and $12 respectively) and an unchanged flow of real product from day to day. Now let the final product produced by these three workers sell for $45. Keynes's wage-unit measure of income, Y_w, would then be ($45/3) or 15, the number of hours of ordinary labour services which the national income could purchase. Suppose next day the same three workers produce the same quantity of real product but that overnight the wage-unit doubled. If expenditures on final product doubled as well, the Y_w would remain unchanged at 15. However, if the wage-unit doubled and national income rose by more (less) than a factor of 2, Keynes's Y_w would register a number larger (smaller) than 15. Again, this is true, even though the same three workers are on the job for three man-hours producing the same quantity of real output!

This example demonstrates that the absolute stability of Keynes's wage-unit measure of national income, Y_w, requires only that expenditures on final product rise in proportion to the wage-unit. Its stability does not require that all wages and all prices rise by equal percentage amounts. In sum, the absolute stability of the totality of Keynes's wage-unit measures requires nothing more than that expenditures on both wages and salaries and final product rise in proportion to the wage-unit. Hence the validity of these measures does not at all depend upon money wages and prices changing in accordance with the wage-theorem.

Keynes recognized that the absolute stability of his measures depended upon proportional expenditure responses to increases in the wage-unit. Early in the *General Theory* he wrote:

> As a first approximation ... we can reasonably *assume* that, if the wage-unit changes, the expenditure on consumption corresponding to a given level of employment will, like prices, change in the same proportion. (*ibid.*, p. 92; emphasis added)

But this slightest hint of a wage-theorem was no more than a quickly dropped illustrative first approximation; an approximation which is not basic either to his wage-unit measures, nor to the theory of the *General Theory*.

Although Keynes recognized the proportionality dependence of his several measures, he nevertheless worked out his theory in terms of wage-units. Despite the fact that his aggregate wage-unit measures were subject to some degree of instability, he did argue convincingly that they were superior to the highly heterogeneous measure units of his day; i.e. the volume of real output, Q, the stock of capital, K, and the general level, P (*ibid.*, pp. 37–44; see also *CW*, V, pp. 47–107). After all, they were Keynes's well-thought-out choice of 'the units of quantity appropriate to the problems of the economic system as a whole' (*CW*, VII, p. 37).

Did Keynes believe that the wage-theorem usually held true?
Keynes provided an unequivocal answer to this question. Prices, he wrote, 'certainly do not change in exact proportion to changes in money-wages' (*CW*, VII, p. 259). His theory of prices (*ibid.*, pp. 222–309) well explains why they do not behave in accordance with the wage-theorem:

> The general price-level depends partly on the rate of remuneration of the factors of production which enter into marginal cost and partly on the scale of output as a whole, i.e. (taking equipment and technique as given) on the volume of employment ... If we allow ourselves the simplification of assuming that the rates of remuneration of the different factors of production which enter into marginal cost all change in the same proportion, i.e., in the same proportion as the wage-unit, it follows that the general price-level ... depends partly on the wage-unit and partly on the volume of employment. (*ibid.*, pp. 294–5)

Short of full employment, increases in effective demand will be spent partly in increasing prices, and partly in increasing output and employment in wage-units. The rise in prices will be due to the tendency for money wages to rise as business improves, to the diminishing returns from given equipment and to the diminished efficiency of newly employed workers. Since differing industries experience differing degrees of diminishing returns, and because industry may draw their workers from different labour pools, some pools having fewer and others more 'specialized or practiced labor' available (*ibid.*, p. 42), prices will rise by differing percentage amounts in response to a demand generated increase in the wage-unit. But in neither the real world nor in the *General Theory* do prices rise and fall by equal percentage amounts. Clearly the *General Theory* does not support Hicks's assertions that Keynes thought the wage-theorem usually held true; that the wage-theorem was a principle very important to Keynes; and that the *General Theory* could not be understood without the help of the wage-theorem.

Does inflation matter?
The assertion most damaging to Hicks's interpretation of Keynes is his statement that 'the view which emerges from the *General Theory* is ... the view that inflation does not matter' (1974, p. 61). Keynes had long known that inflations and deflations do occur, and he knew that they do matter. Furthermore, he well understood why they mattered. His

Tract on Monetary Reform, Essays in Persuasion, Treatise on Money
and, of course, the *General Theory* were in good part devoted to the
analysis of the various causes of price instability, their economic consequences and the setting down of logical policy recommendations for
stabilizing prices and the level of employment.

The view which does emerge from the *General Theory* is that *stability* matters. Chapters 17–21 of Keynes's work make clear his deep
commitment to stability: to the stability of money wages, of prices and
the level of employment (the latter at some high rather than at some
middling or low level). He wrote:

> When there is a change in employment, money-wages tend to change in the
> same direction as, but not in great disproportion to, the change in employ-
> ment; i.e., moderate changes in employment are not associated with very
> great changes in money-wages. *This is a condition of the stability of prices
> rather than of employment.* (*CW*, VII, p. 251; emphasis added)

His prescription for stability, repeatedly voiced in the *General Theory*,
is that prices could best be held firm by stabilizing money wages and the
level of employment. The following statement well illustrates Keynes's
good sense and strong preference for stability. It is his recommendation
for preserving the purchasing power of money in both the short and long
run:

> Thus with a rigid wage policy, the stability of prices will be bound up in the
> short period with the avoidance of fluctuations in employment. In the long
> period . . . we are still left with the choice between a policy of allowing prices
> to fall slowly with the progress of technique and equipment whilst keeping
> wages stable, or of allowing wages to rise slowly whilst keeping prices stable.
> On the whole, my preference is for the latter alternative, on account of the
> fact that it is easier with an expectation of higher wages in future to keep the
> actual level of employment within a given range of full employment than with
> an expectation of lower wages in future, and on account also of the social
> advantages of gradually diminishing the burden of the debt, the greater ease
> of adjustment from decaying to growing industries, and the psychological
> encouragement likely to be felt from a moderate tendency for money-wages
> to increase. (*ibid.*, p. 271)

He noted:

> There are advantages in some degree of flexibility in the wages of particular
> industries so as to expedite transfers from those which are relatively declining
> to those which are relatively expanding. But the money wage level as a whole
> should be maintained as stable as possible, at any rate in the short period.
> (*ibid.*, p. 270)

These passages surely could not have been written by one who believed
'that inflation does not matter'. In sum, Hicks's assertion that Keynes

held the radical view that inflation did not matter is contrary to both the substance and spirit of the *General Theory*.

Does the General Theory *provide a foundation for the wage-theorem?*
Hicks's observation that Keynes developed a good part of his theory on the assumption of fixed money wages is absolutely correct. However, his assertion that Keynes did so just to provide a foundation for the wage-theorem (1974, p. 60) is not correct. Keynes opened chapter 19 of the *General Theory* (the chapter in which he analysed the consequences of decreases in money wages) with his reasons for assuming rigid money wages throughout the first part of his book. They make good sense and are quite distinct from the reason Hicks advanced:

> It would have been an advantage if the effects of a change in money-wages could have been discussed in an earlier chapter. For the classical theory has been accustomed to rest the supposedly self-adjusting character of the economic system on an assumed fluidity of money-wages; and, when there is rigidity, to lay on this rigidity the blame of maladjustment ... It was not possible, however, to discuss this matter fully until our own theory had been developed. (*CW*, VII, p. 257)

Keynes developed his own method of analysis on the assumption of fixed money wages, so that he could then apply a sufficiently developed theory to the analysis of falling money wages.

In this chapter, Keynes examined the employment and output consequences of a reduction of *money wages*. It is to be noted that in conducting his analysis, he most carefully did not assume that money wages fell by equal percentage amounts. Keynes knew better than this. He knew that in real-world capitalist economies money wages do not fall in proportion. Although his expectation was that they would rise in rough proportion, his certainty was that they could not fall in this manner:

> Since there is, as a rule, no means of securing a simultaneous and equal reduction of money-wages in all industries, it is in the interest of all workers to resist a reduction in their own particular case. In fact, a movement by employers to revise money-wage bargains downward will be much more strongly resisted than a gradual and automatic lowering of real wages as a result of rising prices. (*ibid.*, p. 264)

He added: 'Except in a socialized community where wage-policy is settled by decree, there is no means of securing uniform wage reductions for every class of labor' (*ibid.*, p. 267).

Keynes shaped his *General Theory* to conform with the real-world facts that money wages were upwardly fluid but downwardly sticky.

However, he did realize that money wages could be brought down by a sufficiently high level of unemployment. Keynes's celebrated 1925 essay 'The Economic Consequences of Mr Churchill' explained that downwardly sticky money wages could become unglued by a tight money policy. But 'By what *modus operandi* does credit restriction attain this result?' (*CW*, IX, p. 218). His answer was that tight money brought wages down:

> *In no other way than by the deliberate intensification of unemployment* ... The policy can only attain its end by intensifying unemployment ... until workers are ready to accept the necessary reduction of money wages under the pressure of hard facts. (*loc. cit.* emphasis added.)

But both 'The Economic Consequences of Mr Churchill' and the *General Theory* inform us that when downwardly sticky money wages do fall, they do not fall in proportion.

Keynes's chapter 19 analysis led him to conclude that falling money wages would, on balance, neither improve nor worsen the level of employment. Unemployment is due simply to a lack of effective demand. With this established, he wrote:

> There is ... no ground for the belief that a flexible wage policy is capable of maintaining a state of continuous full employment; – any more than for the belief that an open-market monetary policy is capable, unaided, of achieving this result. The economic system cannot be made self-adjusting along these lines. (*CW*, VII, p. 267)

Clearly, Keynes did not write a good part of his *General Theory* just to provide a foundation for the wage-theorem. He wrote his book for quite a different reason.

Conclusion

Hicks concluded his wage-theorem reworking of the *General Theory* with the rather remarkable statement that: 'the wage-theorem is identical with an extreme of the quantity theory of money; for on the quantity theory a change in money supply affects no *real* price-ratios, wages and prices being again adjusted in the same proportion' (1974, p. 72). He adds that the only difference between his interpretation of the *General Theory* and the quantity theory is that 'The quantity theory begins from a change in money supply; the wage theorem begins from a change in the level of money wages' (*ibid.*, p. 73). Thus if Hicks's wage-theorem account of the *General Theory* were to be accepted, then Keynes's magnificent work would collapse into little more than a footnote to the quantity theory of money!

But surely Hicks's interpretation cannot be accepted. The wage–price behaviour of the *General Theory* bears no resemblance whatsoever to the manifestly unreal wage–price behaviour that Hicks mistakenly imputed to Keynes. Keynes was of the real world where prices and wages do not (cannot) rise or fall by equal percentage amounts. Surely Keynes did not, nor does Hicks, nor can any economist who has studied the behaviour of individual prices and wages accept the wage-theorem's specification of wage–price movements. Clearly, Hicks has not rendered an interpretation of Keynes's *General Theory*. Instead he has inexplicably worked a highly misleading line of thought into the *General Theory* and into his own otherwise valuable set of essays, *The Crisis in Keynesian Economics*.

Note

1. *CW* refers to the *Collected Writings of John Maynard Keynes*, ed. D.E. Moggridge, London: Macmillan, 1971– .

References

Hicks J.R. (1974), *The Crisis in Keynesian Economics*, New York: Basic Books.
Keynes, J.M. (1971), *A Treatise on Money*, Vol. V, *Collected Writings*, London: Macmillan.
Keynes, J.M. (1973), *The General Theory of Employment, Interest and Money*, Vol. VII, *Collected Writings*, London: Macmillan.
Keynes, J.M. (1972), *Essays in Persuasion*, Vol. IX *Collected Writings*, London: Macmillan.

11 Unemployment resulting from preferences on wages or prices

S.-C. Kolm

The essence of the problem

Preferences on prices and wages

Keynesianism was invented and applied to decrease 'involuntary' unemployment. Keynes characterizes involuntary unemployment by the property that the wage rate exceeds the marginal disutility of labour: in Keynes's words, 'the equality of the real wage and of the marginal disutility of employment corresponds to the absence of "involuntary unemployment"' (1936, chapter 2, sections IV, I).[1]

Present-day critics of Keynesian theory and policies revive an argument that Keynes attributes to the 'classical school': unemployment is due to 'the refusal of a unit of manpower to accept a remuneration equivalent to its marginal productivity', that is, it is 'voluntary' (*ibid.*, ch. 2, section I, II). Why, say the modern critics, don't the unemployed offer their labour at wages lower than the present ones so as to obtain employment? If they do not, this means that they are not involuntarily unemployed. Thus there is no genuine excess supply of labour. Therefore, the government must not try to reduce such an excess supply. To try to do this by reflation, for instance by monetary expansion, can only result in inflation.

In response to this argument, the other side tries to find reasons why there would be downward inflexibility of wages, which would justify government employment policy, macroeconomic in particular. This question is commonly considered to be the main problem for economic analysis nowadays. Both fixed price models with unexplained wages and prices, and models which assume a priori market clearing, shirk the issue. The theories of rigidities recently proposed, such as 'implicit contract' or 'efficiency wages', are insufficient and unsatisfactory for reasons which are well known. Official 'minimum wages' are not a result of private exchanges. Authors who introduce imperfect competition due to unionized labour have a more powerful tool, and this will be present in this chapter as it is in Keynes. But crucial questions still have to be answered regarding the 'voluntariness', optimality and structure of wage claims and of unionization.

As for Keynes, he devotes two full chapters (2 and 19) to providing answers to these old and new classical questions and makes a number of remarks elsewhere. Keynes's explanations of wage rigidities and floors are multiple, they rely on psychological and social phenomena which are not standard in the description of economic choices and they strike one by their realism, relevance and importance. His emphasis on the effect of relative wages is one of the most frequently noticed, although the reasons he gives for it are not sound.

Nevertheless, a large amount of observations, from a plethora of casual ones to elaborate studies by many authors, show the importance of relative wages both in people's feelings and in the processes of wage determination (see references). Furthermore, the direct attachment to relative wages tends to occupy a relatively more prominent place in people's interests when the rising level of welfare satisfies the more urgent consumption needs. Attachment to relative wages has two 'unclassical' structural effects. On the one hand, the wage-earner sees importance in the level of his wage not only through its effect on his wage income (whether nominal or real). On the other, he also attaches importance to others' wages and to the general pattern of wages. As a result of this latter structure, this phenomenon does not check workers' willingness to decrease their wages if all wages move down together. But the initial question was why don't unemployed workers lower the wage they would accept. Fully employed incumbents have no reason to voluntarily participate in a general wage cut. And not only are they much more numerous, but their wages are the only ones in existence, and which can serve as a reference point. (Thus, the eventual difficulty of collective agreement between numerous wage earners is not even relevant.) The reasons why one directly attaches importance to a general wage pattern or to relative wages or to others' wages are feelings of jealousy, benevolence, justice, fairness, appropriateness, normalcy, status, unwillingness to 'steal' colleagues' employment, etc. Keynes probably also had this in mind; at least we are sure that he was quite prepared to see the economic importance of such phenomena, given his previous mention of status or imitation-related consumption in his pamphlet, *Economic Prospects for our Grandchildren.*

Unclassical preferences on one's own wage can also exist without comparison with others' wages for various reasons which can also be classified under headings of attachment to social status or social norms. People may, for instance, refuse a lower wage or prefer a higher one for reasons of prestige, pride, honour or fear of loss of face, because they feel it is 'what they are worth' or what corresponds to their education and experience, because it is what they received before, because they feel that they (or civilized men) are entitled to some level of work compensation or of living or just because this pay is felt as normal, correct, just, fair, customary, traditional, etc. Also if we consider several successive periods, one may have preferences on one's wage level in one period because it influences the wage level, and thus the income, in further periods not only for reasons of habit or of what is due, but also because the former wage classifies the labour and is taken as information on its quality (this signalling effect could be classified as a kind of status effect).

The desire to work and to earn an income may overcome these feelings and the resistance to wage decreases they induce. But it may be only after a delay. And the relative importance of these norm and status effects are certainly boosted by the existence of unemployment compensations – often substantial – as well as by the increase in the general level of well-being and of collective services (social insurance, medical care, etc.) or the more frequent existence of second wages in families.

To put prices in utility functions, or as dimensions of the space on which individual preference orderings are defined, has drastic consequences. With parametric prices ('perfect competition', in this sense), general equilibria exist under the traditional conditions for the quantity variables. But these equilibria are no longer Pareto optima in general. Thus Pareto optima are no longer competitive equilibria. At the prices they contain, they display *disequilibrium*. In particular, with positive direct valuation of wages, Pareto optima will tend to have excess supply of labour – unemployment, in this sense.

On the involuntariness of unemployment
Is unemployment resulting from preferences on wages voluntary or involuntary? This is the vocabulary and the distinction of the ongoing discussion. But this distinction is ambiguous and misleading for a number of reasons of which the following are only a sample.

First of all, the distinction between voluntary and involuntary unemployment is used in order to conclude that the government must not or must intervene and do something about this unemployment, through macroeconomic policy in particular. The idea is that voluntary unemployment freely manifests workers' preferences, it respects Pareto optimality and the government should not intervene or try to influence in such situations. However, it may be that unemployment can be classified as voluntary, and yet that a reflation can both decrease it (without any illusion on prices) and be beneficial to everybody. We could give several examples of such a situation, some being caused by well-known phenomena (excess supply on product markets, labour supply curve with horizontal threshold section, direct preferences on wages which can also render optimal some involuntary unemployment – see below –, imperfect competition, etc.).

Imperfect competition provides a series of problems about the use of concepts of voluntary or involuntary unemployment. When an 'association', 'combination' or union has chosen or influenced a wage, monopolistically or in bilateral monopoly with employers or otherwise, this level is generally given for each wage-earner. Then if the labour supplied at this wage is not all employed, which is generally the case, what remains looks very much like involuntary unemployment even if workers agree with the union's action. In fact, Keynes discusses labour combinations and unions and considers this result as involuntary unemployment.

The labour market thus provides an example of a very important phenomenon in the logic of a society which I called 'social multi-level voluntariness'. That is the simple fact that a person enters into a voluntary agreement with others but, then, when he considers acting by himself, would prefer to do something else than what the agreement says. The situation is, for this person, voluntary at the collective level, but 'involuntary' at the level of purely individualistic autonomous action. According to the specificities of the social situation, this 'involuntariness' may not be apparent by being melted and imbedded in the collective decision, or it may become very conspicuous. The latter case prevails, for instance, when there is a sufficient delay between the collective agreement and the individual's abiding by it, or when force is used to constrain the individual to do his part of the contract, or when the agreement has been implicit only.

There is still another category of problems which mars the distinction between voluntary and involuntary unemployment, which are deeper and of a psychological or sociological nature. It is often not easy to know what is voluntary and what is not. Some people do not even believe in the existence of free will. Even if we do not go to such an extremity, we must consider a number of questions. Imperfect, changing or asymmetric information (including one's own preferences) raise several others. Furthermore, any human action has both voluntary and involuntary causes. The distinction between what shapes pre-ferences and what pertains to constraints is often ambiguous, arbitrary or impossible. That is especially so if one considers physiological and psychic constraints – the physiological causes of various desires, the stock of knowledge (which includes memories of past experiences, knowledge of life-styles, etc.), the capacities for mental processing of information, the ability to will one's own existing tastes, whatever their causes etc., are given at each moment of time. A structure of preferences is a constraint, and a self-imposed constraint – a common behaviour – is a preference. Furthermore, choice theory would classify as voluntary actions resulting from psychic states which make this denomination very dubious such as compulsion, impulsion, inadvertence, weakness of the will, *akrasia*, unconscious acts and subconscious decisions, etc.

Finally, norms, our central topic, present this ambiguity in the extreme with the essential extra dimension of mobilizing the various kinds of influence of society on individuals' choices. They can be manifested through preferences or as constraints on choices and actions, or both. They often imply preferences on some other people's actions or states, and these preferences can themselves be norms and determine actions of various kinds. Society (or the others) can induce an individual to obey norms through a full spectrum of interdependent means of influence, ranging from persuasion, education, indoctrination, to various kinds of social pressure, including approval, disapproval, fame and reputation, honours or blame, material advantages or inconveniences of various kinds, rewards and punishment as well as sheer social constraints, with various degrees of internalization (in a sociological sense) by the actor. In our present topic a standard labour supply curve may be superimposed with a normatively determined wage floor having priority. If this norm acts as an external constraint on the actor, and if this constraint is effective (binding) and creates unemployment, one could agree to call the latter involuntary. On the other hand, if this norm is internalized and voluntarily adhered to without the need of force or the approval or blame of watchers, we would call it, and the eventually ensuing unemployment, voluntary. But there are still other, intermediary, cases, where others' approval or blame, sense of duty to obey legal norms, and many other things, can intervene. All this means that the choice to call a resulting unemployment voluntary or involuntary is just a matter of discussion, in reality a sterile and useless one.

The main analytical results shown in the simplest model

The meaning of the model
We want to explain how norm and status effects of wages affect actual employment, optimal employment and the discrepancy between them, and we want to know if fiscal policy can make actual employment

optimal if they otherwise differ. These effects of the fact that economic agents have direct preferences on prices (including wages) are quite original and have not yet been studied by economists, in spite of the actual pervasiveness of this situation. For this analysis a formal model is necessary. The definitive answers to such questions would lie only in a complete, disaggregated micro model, which will be published elsewhere, but we begin here by presenting the essence of these answers in an aggregative macroeconomic framework which however must keep some micro features such as a utility function (since 'employment' is not a sufficient objective).

The agents are, first, the wage-earners and the firms' owners (this is a 'class' society); secondly, there may be collective agents which defend the interests of these categories, the essential one being a labour union, with also the possibility of a union of employers (formal or informal); and at a third level, there is an optimizing government whose correct action we want to determine. The optimum concept is only Pareto optimality, with the possibility of various transfers through public finance.

Wage-earners have preferences on their income, their labour and also directly on their wages for the norm, status or signalling effects. Firms are profit maximizing and essentially classical (as in Keynes). The structures of the labour market can be of competition or monopoly on each side of the market, which makes four cases, including bilateral monopoly. Monopoly on the employers' side can mean either that there is only one firm or that the employers 'combine' on this market whether through an institutionalized union or just an agreement, or even an implicit one. Monopoly on the labour-supply side is the act of a labour union. To describe the behaviour of this union, the microeconomic analysis – not presented here – develops the theory of the 'efficient union', meaning that the union cannot act in opposition to the wishes of all the members of its constituency (here the workers, which does not necessarily imply that they all are union members), from which we deduce that it will not make a choice if there exists another possible one that all these persons prefer. We add that the union can make some transfers between these people, directly through contributions and solidarity support, or indirectly by inducing the employers or public bodies to do it (in particular, unemployment compensations are often set up in this manner). A consequence of this behaviour in the present macro model is that the union obeys the preferences of the wage-earners, whatever the reasons for them (including norm–status effects). Furthermore, the reality of labour markets shows two kinds of behaviour when these collective agents intervene: either they determine the wages and let the individual agents determine the quantities of employment at these wages (with, in particular, the possibility of unemployment which thus is 'individually involuntary') or these collective agents choose both the wages and the quantities of employment. In the aggregate analysis this question will intervene only once, on the firms' side; but it is implictly present as two possible interpretations of the behaviour of the union (which knows what the wage-earners would choose to do when it determines the wages).

An important result of the microeconomic analysis is that perfectly competitive supply of labour makes workers behave as wage-takers even in the presence of direct preferences on the wage levels.

The conclusions of the model will be derived from conditions of Pareto optimality under all the constraints of the problem which will be technology (production function), structure of preferences, and market structure and behaviour with the various cases. To derive them macro-economically, the explicit macro-model aggregates firms on the one hand, and workers on the other, with a utility function for the latter. The use of such a global utility function is justified to describe workers' individual behaviour, or by the transfers performed or induced by the union or by the government (as the disaggregated analysis shows).

Finally, aggregate analysis leaves us with one type of labour and thus one wage level, which has consequences for these two types of variable. Unemployment will appear as some lower aggregate employment, and therefore as partial global unemployment, whereas it consists in some people being fully unemployed, while some others may suffer from partial unemployment (labour time lower than the 'full employment' one); only the micro analysis can distinguish and sort out who becomes fully unemployed. Secondly, to have only one wage level precludes the explicit consideration of preferences on relative wages; but there also exists direct preferences on wages for norm, status or signalling reasons which do not come from preferences on relative wages; furthermore, a desire for a higher global wage level can describe the result of preferences on relative wage levels when individual wage-earners influence their own wages while taking the others' as given (a Nash non- cooperative solution), with the unique wage level being either the result of this process or an average of various different wages; again, only the microeconomic model describes completely this question.

Labour supply
We call ℓ the quantity of labour and w the wage rate. We assume $\ell > 0$ since only cases with some aggregate labour are relevant (but in the disaggregated model the labour of the totally unemployed is zero). $w\ell$ is wage income of wage-earners and the wage bill for firms. The good produced or consumed has a price equal to 1 (therefore w is

the real wage). Wage-earners have the utility function u(wℓ, ℓ, w). The first argument represents goods bought with income (we can assume they are consumed). The second and third arguments represent preferences on labour and on the wage level for reasons other than the fact that they produce income. As for labour, the classical consideration is that of its 'disutility' because of its painfulness for any reason – the first being that it takes time which would otherwise have been devoted to leisure (by definition). This makes u a decreasing function of its second argument. We shall discuss later other reasons which influence this sensitivity of u to ℓ and which are of great importance. The third argument represents the direct preferences on w for the status or norm reasons which are our primary concern here. If some status or norm sentiment applies to wage income rather than to wage level, it is described by the first argument, which then has several reasons to influence u (but norms or status effects often act through w rather than through wℓ, as has been discussed above). In accordance with previous discussions, u is a non-decreasing function of this third argument, w. A 'preference for inconspicuousness' might provide some effect of w or of wℓ in the other direction, but they certainly must not be considered as important and thus dominant.

We assume that u is differentiable and we call u_1, u_2, u_3 its first derivatives. In accordance with previous discussions, we assume $u_1 > 0$, $u_2 < 0$ for the time being, and $u_3 \geq 0$. We then call $a = -u_2/u_1$ and $b = u_3/u_1$, thus with $a > 0$ and $b \geq 0$; a is the monetary marginal disutility of labour, and b is the monetary marginal value of the wage *per se*, or the *status or norm effect*. The difference $w - a$ is the *wage gap*. As we recalled above, Keynes defined the existence of involuntary unemployment by the fact that there is a positive wage gap.

If wage-earners are price- and wage-takers, so that the supply of labour is competitive in this specific sense, they take the wage rate w as given and choose to supply the quantity of labour ℓ which maximizes u, i.e. which satisfies $a = w$. The equation in ℓ and w, $a(\ell, w) - w = 0$ defines the wage-taking labour supply curve $\ell = \ell_s(w)$.

With monopolistic (unionized) labour supply facing a competitive labour demand $\ell_d(w)$ (with $\ell'_d < 0$), so that $\ell \leq \ell_d$, labour chooses ℓ and w which maximize u, given this relation, i.e. which satisfy $\ell = \ell_d(w)$ and:

$$(w - a)\, \ell'_d + \ell + b = 0 \tag{1}$$

This condition explicitly depends upon the status-norm effect of wages b.[2] Given the signs of ℓ, b and ℓ'_d, it implies $w > a$: there is a positive wage gap and thus 'involuntary unemployment' in Keynes's definition.

As a matter of example in order to discuss the effect on employment of the norm and status effect, assume that b is constant (locally), that a depends only on ℓ – a plausible assumption and then we write a = a(ℓ) – and that a specification of u has the form u = wℓ – a(ℓ)·ℓ + bw. Differentiating equation (1), we find the sensitivity of employment to the norm-status effect:

$$d\ell/db = -[2 - a'\ell'_d - (\ell + b)\ell''_d/\ell'^2_d]^{-1}$$

Normally $\ell'_d < 0$ and $a' \geq 0$, such that $d\ell/db \leq 0$ if in addition $\ell''_d \leq 0$.

In the 'linear case' when u and ℓ_d are linear, that is $a' = 0$ and $\ell''_d = 0$, we have $d\ell/db = -1/2$. If, then, $\ell_d = -\alpha w + \beta$, where α and β are positive constant, we obtain $\ell = \frac{1}{2}(\beta - \alpha\, a - b)$. The difference with the case without status-norm effect (b = 0) is that employment is lower by b/2. This amount can be called the status-norm unemployment. We, therefore, have the property that *in monopolistic (unionized) labour supply and competitive labour demand, in the linear case the status-norm unemployment is half the status-norm effect.*[3]

Labour demand
With labour ℓ, firms produce the quantity f(ℓ) of product, and their profit is P = f(ℓ) − wℓ (this profit includes return to capital, it is profit in Marx's definition). Firms maximize P under the production and market conditions.

With wage-taking, 'competitive' labour demand, w is given to them and they choose demand ℓ such that f′ − w = 0 (and f″ ≤ 0). This defines the competitive labour demand curve $\ell_d(w)$ which is the inverse function of f′.

With a monopolistic labour demand facing a wage-taking labour supply $\ell_s(w)$ with $\ell \leq \ell_s$, the firm(s) choose ℓ and w such that $\ell = \ell_s$ and

$$(f' - w)\cdot\ell'_s - \ell = 0 \quad \text{or} \quad f' - w = \ell/\ell'_s$$

which implies w < f′ with normal $\ell'_s > 0$.

With wage-taking on both sides of the labour market, w = a = f′.

The labour market structure which remains to be considered is bilateral monopoly. If we assume, as is reasonable, that the issue of this bargaining in the two variables ℓ and w is efficient, that is, Pareto-optimal for wage-earners (union) maximizing u and firms' owners maximizing P, then:

$$\frac{\partial u}{\partial \ell} \Big/ \frac{\partial u}{\partial w} = \frac{\partial P}{\partial \ell} \Big/ \frac{\partial P}{\partial w}$$

which comes out as:

$$\frac{b}{\ell} = \frac{f' - a}{w - f'} \tag{2}$$

Without status-norm effect, i.e. if $b = 0$, the condition is $f' = a$. The effect of a status-norm effect $b > 0$ is to drive a wedge between f' and a, that is, between demand and supply marginal values. $b/\ell > 0$ imply that f' is in between w and a; $b > 0$ imply $w > f' > a$. There is a positive wage gap and thus involuntary unemployment in Keynes's sense. Given this w, we have $\ell_d < \ell < \ell_s$. That is to say, for wage-taking units, there is both *excess supply of labour and excess employment in firms*. This excess supply of labour, $\ell_s - \ell$, is the involuntary unemployment.[4]

If there is only one firm, this excess employment (at given wage) is an understandable issue of the bargaining. If there are several employing firms which join for the bargaining, the situation can be similar to the one we have described above for labour and labour unions. Given the wage decided upon, firms would like to have globally a smaller workforce than the employment decided by the agreement. Firms may have agreed to keep a larger labourforce than they would like to have at the agreed-upon wages, first, as an engagement towards the other firms, and secondly, as an engagement towards labour (union here). But wage-taking firms who keep their individual right to hire and fire tend to choose employment such that globally $\ell = \ell_d(w)$. While involuntary unemployment seems to be very common, such over-employment by private firms on the contrary is not the usual situation (in places where pressures by unions, government, convention, or society at large have prevented firings or imposed hirings, this either has been accompanied by a decrease in the effective wage cost – through a decrease in the wage rate or in employees' premiums or in social charges or thanks to subsidies – or it has been provisional, or it was labour time-sharing, or a mixture of these modalities). Therefore, a standard situation is that in which this employer's right imposes on the economy a constraint $\ell \leqslant \ell_d(w)$, the consequences of which we shall consider.

Optimality
The social optimum satisfies Pareto optimality with the possibility of lump-sum transfers. We determine the conditions for this Pareto optimality in this section. As for the constraints, apart of course from the production function, we consider especially the most relevant case where it is not possible to impose on firms more employment than they want at the prevailing wages and prices (a similar condition for workers would not be binding). Apart from this free exchange

constraint, what we consider here is a first-best optimum. In particular, it is 'financially first best' thanks to these exclusively lump-sum taxes or subsidies which these transfers can be. The result will be different than that in all the market structures previously considered. In the next section we show that some other, non-lump-sum, taxes or subsidies, in particular ones which vary with incomes, enable the main market structures to achieve this first-best optimum.

This Pareto optimality can be described by the maximum of some 'social welfare function':

$$W[u(w\ell + \tau, \ell, w), P - \tau]$$

where W is an increasing function of its two arguments, and τ – which can have any sign – is the transfer between owners' and earners' incomes. We recall that $P = f(\ell) - w\ell$.

If w were a free variable, the solution would be a = f' and b = 0; if b > 0 whatever w, i.e. there is no satiety in preferences for higher wages for status or norm reasons, the solution would be w = +∞ (or very large) and $\tau = -\infty$ (very large transfer from wage-earners): it is always beneficial to have a higher w, with a lump-sum transfer of the higher income to cover the larger labour cost to firms.

But as we have seen, the interesting case is that where firms, being profit-maximizing wage-takers free to choose their work-force, choose employment ℓ which satisfies $w = f'(\ell)$, that is, the inverse $\ell = \ell_d(w)$. Maximizing W given this relation, gives $w - a + b f'' = 0$. We also must have $f'' = 1/\ell'_d < 0$. This shows that the status-norm effect (b > 0) makes it optimal that there is a positive wage gap (w − a > 0), and therefore involuntary unemployment in Keynes's sense:

With a status-norm preference on wages, some involuntary unemployment is optimal.

The optimal wage gap is:[5]

$$w - a = -bf'' \tag{3}$$

Therefore, the wage-taking equilibrium situation (w = a = f') is not optimal if there is a status-norm preference on wages.

The labour monopoly situation is not either since, from equation (1), the wage gap in this case is:

$$w - a = -(\ell + b)f''$$

This shows that *employment is higher than optimal with wage-taking equilibrium and lower than optimal with monopoly labour.*

This also shows that *the wage rate is lower than optimal with wage-taking equilibrium and higher than optimal with monopoly labour.* Therefore, the optimum can be achieved by a *minimum wage, a wage floor*, in the case of competitive labour, and by a *maximum wage*, a *wage ceiling*, in the case of monopoly labour.

As an example, in the linear case (a and b are constant, $\ell_d(w) = -\alpha w + \beta$), $\ell'_d = 1/f'' = -\alpha$ and using indexes c,o,m for the competitive, optimal and monopoly union cases:

$$w_c = a, \quad \ell_c = \beta - \alpha a$$
$$w_o = a + b/\alpha, \quad \ell_o = \beta - \alpha a - b$$
$$w_m = \tfrac{1}{2}[a + (b + \beta)/\alpha], \quad \ell_m = \tfrac{1}{2}(\beta - \alpha a - b)$$

We see that *the status-norm effect decreases optimal employment by its amount* and that $\ell_o = \ell_c - b = 2\ell_m$.

The efficiency of global balanced fiscal policy

Can these non-optimalities in the global situation and, in particular, in the employment level caused by these preferences on wages be corrected by a global fiscal policy? The instruments of such a policy are taxes and subsidies on and to incomes, a priori depending upon incomes, and which, all reckoned, constitute a balanced public budget.

A priori, such a structure constitutes a constraint which makes the optimum unreachable and allows only the possibility of a 'second-best' optimum relative to this constraint. However, we shall see that these tools allow to reach the 'first-best' relative to this constraint, provided the utility function has the property called 'constant marginal utility of income' which is classical and well discussed. This property is that there exists a specification of the ordinal $u(y, \ell, w)$ of the form $y + v(\ell, w)$.

Furthermore, taxes on profits or subsidies to them do not change the behaviour of profit-maximizing firms as long as the profit after tax and subsidy remains an increasing function of the profit before them (in this model without uncertainty, nor consideration of failures). It is, therefore, taxes on earned incomes or subsidies to them which will influence the w and ℓ chosen by the market whatever its structure.

The general problem is to set tax and subsidies schedules. Given these schedules and the prevailing type of market structure, the agents determine w and ℓ, which therefore depend upon this fiscal structure. Then these schedules are chosen so as to maximize a Social Welfare Function dependent upon utilities with incomes after taxes and subsidies, and therefore dependent upon these schedules both directly and because they influence the prevailing ℓ and w.

We consider taxes and subsidies both proportional and additive to incomes. The proportional ones have rates π for earned incomes and ϱ for profits, and the additive ones are lump-sum transfers τ for wage-earners and θ for profits. We write π, ϱ τ and θ negative for taxes (withdrawal from income) and positive for subsidies (additions to income). The after-tax-subsidy wage income is $(1 + \pi)w\ell + \tau$, so that the after-tax-subsidy utility of wage-earners is:

$$E = (1 + \pi)w\ell + \tau + v(\ell, w)$$

Owners receive the after-tax-subsidy profit:

$$O = (1 + \varrho)(f - w\ell) + \theta$$

The public budget constraint is:

$$\pi w\ell + \tau + \varrho(f - w\ell) + \theta = 0 \qquad (4)$$

The Social Welfare Function is $W(E, O)$ and its first derivatives (positive) are written W_1 and W_2.

The two partial first derivatives of $v(\ell, w)$ are $v_1 = -a(\ell, w)$ and $v_2 = b(\ell, w)$.

In all cases we have:

$$f'(\ell) = w \qquad (5)$$

In the competitive case wage-earners choose ℓ which maximizes E, given w, π and τ. It thus satisfies:

$$(1 + \pi)w - a = 0 \qquad (6)$$

which, with equation (5), determines ℓ and w as functions of π.

In the labour union monopoly case the union chooses w and ℓ, which maximizes E given equation (5) and given π and τ. It thus satifies:

$$(1 + \pi)(f' + \ell f'') - a + bf'' = 0 \qquad (7)$$

which, with equation (5), determine ℓ and w as functions of π.

Then, in each case, we put these ℓ and w in E and O, and E and O in W, which we then maximize for the fiscal parameters π, p, τ, θ under the public budget constraint (4). We see that since these ℓ and w do not depend upon τ or θ, those two parameters enter only directly and thus additively in E and in O. Therefore, when we maximize W for τ and θ under the constraint (4), we obtain $W_1 = W_2$. But this implies that the first-order conditions for the maximum of W are the same as the first-order conditions for the maximum of $E + O$ under the same constraint. Now, given this condition (4):

$$E + O = f(\ell) + v(\ell, w) \qquad (8)$$

Now the 'first-best' solution with the possibility of lump-sum transfers, as obtained in the preceding paragraph, results from the maximization of:

$$W[w\ell + v(\ell, w) + \tau, f(\ell) - w\ell + \theta]$$

with $\tau + \theta = 0$, for τ, θ, ℓ, w with eventually a relation like (5) between ℓ and w. The first-order condition for τ and θ is $W_1 = W_2$. Then, as above, the first-order conditions for the maximum of W are the same as those for the maximum of the sum of its arguments, $w\ell + v + \tau + f - w\ell + \theta = f(\ell) + v(\ell, w)$.

This proves that the fiscal policy can reach the first-order optimum, that is, *this fiscal structure of global taxes and subsidies on incomes, globally balanced, do not impose a binding constraint on the social optimum.*[6]

We also note that in the cases considered above where ℓ and w depend upon π, they do not also depend upon ϱ, so that the tax or subsidy rate on profits can be anything. For instance, it can be $\varrho = \pi$, so that all incomes are taxed or subsidized at the same rate whatever their sources, or it could be $\varrho = 0$.

The tax-subsidy solution

Maximizing expression (8) with relation (5) gives the optimality condition:

$$f' - a + bf'' = 0 \quad \text{or} \quad w - a + bf'' = 0 \tag{3a}$$

If we call $e = w\ell'_d/\ell = w/\ell f''$, the elasticity of the demand for labour $\ell = \ell_d(w)$, comparing equation (3a) with equations (6) and (7) respectively, gives the optimizing values of the tax-subsidy rate π in the perfect competition and in the labour union monopoly cases:

$$\pi_c = b/\ell e \tag{9}$$

and:

$$\pi_m = -1/(1 + e) \tag{10}$$

where w and ℓ have their optimal values.

We have $\pi_c < 0$ since $e < 0$: the optimal fiscal action in the competitive case is an income tax, and subsidies must come by lump-sum transfers τ.

Expression (10), which is also $1 + \pi_m + e\pi_m = 0$ imply, since $e < 0$, either $\pi_m > 0$ – a proportional income subsidy –, or $1 + \pi_m < 0$ – a marginal tax rate above 100% –, plus lump sum subsidies or taxes. These cases occur according to whether $1 + e \lessgtr 0$, that is $1 + a$ $\ell_d/\ell - b/\ell \lessgtr 0$; in particular, a sufficiently large status-norm effect b requires the proportional income subsidy.

We also notice that π_c depends explicitly on b and is zero when $b = 0$: the tax in the competitive case must directly implement the required consequence of the status-norm effect. On the contrary, π_m does not depend upon b (nor upon a) otherwise than through their effect on ℓ and w. This means that in the labour union monopoly case, the fiscal instrument only corrects the monopoly effect; the status-norm effect then takes care of itself; however, it can do that only because there is monopolistic sensitivity to wage elasticity rather than competition.

A norm and status economy

Equations (1), (2) and (3) show that the same situations, the same achieved or optimal w and ℓ, can be obtained with higher status or norm effects of wages, b, if a is smaller. And a can be lower because the negative appreciations of working are lower or because the positive ones are higher. Since we introduced status or norm appreciations of wages, we must also consider status or norm appreciations of occupations. More generally, status as income earner, social identity, the fact of being needed, useful or desired, social integration, social relations, occupation and structuration of time, meaningfulness of life, self-actualization or achievement, not being rejected, normalcy and conformity, etc., are all very important reasons for desiring to work, independently from the income received for working. Absence of integration and participation is often presented as the scourge of youth worklessness. Unemployment makes many people despair in spite of their receiving abundant financial compensation (and compulsory retirement shows the same effect). In parallel, present technical progress in advanced economies decreases work painfulness and increases the proportion of jobs with expertise and responsibility. All this increases intrinsic utility of labour and decreases its disutility. That is, it decreases a. And for all these reasons, this trend is certainly globally on the rise. If we add unemployment compensations and the general increase in wealth, we see that the nature of the costs of unemployment, or the relative importance of their various elements, certainly differ from what they were a few decades ago. These pairs of low a and high b picture a society where the social effects of work and wages become relatively quite important compared to their standard effect of providing income.

The earners' direct preferences on wages for norm or status reasons have a very strange situation in the history of thought. Very few generalist economists mention them, whereas very few specialists of wages and pay fail to point out their importance and several present factual analyses of the corresponding norms (see References). As for economic analysis, Frank's study of the status preference on relative wages within workgroups (not explicit in the model presented above) is more elaborate than others' remarks, and a number of economists mention – and Ackerlof models – wage norms on the labour-demand side, which seems much less important than norm, status (and signalling) effects on the labour-supply side (a firm may promote more its local status by hiring than by paying more, and competition checks its eventual desire to pay more). Nevertheless, all these views are on the right general track, which is to introduce in economic analysis more psychological, social and ethical considerations since, short of this, what will remain unexplained is not only unemployment, but as well such crucial questions as the cost of inflation, the growth of productivity, the cost of external indebtedness and all the aspects of the normative dimension; that is to say, a very large part of what economics seeks out to explain.

Notes

1. This paper has benefited from remarks by Professors Mahomed Dore, Mario Nuti and Felix Fitzroy.
2. In the disaggregated model, the b here is the sum of similarly defined b_i's for the various wage-earners i's, a sum which is unweighted if income is redistributed as required between these individuals. A similar remark will hold for the further uses of b. This property manifests the fact that the wage level is a 'public good' for the wage-earners, as, more generally, all prices are 'collective concerns'.
3. To take another example, if utility is of the form $u = w\ell.\ell^{-A}w^B = w^{1+B}\ell^{1-A}$, where A and B are constant with $A > 0$ and $B > 0$, maximization with $\ell = \ell_d(w) > 0$ gives the first-order condition:

$$-w\ell_d'/\ell = \frac{1+B}{1-A}$$

   if $\ell > 0$, which implies $A < 1$ (for $A > 1$, $\ell = 0$ is chosen). The norm-status effect of wages is here described by B. It does not exist when $B = 0$. Its effect is thus to add $1/(1 - A)$ times its value to the (absolute value) elasticity of the demand for labour.
4. If $u = w\ell + v(\ell, w)$, the bargaining is in a situation where a Nash solution is relevant. If p and q are the relative bargaining power of wage-earners' union and of owners, at this solution $u^p P^q$ is maximum, which gives in addition to condition (2) the condition $u/P = (p/q) (1 + b/\ell)$. This gives the relative benefits to the two groups as a function of their relative bargaining power and of the status-norm effect (the presence of which boosts this relative bargaining power by b/ℓ).
5. This is the Pareto optimality (first-order) condition for the optimum. Therefore, we have mentioned several Pareto optimality conditions; they differ as to the variables and constraints. Formula (2) is for variables w and ℓ and no τ. The case $f' = a$ and $b = 0$ or w very large is for the three variables w, ℓ and τ. Formula (3) is for variables ℓ or w tied by $w = f'(\ell)$ and τ.
6. For space and simplicity, we do not write explicitly the second-order conditions.

References

Ackerlof, G.A. (1984), *An Economic Theorist's Book of Tales*, Cambridge: Cambridge University Press.

Annable jr. J. (1984), *The Price of Industrial Labor*, Lexington: Lexington Books.

Behrend, H. (1973), *Incomes Policy, Equity and Pay Increase Differentials*, Edinburgh: Scottish Academic Press.

Brown, J.A.C. (1954). *The Social Psychology of Industry*, Harmondsworth: Pelican.

Fogarty, M.P. (1961), *The Just Wage*, London: Chapman and Hall.
Frank, R.H. (1984), "Are workers paid their marginal product?", *American Economic Review*.
Frank, R.H. (1985), *Choosing the Right Pond; Human behavior and the Quest for Status*, New York: Oxford University Press.
Hahn, F. (1984), "Economic theory and Keynes' insights", Economic Theory Discussion Paper, n°72, Cambridge: University of Cambridge, January.
Hicks, J. (1975), *The crisis in Keynesian economics*, Oxford.
Jaque, E. (1967), *Equitable Payment*, Harmondsworth: Penguin.
Kahneman, D., Knatsch, J. and Thaler, R. (1986), "Fairness as a constraint on profit-seeking: entitlements in the market", *American Economic Review*, September.
Kaldor, N. (1985), *Economics without Equilibrium*, Cardiff: University College Cardiff Press.
Keynes, J.M. (1936), *The General Theory of Employment, Interest and Money*, London: Macmillan.
Keynes, J.M. (1971–), *Collected Writings of John Maynard Keynes*, ed. D.E. Moggridge, London: Macmillan, 1971– .
Kolm, S.-Ch. (1969a), *L'Etat et le système des prix*, Paris: Dunod.
Kolm, S.-Ch. (1969b), *Le service des masses*, Paris: Dunod.
Kolm, S.-Ch. (1971), "La taxation de la consommation ostentatoire", *Revue d'économie politique*, I.
Kolm, S.-Ch. (1984a), *La bonne économie (la Réciprocité générale)*, Paris: Presses Universitaires de France.
Kolm, S.-Ch. (1984b), *Sortir de la crise*, Paris: Hachette.
Kolm, S.-Ch. (1984c), *Le libéralisme moderne*, Paris: Presses Universitaires de France.
Kolm, S.-Ch. (1985), *Le Contrat social libéral*, Paris: Presses Universitaires de France.
Kolm, S.-Ch. (1986a), "L'Etat doit-il avoir des politiques de l'emploi, de stabilisation, macro-économique", Discussion Paper, n°48, CERAS.
Kolm, S.-Ch. (1986b), "Chômage et inflation résultant des effets de norme et de statut des salaires et des prix", Discussion Paper, n°51, CERAS.
Kolm, S.-Ch. (1986c), "Prix et normes", Discussion Paper, n°51, CERAS.
Kolm, S.-Ch. (1987), *L'homme pluridimensionnel*, Paris: Albin Michel.
Lupton, Bowey (1983), *Wages and Salaries*, (2nd edition), Gower.
Malinvaud, E. (1984), *Mass Unemployment*, Oxford: Basil Blackwell.
Marx, K., *Wages, Prices and Profits*, (any edition).
Okun, A.M. (1981), *Prices and Quantities, A Macroeconomic Analysis*, Oxford: Basil Blackwell.
Patchen, M. (1961), *The Choice of Wage Comparisons*, Englewood-Cliffs: Prentice Hall.
Pigou, (1933), *The Theory of Unemployment*, London.
Pigou, (1945), *Lapses from Full Employment*, London.
Richardson, R. (1971), *Fair Pay and Work*, London: Heineman.
Schnapper, D. (1981), *L'épreuve du chômage*, Paris, ed. Gallimard.
Schultze, C.L. (1985), "Microeconomic Efficiency and Nominal Wage Stickiness", *American Economic Review*, vol. 75, pp. 1–15.
Solow, R. (1980a), "On theories of unemployment", *American Economic Review*, vol. 70, pp. 1–9.
Solow, R. (1980b), "Alternative approaches to macroeconomic theory: a partial view", *Canadian Journal of Economics*, vol. 12, pp. 339–54.
Trevithick, J. (1976). "Money wage inflexibility and the Keynesian labor supply function", *The Economic Journal*, vol. 86, June.
White, H. (1981), *The Hidden Meaning of the Pay Conflict*, Macmillan.
Williams, P. (1981), *Fairness, Collective Bargaining and Incomes Policy*, Oxford: Clarendon Press.
Wootton, B. (1955), *The Social Foundations of Wage Policy*, London: George Allen and Unwin.

PART IV

MONEY AND
INTEREST RATES

12 Keynes's treatment of interest

Basil J. Moore[1]

> In both books [the *Treatise* and the *General Theory*] the interest rate is a phenomenon of money ... Keynes ... comes to his decisive innovation, the sundering of the investment incentive from the urge to save, by discarding the notion that the interest rate is determined by the interaction of these two, and therefore coordinates them. Instead he makes the interest rate to spring from and to manifest liquidity preference, and so investment can be insufficient to match the potential saving gap out of a full employment income ... The *General Theory*'s most momentous, radical and decisive service was to release the interest rate from its imprisonment in the mutual self-determinating equilibrium system of prices of goods in terms of goods, and to make it a response to uncertainty. (G.L.S. Schackle, 1983, pp. 365–6)

As has been made clear from student notes of his early 1930s lectures at Cambridge, Keynes's central intent was to develop a theory of a monetary economy, where 'monetary disturbances don't wash out over the long period. The introduction of money leads to a different long period conclusion' (Dimand, 1986, p. 4). In the *General Theory* one of Keynes's principle motivations was to refute the loanable funds theory of interest. He interpreted this as the theory which regards the rate of interest as 'the factor which brings the demand for investment and the willingness to save into equilibrium with each other' (Keynes, 1936, p. 175). Keynes believed that this conflicted directly with his theory of effective demand. He rejected it because he believed the ability to save depended on the amount of investment, so that supply and demand curves for loanable funds were not independent. As a result, one 'could not obtain a determinate conclusion without introducing some additional equation or datum' (*CW*, XXIX, p. 228). This led Keynes to argue that the rate of interest was determined by monetary and not by real phenomena. He expressed this by proposing in the *General Theory* that interest rates were determined by the supply and demand for liquidity. The modern portfolio balance approach is a direct generalization of Keynes's liquidity preference theory of interest.

In chapter 14 of the *General Theory*, 'The Classicial Theory of the Rate of Interest', Keynes accepted the classical argument that in equilibrium the rate of interest will be equal to the marginal efficiency of capital. But he explicitly reversed the classical direction of causality. He argued that:

> the output of new investment will be pushed to the point at which the
> marginal efficiency of capital becomes equal to the rate of interest; and what
> the schedule of the marginal efficiency of capital tells us, is, not what the rate
> of interest is, but the point to which the output of new investment will be
> pushed, given the rate of interest. (Keynes, 1936, p. 184)

In his appendix to this chapter, Keynes attempted to refute the classical
and neo-classical view of the rate of interest as equating the demand
and supply of real capital or loanable funds. He first argued that there is
no 'consecutive' discussion of interest in Marshall or Pigou. 'Interest', as
a monetary phenomenon which belongs to a monetary economy had, he
argued, no business even being in Marshall's *Principles* which takes no
account of money (*ibid.*, p. 189).

Ricardo's classical statement on interest was so clear-cut and so
diametrically opposed to his own that he was forced to meet Ricardo's
argument head on:

> The interest of money is not regulated by the rate at which the Bank will
> lend, whether it be 5, 3 or 2 percent, but by the rate of profit which can be
> made by the employment of capital, and which is totally independent of the
> quantity or of the value of money. Whether the Bank lent on million, ten
> million, or a hundred millions, they would not permanently alter the market
> rate of interest; they would alter only the value of the money which they thus
> issued. (Ricardo, *Principles*, as quoted in *ibid.*, p. 190)

Keynes's cautious response is that this must be interpreted as a long-run
argument. As a result, granting the usual classical assumption of full
employment, there is only one rate of interest compatible with long-
period full employment.

Keynes then emphasizes the critical difference between assuming that
monetary policy constitutes *fixing the money supply* or *fixing the rate of
interest*:

> If . . . Ricardo had argued that it would make no permanent alteration to the
> rate of interest whether the quantity of money was fixed by the monetary
> authority at ten millions or at a hundred millions his conclusion would hold.
> But if by the policy of the monetary authority we mean the *terms* on which it
> will increase or decrease the quantity of money, i.e. the rate of interest at
> which it will . . . increase or decrease its assets – which is what Ricardo
> expressly does mean in the above quotation – then it is not the case either
> that the policy of the monetary authority is nugatory or that only one policy is
> compatible with long-period equilibrium . . . Assuming flexible money-
> wages, the quantity of money as such is, indeed nugatory in the long period;
> but *the terms on which the monetary authority will change the quantity of
> money enter as a real determinant into the economic scheme.* (*ibid.*, pp.
> 190–1; emphasis added)

Keynes points out that Ricardo overlooked the fact that the marginal efficiency of capital would change according to the amount invested, or alternatively expressed, that the amount of investment undertaken would depend on the ruling lending rate charged. But he went on to observe that, if following Ricardo both the quantity of employment and the psychological propensities of the community were assumed given, then it would follow that there is only one possible rate of accumulation of capital, and consequently only one possible value for the marginal efficiency of capital. He concluded generously:

> Ricardo offers us the supreme intellectual achievement, unattainable by weaker spirits, of adopting a hypothetical world remote from experience as though it were the world of experience, and then living in it consistently. With most of his successors common sense cannot help breaking in – with injury to their logical consistency. (*ibid.*, p. 192)

Keynes's infamous chapter 17, 'The Essential Properties of Interest and Money', opens as follows: 'It seems then, that the rate of interest on money plays a peculiar part in setting a limit to the level of employment, since it sets a standard to which the marginal efficiency of a capital asset must attain if it is to be newly produced' (*ibid.*, p. 222). He then proceeded to argue that all asset prices will adjust until their expected marginal efficiency, i.e. the own rates of return on all assets, are brought into equality. All pecuniary and non-pecuniary services on assets must be included in the return, which he proceeded to analyse in terms of the physical or pecuniary yield, carrying costs and liquidity premium.

Throughout this chapter, Keynes enumerated a multitude of reasons why the rate of interest does not adjust automatically to restore monetary equilibrium at full employment. Money is unique in having a high liquidity premium and low carrying costs. Money has zero or negligible elasticities of production, employment and substitution by the private sector. These arguments were all designed to show why, for money alone, its marginal efficiency need not fall in response to an increase in demand:

> The money rate of interest, by setting the pace for all the other commodity-rates of interest, holds back investment in the production of these other commodities without being capable of stimulating investment for the production of money, which by hypothesis cannot be produced ... Unemployment develops, that is to say, because people want the moon; men cannot be employed when the object of desire (i.e. money) is something which cannot be produced and the demand for which cannot readily be choked off. (*ibid.*, p. 235)

Keynes was forced into these somewhat unconvincing and metaphorical arguments about the exogeneity of own rates of return on money by his failure to emphasize in the *General Theory* the crucial difference be-

tween a commodity money and a credit money economy. His fundamental logical mistake was his willingness to regard 'the quantity of
money as determined by the action of the central bank' (*ibid.*, p. 247).
His famous properties of money, enumerated above, refer only to
commodity or fiat money. Zero elasticities of production or substitution
by the private sector obviously do not apply to credit money. Had he
instead incorporated into the *General Theory* his earlier insights in the
Treatise, that central banks set the level of interest rates, rather than
the quantity of the money supply, so that the supply of credit money
becomes endogenously demand determined, he would have been able
to reach his central conclusion that interest rates are a monetary and not
a real phenomenon, so that the return on money is exogenous and
'rules the roost', much more simply and persuasively. One year later, in
his 1937 discussion of the 'Finance Motive', Keynes was pushed by his
critics to recognize the endogeneity of credit money via the overdraft
system.

Keynes's position on the efficacy of monetary policy changed sharply
from the *Treatise* to the *General Theory*. When Britain left the gold
standard in September 1931, Keynes promptly wrote a letter to *The
Times* withdrawing his earlier support for tariffs to offset the overvaluation of sterling, on the grounds that an expansionary monetary policy
had at last become a possibility (Dimand, 1986). Over the subsequent
year the bank rate was lowered rapidly from 6 to 2 per cent, and the
interest rate on savings deposits which was tied to the bank rate fell to
0.5 per cent. In his final lecture in the fall term of 1932, Keynes stated
his belief that interest rates in Britain had probably reached their minimum level, and first used the term 'liquidity trap' to describe this phenomenon (*ibid.*).

Keynes explained the liquidity trap in the *General Theory* as caused
by an increase in the speculative demand for money balances as interest
rates fell to historically unprecedentedly low levels. He argued that
some positive floor level of interest rates existed at which the speculative
demand for money would rise indefinitely. Implicitly he was assuming
that interest rate expectations were regressive. As the level of interest
rates fell investors would feel increasingly confident that future interest
rates could only rise, so that the anticipated downside risk of capital
losses on holding bonds would more than offset their low interest yield.
Once this situation was reached, interest rates would not fall below this
level, no matter how much the central bank flooded the banks with
reserves.

The liquidity trap was thus explained by the demand for money
becoming infinitely interest elastic at some positive floor level of interest

rates. This at least is the version of the story that appears in the textbooks, even though Keynes explicitly states in the *General Theory* that 'Whilst this limiting case might become practically important in the future, I know of no example of it hitherto' (*CW*, VII, p. 207).

One problem with Keynes's explanation is that it does not apply to short-term rates, where capital losses do not occur if future rates rise. Although never explicitly stated, liquidity preference must thus refer only to long-term interest rates. In fact the level of short-term market interest rates continued to decline as the depression persisted. After 1932, the level of market short-term interest rates in both the UK and the USA fell below 1 per cent, and by 1939 rates on 90-day Treasury Bills in the USA had fallen to 0.02. Nevertheless, long-term rates and administered bank lending rates in either country never fell below 2.5 per cent. Moreover, at the extremely low level to which rates on short-term securities were reduced in the USA, banks voluntarily chose to hold enormous quantities of excess reserves, exceeding in amount the Federal Reserve's entire security portfolio.

In the *Treatise*, Keynes had stated that 'the Central Bank lacks direct control over the quantity of money ... the governor of the whole system is the rate of discount' (*CW*, V, p. 211). If central banks are regarded as setting the level of short-term interest rates rather than the money supply, a very much simpler explanation for a positive floor level of bank interest rates is available, one which does not necessitate any assumption about the behaviour of money demand. Due to the zero nominal return on currency, the nominal interest rate banks pay on demand deposits, a close substitute for currency, cannot fall below zero. The rate on savings deposits ordinarily must somewhat exceed zero in order to compensate holders for any imposed sacrifice of liquidity. Keynes was thus quite correct in arguing that the rate on savings deposits could not be pushed much below the level of 0.5 per cent already reached in 1932.

Given the spread required to cover the costs of bank intermediation, whose minimum value was of the order of 2–3 per cent, this implies in turn that the minimum administered nominal lending rates charged by banks can never fall below 2–3 per cent. Banks must be able to cover their variable costs for providing intermediation services and earn the required return on their equity capital if they are to remain in business.

The zero return on currency thus imposes a minimum positive floor to bank deposit rates, and since bank lending rates in oligopolistic markets may be viewed as administered at some mark-up over their deposit rates, a proportionately higher positive floor level of bank lending rates.

In 1933 less than two years after Britain had left the gold standard,

Keynes reversed himself and again recommended a protective tariff policy to stimulate aggregate demand (Dimand, 1986, p. 9). His pessimism over the effectiveness of cheap money policy as a means of stimulating increased borrowing in the extreme slump conditions of the 1930s was surely justified. From 1929 to 1933 the consumer price level fell by approximately 25 per cent in both the UK and the USA. To the extent this experienced deflation led to the extrapolative expectations of continuing future deflation, low nominal interest rates would not represent cheap money to prospective borrowers, or low returns to prospective leaders. Anticipated deflation raises the *ex ante* real cost of borrowed funds, and the *ex ante* real return on money balances, thus depressing effective demand for currently produced goods and services.[2]

Conversely, in contemporary situations of cost inflation a policy of low nominal interest rates will be much more effective in stimulating aggregate demand. With anticipated inflation, both the *ex ante* real cost of borrowing and the *ex ante* real return from holding money will be reduced below the nominal interest cost. As a result, in inflationary situations central banks are easily able to engineer *negative ex ante* real rates of interest by reducing nominal interest rates towards their positive floor level. Their ability to stimulate the level of aggregate demand is thus very much greater, compared with their power in depression situations experiencing deflationary price declines.

Keynes later summed up his position as follows:

> 'Put shortly, the orthodox theory maintains that the forces which determine the common value of the marginal efficiency of various assets are independent of money, which has, so to speak, no autonomous influence, and that prices move until the marginal efficiency of money, i.e. the rate of interest, falls into line with the common value of the marginal efficiency of other assets as determined by other forces. My theory, on the other hand, maintains that this is the special case and that over a wide range of possible cases almost the opposite is true, namely, that the marginal efficiency of money is determined by forces partly appropriate to itself, and that prices move until the marginal efficiency of other assets fall into line with the rate of interest. (*CW*, XIII, p. 420)

Because Keynes in the *General Theory* proceeded on the assumption that the money stock was exogenously set by the monetary authorities, his liquidity preference theory of the determination of interest rates unfortunately appeared to be indeterminate. On his own logic the demand for money and the level of interest rates would vary with the level of income, and so would feed back to affect investment spending. It was this circularity which Hicks's IS/LM analysis was designed to rescue, but which by an internal logic of its own has developed into the 'neo-classical synthesis'. The IS/LM analysis concluded that in long-run equilibrium, assuming full wage and price flexibility, interest rates would continue to adjust through the real-wealth effect until full employment was attained. This was unfortunately the very neo-classical result, that in the long run money is neutral and interest rates are determined entirely by real forces, which Keynes had been at utmost pains to deny:

> But if what these two quantities (saving and investment) determine is, is not the rate of interest, but the aggregate volume of employment, then our outlook on the mechanism of the economic system will be profoundly changed. A decreased readiness to spend will be looked on in quite a different light if, instead of being regarded as a factor which will, *cet par.*, increase investment, it is seen as a factor which will, *cet par.*, diminish employment. (Keynes, 1936, p. 185)

The logic of Keynes's own analysis would seem to demand that the rate of interest be exogenously determined from outside his system. For if interest were to act as an equilibrating mechanism, so that 'a decrease in spending will tend to lower the rate of interest, and an increase in spending, to raise it' (*ibid.*, p. 185), we are back in a Say's law world, at least in so far as long-run equilibrium is concerned.[3] As Passinetti has noted,

> What this theory [of effective demand] requires as far as the rate of interest is concerned, is not that the rate of interest is determined by liquidity perference, but that it is determined *exogenously* with respect to the income generating process. Whether, in particular, liquidity preference or anything else determines it, is entirely immaterial. (Passinetti, 1974, p. 47)

In his correspondence with Hicks concerning 'Mr Keynes and the Classics', Keynes responded, 'I . . . really have next to nothing to say by way of criticism'. But he then continued:

> From my point of view it is important to insist that my remark is to the effect that an increase in the inducement to invest *need* not raise the rate of interest. I should agree that, unless the monetary policy is appropriate, it is quite likely to. In this respect I consider that the difference between myself and the classicals lies in the fact that they regard the rate of interest as a non-monetary phenomenon, so that an increase in the inducement to invest would raise the rate of interest irrespective of monetary policy, – though they might concede that monetary policy was capable of producing a temporary evaporating effect. (*CW*, XIV, pp. 79–80)

This passage suggests that even immediately after the *General Theory*, Keynes as in the *Treatise* still viewed short-term interest rates as determined in the real world essentially by the policy of the monetary authorities, in spite of the fact that he had just emphasized liquidity preference as his brand-new general explanation of interest rates in the book. One year before his death, in his minutes for the National Debt Inquiry, Keynes argued as follows:

> The monetary authorities can have any rate of interest they like ... Up to the point when inflation begins ... a lower rate of interest tends to increase employment ... If, after the war, we need more saving to provide more investment, we have to reduce the rate of interest up to the point of full employment. Thereafter the old rules apply: we have to raise the rate of interest to prevent inflation ... Historically the authorities have always determined the rate at their own sweet will, and have been influenced almost entirely by balance of trade reasons and their own counter-liquidity preference. (*CW*, XXVII, pp. 390–2)

It seems clear that in the *General Theory* Keynes intended that the long-run rate of interest should be treated as one of the key determinants of the level of investment spending, and as a largely exogenous factor determined by monetary forces. As Hicks has noted, 'From the point of view of the theory, an exogenous element cannot be an effect. It can only be a cause' (1979, p. 22). But because Hicks insisted that the rate of interest must be viewed as determined endogenously in the ruling neo-Walrasian general equilibrium paradigm, this central notion of uni-directional causality became lost in his IS/LM interpretation of Keynes. In abandoning Keynes's partial equilibrium method, and no longer treating interest as an exogenous variable, Hicks fundamentally if unintentionally distorted the meaning of Keynes's theory. As a result, Keynes's brilliant formulation of the non-neutral processes by which the level of interest affect real activity have been obscured and nearly entirely overlooked.

This central message of Keynes has become completely unintelligible in the 'neo-classical synthesis' of mainstream Keynesian analysis. By taking the money stock as exogenous, as is appropriate only for a commodity or fiat money world, it is easy to demonstrate that full employment equilibrium with a unique real rate of interest necessarily follows from the assumption of perfect price and wage flexibility. As a result, in long-run equilibrium money becomes neutral, and real factors alone determine the level of interest rates. However, once it is recognized that in all credit money economies it is the level of nominal interest rates, rather than the nominal money stock, which is exogenously determined by the central bank, monetary non-neutrality follows simply and directly. The terms on which credit money is issued have real effects in both the short and long run.

Notes

1. This chapter has been excerpted from a forthcoming manuscript, Horizontalists and verticalists: the macroeconomics of credit money'.
2. This may explain why US banks were willing to purchase Bills, even when their nominal returns had fallen to one or two basis points. If any deflation is anticipated, their *ex ante* real return becomes, in effect, the expected deflation rate.
3. This has been the contribution of the 'neo-classical synthesis'.

References

Dimand, R.W. (1986), 'The road to the *General Theory*: Keynes' lectures on the monetary theory of production, 1932–33', Carleton University, mimeo.

Hicks, J.R. (1979), *Causality in Economics*, Oxford: Blackwell.

Keynes, J.M. (1936), *The General Theory of Employment, Interest and Money*, London: Macmillan.

Keynes, J.M. (1973a), *The General Theory and After, Part I, Preparation*, London: Macmillan.

Keynes, J.M. (1973b), Vol. XIV, *The General Theory and After. Part II, Defense*, London: Macmillan.

Passinetti, L. (1974), *Growth and Income Distribution: Essay in Economic Theory*, Cambridge: Cambridge University Press.

Shackle, G.L.S. (1983), 'Levels of simplicity in Keynes's theory of money and employment', *South African Journal of Economics*, 51(3), September, 357–367.

13 Keynes and stable money
T.K. Rymes[1]

Introduction

The idea that to Keynes, in Keynes or in Keynesian economics (all three are different) 'money did not matter' must be one of the strangest developments in modern economic thought. Professor Friedman, in his presidential address to the American Economic Association, argued that for two decades following '... Keynes's rigorous and sophisticated analysis' it was believed by almost all in the economics profession that 'Money did not matter' (Friedman, 1968, p. 96). Scholars are puzzling over this development (cf. Ascheim and Talvas, 1979; Talvas, 1981; Rotheim, 1981; Nell, 1983; Kregel, 1985). Davidson (1972, 1978), Minsky (1975), Dow and Earl (1982) are often cited as those, writing in the Keynesian tradition, who maintain that money does indeed matter.

The idea that 'money did not matter' to Keynes is obviously false. He was, above all, a monetary theorist. While the theory of the supply of money was not front and centre in the *General Theory*, by Keynes's own statements we know that the central problem confronting him was the determination of the rate(s) of interest in a monetary economy.

In his notes on Keynes's lectures for Michaelmas Term, 15 October 1934, where Keynes is setting out the content of his lectures entitled 'General Theory of Employment', Bryce reports Keynes as saying: '... it is the theory of the rate of interest that is at [the] bottom of the trouble' (Rymes, 1986d). Keynes himself argued earlier:

> The divergence between the real-exchange economics and my desired monetary economics is, however, most marked and perhaps most important when we come to the discussion of the rate of interest and to the relation between the volume of output and the amount of expenditure. (Keynes, 1931)

Furthermore, while it might appear that 'the essential properties of interest and money' in the *General Theory* was an afterthought, it is clear from Keynes's own summaries of his theory in his paper in honour of Irving Fisher and the famous *Quarterly Journal of Economics* article that it was central (cf. Keynes, 1936b, 1937). It is commonplace that the *General Theory* represented the final part of a long struggle for Keynes to escape from the clutches of the quantity theory of money.

The traditional quantity theory asserts that, in the long run, 'money does not matter', i.e. money is 'neutral'. Nowadays, with rational expectations, money is neutral even in the short run. Super-non-neutrality arises if, and only if, it is possible for authorities to engineer, via lump-sum taxes or transfers, alternative rates of inflation which affect the size of the Bailey trapezoids under the general equilibrium demand schedules for real fiat money balances. Since the money is fiat, the old and new quantity theories imply either impotent monetary authorities[2] or mischievousness on their part which requires them to be subject to constitutional rules (Lucas, 1986; Brennan and Buchanan, 1986). Keynes was certainly aware that the quantity theory implied that 'money did not matter' (cf. his critiques of the real exchange or neutral economics), and he also knew that monetary authorities believed that, with respect to the volume of employment and output, their hands were tied. Since Keynes gave his life to the establishment of international monetary authorities such as the IMF, it is doubtful though if even he could have imagined the modern attacks on the potency of monetary authorities and the democratic implementation of monetary policies which is entailed in the constitutionalist assault on discretionary central banks.[3]

Keynesian theory of the discretionary services of monetary authorities
What, then, is the Keynesian theory of money such that 'money matters', and such that monetary authorities and discretionary monetary policy, as distinct from monetary rules, are important? Money, we shall argue, earns a liquidity premium *par excellence* because its service is really the service of the monetary authorities which is the conventional collective 'inconclusive solution' (O'Donnell, 1982, p. 27) to the problem of instability. The full development of the Keynesian theory of money awaits a satisfactory development of the Keynesian theory of banking.[4] Yet the essence of the argument can be captured if the technical details of banking are pushed into the background and one concentrates solely on fiat money.

One starts with the modern neo-classical monetary theory because it clearly illustrates the importance of super-non-neutrality vs neutrality in the traditional quantity theory of money. This theory employs temporary general equilibrium analysis just as Keynes's *General Theory*, particularly as set out in chapter 17, is temporary general equilibrium theory.

Consider the simplest world of the usual one commodity and one fiat money. Temporary equilibrium entails that the real net rates of return to the two assets, commodity (stocks) and money, are equalized; i.e. at full employment:

$$r_k = \frac{\partial C}{\partial K} \underset{-}{(K,} \underset{+}{M/P)} - \delta =$$

$$\frac{\partial C}{\partial M/P} \underset{+}{(K,} \underset{-}{M/P)} + i - \delta_M - p = r_{M/P}$$

The real net rate of return to capital is the gross marginal physical product of the services of capital[5] less the rate of depreciation. The real product of the services of real money or what is the same thing, the services of the authorities[6] plus a nominal rate of interest, if paid by the authorities, minus the service charges, expressed as a rate, on money balances levied to pay for the services of the authorities minus the expected rate of inflation. Rewrite these equations as nominal rates of return. Introduce Keynes's notation to see that they are indeed the temporary equilibrium analysis of chapter 17 of the *General Theory*; i.e.:

$$R_K = \frac{\partial C}{\partial K} (K, M/P) - \delta + p = \frac{\partial C}{\partial M/P} (K, M/P) + i - \delta_M = R_{M/P}$$

may be rewritten as:

$$R_K = q_K - c_K + a = q_M - c_M = R_{M/P}$$

where q_K and q_M are the *own-expected yields* on capital and money, c_K and c_M are the depreciation or service charges or *carrying costs* of capital and money and a is the expected rate of inflation of the money price of commodities. In Keynes's language, $\partial C/\partial K$ ($\cdot$) $- \delta$, the net marginal physical product of capital, is the own-rate of interest on capital, while $\partial C/(\partial M/P)$ ($\cdot$) $+ i - \delta_M$, is the own-rate of interest on money. Note that there is as yet no liquidity premia in these formulations of rates of return. Given K, M and i, δ, δ_M and p, temporary equilibrium occurs when there is a price of capital, p, the price level of non-monetary goods such that the two net rates of return are equal. If the two rates of return were equal to the steady-state rate of return, designated as $n + n' + \varrho$, where n is the rate of growth of the population, n' the rate of Harrod neutral technical progress and ϱ the rate of pure time preference, then there would be no further capital or real money accumulation. In the case of *stability*, all temporary equilibria seek the steady state (see Figure 13.1).

In Figure 13.1 the locus $\dot{K} = 0$ is the set of all Ks and M/Ps such that $r_K = n + n' + \varrho$ and the locus $\dot{M}/P = 0$ is the, in general, different set of Ks and M/Ps such that $r_{M/P} = n + n' + \varrho$.

A unique steady state is the set K* and M/P*. Consider an initial

Figure 13.1

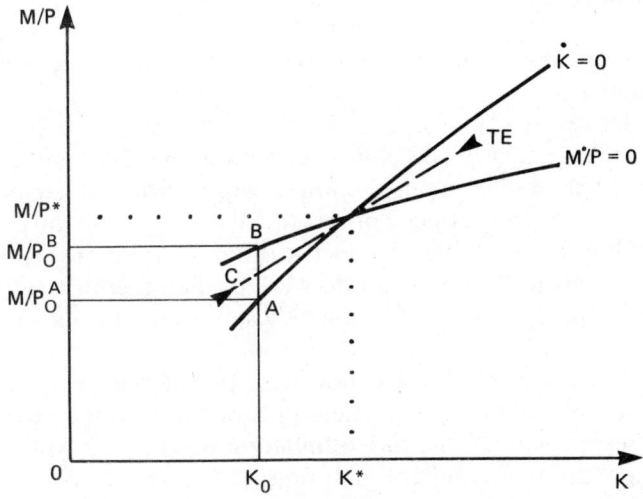

lower capital–labour endowment, K_0. From the generalized diminish-ing return technology, a lower K entails a higher r_K and a lower $r_{M/P}$. Portfolio balance will require a higher price level and lower real-money balances. Suppose the higher price level, P_0^A, entails so lower a stock of real-money balances that the net rate of return to capital is again the steady-state rate, the point A on the $\dot{K} = 0$ locus. That price level could not be a temporary equilibrium price level, however, since the net rate of return on money would be *above* the steady-state rate (given K_0, the level of real-money balances at A entails a point *below* the $\dot{M/P} = 0$ locus).

If a higher price level, P_0^B, entails not quite so low a level of real-money balances, so that now the net rate of return to money balances is again the steady-state rate (the point B on the $\dot{M/P} = 0$ locus), then neither can that price level entail a temporary equilibrium. However, a higher price than the one entailed at B but lower than at A, will bring the net rates of return into equality, at a level above the steady-state rate. That price level is indicated by the point C on the temporary equilibrium locus, TE. With the endowment K_0 and real-money bal-ances indicated by the height of C, the economy may accumulate real-capital and greater real-money balances such that the price level must be lower and lower as the economy seeks the steady state through a sequence of temporary equilibria. Thus whatever the initial endow-ment K, for every M given i, δ, δ_M and p, there will exist price levels such that temporary equilibria will be observed, all such equilibria being attracted to the steady state, even if the steady-state equilibria should themselves be changing.

The neo-classical non-discretionary services of the monetary authorities: a digression

Neither the steady-state solution nor the sequence of temporary equilibria are independent of the policy rule of the monetary authorities. A different level of the nominal money supply will, of course, affect neither – it will merely effect a proportional difference in the price level. If the authorities are able to effect a different real rate of return on money, i.e. the authorities can effect $i - p$, then the $\dot{M/P} = 0$ loci, the temporary equilibria loci and the steady states are affected, as is illustrated in Figure 13.2.

Suppose the authorities had not been paying a rate of interest on money fiat, but had been so engineering a rate of growth of the nominal money supply such that the rate of inflation was zero. It will be noticed that the steady state is suboptimal; that is:

$$R_M^S = \frac{\partial C}{\partial M/P} (K, M/P) - \delta_M > 0$$

the value of the gross marginal physical product of the services of real-

Figure 13.2

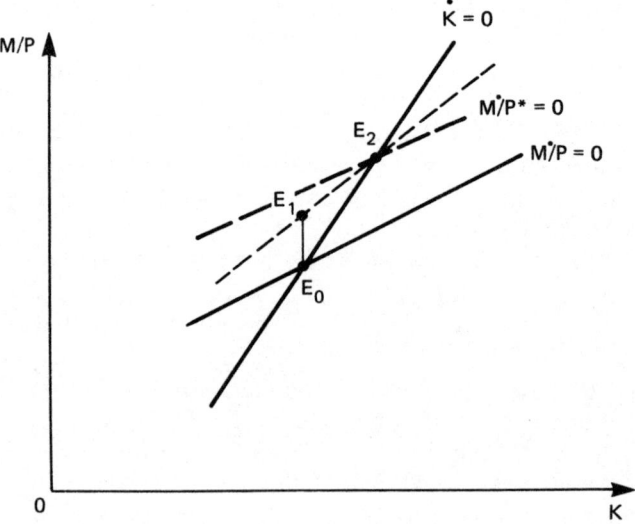

money balances or the services of the monetary authorities in contributing to the steady-state flow of consumption is greater than the service charge. The marginal conditions for a Paretian efficient allocation do not hold. Notice also that the service charge by the authorities implies that the services rendered are private, i.e. individuals, by holding more money, will reap additional benefits but will have to pay more service charges. All individuals taken together determine the price level, so that the amount of real-money balances in the economy is such that the gross marginal physical product of money balance exceeds the service charge, expressed as a rate, by the steady-state net rate of return.

Let the authorities pay i equal to R^S.[7] The resulting excess demand for cash is eliminated when the price level is lower and real balances greater until the gross marginal physical product of real-money balances is lower and the gross marginal physical product of capital is higher, so that the point E_1 on the new temporary equilibrium locus prevails. At that point, however, the equal net rates of return exceed the steady-state rate, capital and real-money balances accumulation proceeds through a sequence of temporary equilibria until a new steady-state equilibrium, E_2, prevails.[8]

The net rate of return on money:

$$R_M^S = \frac{\partial C}{\partial M/P} (K_2, M/P_2) + i - \delta_M$$

implies, since $R_M^S = i$, that $\partial C/(\partial M/P) (K_2, M/P_2) - \delta_M = 0$; i.e. that Paretian optimality has been achieved. The authorities are following the Friedman–Lucas optimum money-supply policy rule (Friedman, 1969; Lucas, 1986).

The authorities are rendering a service which is obtained by holding, and utilizing the services of, real-money balances. The authorities charge for that service. In the Paretian efficient temporary and steady-state equilibria, the service price equals the value of the marginal physical product of that service. The service charge levied by the authorities equals the marginal cost to the authorities of providing that service – and there would, in the context of the model so far, be no reason for the authorities to price otherwise for their services.

If the cost to the authorities of providing the service were zero, then with $i = R_M^S$, the price level would be such that the gross marginal product of real-money balances would be zero. The cost of producing or printing another unit of fiat money might well be zero but the authorities must incur such costs as those of enforcing against counterfeiting (See Klein, 1978). That cost which is the cost of defending the property right of the authorities in the provision of fiat money and is part of Keynes's carrying cost associated with any asset would be positive, so that it would be the net marginal physical product of money balances, $\partial C/(\partial M/P)$ $(K_2, M/P_2) - \delta$, which would be zero in the efficient equilibrium.

So far no reason has been provided as to why the provision of monetary services must be handled by authorities. Private issuers of money would have the same problem of enforcement against counterfeiting. Private users of private moneys, again more precisely users of the services of private issuers, would earn the competitively determined real interest rate of their money balances and would pay a service charge sufficient to cover the costs of the private issuers in providing such services, such costs being no different from those incurred by the authorities. Issuers of private money could form their own collectivity to enforce against cheating or the control of counterfeiting, which any one private issuer might not find it profitable to do (e.g. the Canadian Bankers' Association was formed prior to the birth of the Bank of Canada to regulate Canadian private banks).

If it is the case that the services obviating instability in the value of money arising out of counterfeiting or the private production of costless money can be privately produced, then it follows that there will be no fiat money. The price level defined in terms of such money would be undefined. There would exist a number of privately produced moneys (and the private issuers might form an association monitoring the rate of exchange among such monies). Relative service charges as a part of well-defined general equilibria relative values would be observed. *There would be no such thing as a monetary theory of value.* This stems from the assumption of stability.[9]

If private banking were introduced into the analysis, the fiat money would be reserves of the banks with the authorities. The services provided by authorities, for which service charges could be levied, would then be, for example, inter-bank clearing arrangements and deposit insurance.

The problem of instability and discretionary policy

There is nothing in the model which assures stability, rather it is assumed. Suppose instability in the rational expectations saddlepoint sense, shown in Figure 13.3, is assumed.[10]

Again, consider a lower capital–labour endowment K_0. Given M, i, δ_M and p, the price level which ensures temporary equilibrium at the point C is associated with real rates of return to capital and money which lead away from the steady state, involving higher and higher price levels or the economy degenerating into decumulation and hyperinflation. The

Figure 13.3

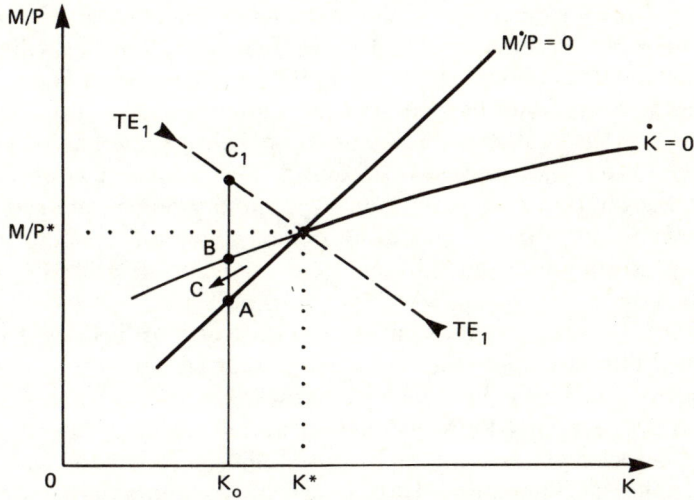

authorities now have an immediate role to play in preventing such instability. How? The problem is that, under initial conditions K_0, the community cannot be persuaded to hold the available money supply – the attempt to go from money to goods is associated with the de-stabilizing rise in the price level. By promising at some time to break its monetary rule, $i - \delta_M - p$, the authorities, by paying higher rates of interest on money, by levying lower service charges or by *promising* to ensure a lower rate of inflation *temporarily*, can ensure that the community can be persuaded to hold more money, not less, and so bring about the lower not a higher price level associated with the point C_1 on the temporary equilibrium locus TE_1.

The temporary equilibrium locus TE_1 is the stable arm. The rational expectations saddlepoint equilibrium argument entails, since the economy maintains itself as a monetary economy, that the community knows the authorities will behave in the discretionary way requisite for stability (see Begg, 1982; Sheffrin, 1983). The crucial point is that, if the community is convinced the authorities will so behave, the price level will immediately be that associated with the stable arm. It is the belief that the authorities will so behave to stabilize the monetary economy, which it is not in the interest of any private supplier of money to do, *which gives fiat money its liquidity premium*. Confidence that the monetary authorities will so behave may be sufficient so that, *ex post*, just as Keynes argued, there will be nothing to show for the liquidity premium. There wll be nothing measurable – i.e. priceable – associated with the liquidity premium.

With rational expectations, the community is confident that the authorities will so behave, and will know that the authorities will do so temporarily. The economy, from C_1, seeks the steady-state E by virtue of the authorities modifying their money-supply policies such that the economy exhibits real-capital accumulation and a sequence of higher price levels such that real-money balance decumulation is observed. Without the temporary or discretionary monetary policy, the economy would exhibit instability. The discretionary monetary policy, which promotes the stability of the monetary economy, is the crucial role the authorities play!

Consider an initial equilibrium wherein the authorities might try to follow the optimum money-supply rule such that, as illustrated in Figure 13.4, the $M/P = 0$ schedule is shifted upward.

In the case of stability there will be an initial fall in the price level, followed by a sequence of temporary equilibria of capital and real-money capital accumulation. In the case of instability, however, the initial fall in the price level would result in a process of accumulation of capital and real balances through ever lower prices. To attempt to establish the optimum money-supply rule would set in motion the problem of instability. To prevent such instability, the authorities must

Figure 13.4

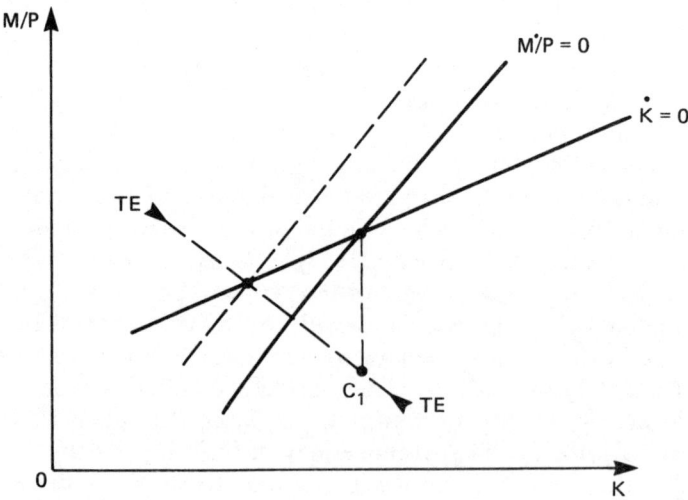

then engage in the discretionary act of making money less attractive to hold, so that the price level would initially be higher on the new temporary equilibrium locus, i.e. at the point C_1 on stable arm, TE, and a process of capital decumulation and real-money accumulation set in motion along the stable arm.

With potential instability, the attempt by the authorities to pursue a rule, in the face of any perturbation, implies the need on the part of the same authorities to change the rule – to act in a discretionary way with respect to the real rate of return on money – to ensure stability.

A number of cases can be considered. Temporary and stable equilibria can be changed because of non-neutral revisions in technology. One could thus analyse the effects – assuming, first, stability, and secondly, instability – of shifts in the $\dot{K} = 0$ and $\dot{M/P} = 0$ loci.

Consider a familiar case. With instability, suppose the disturbance is in terms of the expected marginal physical product to money balances such that, in the first instance, the $\dot{M/P} = 0$ locus is lower, and in the second instance, is higher, as illustrated in Figure 13.5.

In the first instance, where the community wishes to hold less money, if the authorities stand pat, the price level is increased and gets higher and higher without bound. The community knows, however, that the authorities will prevent the hyperinflation from occurring by raising sometime the rate of return on money, thereby breaking its monetary

Figure 13.5

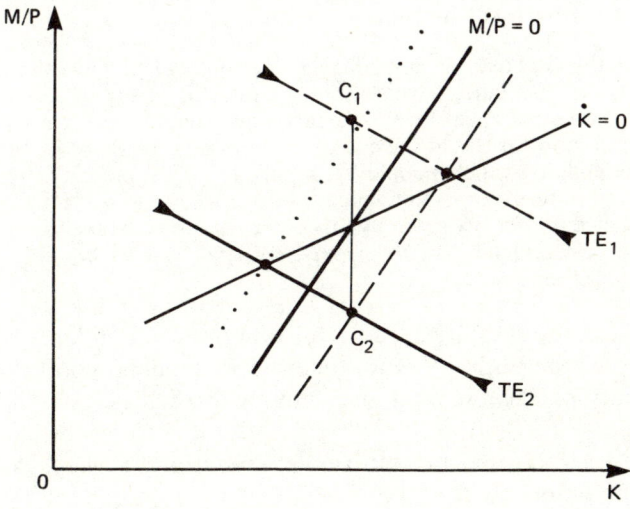

rule and so ensuring that there will be a lower, not a higher, price level associated with the temporary equilibrium on the stable arm, i.e. the point C_1.

Conversely, should the community initially increase its demand for money and the authorities stand by their rule, then the initial lower price level will be associated with an unstable sequence of even lower and lower price levels and hyperdeflation. This analysis is similar to Keynes's parable of the 'banana plantation' in the *Treatise*. Again, though, the community knows this will not be permitted by the authorities. The community expects that, at some time, the authorities will so lower the rate of return on money such that initially the price level is higher, not lower, i.e. the point C_2 on the stable arm TE_2.

The liquidity premium: tentative conclusions

The basic problem confronting the authorities can now be examined. In both the rational expectations stable and saddlepoint equilibria cases, the outcome is stability in the price level or in the real value of money. In the case of stability, the outcome is automatic and there would appear to be no role or rationale for authorities. In the case of saddle-point equilibrium, stability in the price level is brought about by confidence in the community that the authorities will act in a discretionary way to ensure such stability (see DeLong and Summers, 1986).

Stability in the price level expressed in terms of money is what provides money with its characteristic of a general store purchasing power. The fact that the community has this 'power of disposal' over money yields money its liquidity premium. Keynes defined the liquidity premium for any asset as that:

> power of disposal over an asset during a period [which] may offer a potential convenience or security, which is not equal for assets of different kinds, though the assets themselves are of equal value. There is, so to speak, nothing to show for this at the end of the period in the shape of output, yet it is something for which people are ready to pay something. The amount (measured in terms of itself) which they are willing to pay for the potential convenience or security given by this power of disposal (exclusive of yield or carrying cost attaching to the asset), we shall call its liquidity premium. (Keynes, 1936a, p. 226)

Confidence in the stability of the value of money – confidence, that is, in the ability of the authorities to generate that public good through its discretionary policies, is what gives money the highest liquidity yield of all assets.

Return to the stated net returns to capital and money. Add in the liquidity premium on money, ℓ:

$$r_k = \frac{\partial C}{\partial K} (K, M/P) - \delta$$

$$= \frac{\partial C}{\partial M/P} (K, M/P) + i - \delta_M - p + \ell = r_{M/P}$$

It immediately follows that, whatever the rule $(i - \delta_M - p)$ the authorities might be following, the level of prices, the real net rates of return to capital and money and hence the temporary equilibrium amounts of real capital and fiat money accumulation cannot be ascertained independently of the liquidity premium on money. Since no one knows what kind of stability the economy exhibits, the monetary authorities must be concerned with price stability. This is why the elasticity of production of real-money balances is so low, and sets aside the criticisms of Keynes by Friedman and Lerner on this point and weakens the logic of the possibility of equilibrating 'Pigou effects' (See Friedman, 1972; Lerner, 1952). Thus downward variation in prices and money wage rates do not necessarily ensure full employment as a temporary equilibrium because with no intervention the variation may yield hyperdeflation and the monetary authorities, charged with the prevention of instability in the value of money, will not permit the variation to occur in the first instance. The Keynesian problem, of less than full employment temporary equilibria at seemingly 'sticky' money wages and prices, has then a logical non *ad hoc* basis.

Since the provision of monetary stability is not a resource using activity such as policing against counterfeiting, it is not possible for the authorities to set a service charge to price fiat money services efficiently in the Paretian sense. Consequently, the whole set of relative prices in a Keynesian monetary economy will have embedded in them rates of return which will partly reflect the liquidity premium on money (cf. Townshend, 1937). The Keynesian set of relative prices will be equal to the quantity theory general equilibrium set of relative prices if, and only if, the liquidity premium on money is zero. Such a zero premium, however, will pertain only to fiat money economies for which stability is assumed – economies for which as well it is not possible to imagine why fiat moneys and monetary authorities exist in the first place. Once one contemplates a rational expectation saddlepoint equilibrium, however, a reason for fiat money and discretional monetary authorities immediately exists. The liquidity premium reflects the confidence of the community in the authorities in their ability to protect the value of money. In any sequence of Keynesian temporary equilibrium the liquidity premium will always be positive (and will be embedded in all Keynesian relative prices) and implies that such a sequence can never terminate or be deemed to approach the quantity theory of money steady state. Money matters, always! We have the beginnings of a Keynesian monetary theory of value.

Notes

1. This is a revision of a paper presented at the Conference on 'Keynes and Public Policy after Fifty Years', Glendon College, York University, 26–28 September 1986. In earlier unpublished Carleton Economic Papers 74–12, 'Keynes and "the essential properties of interest and money"', and 80–09, 'Sraffa and Keynes on interest rates', I set out hints of the idea in this chapter. Those earlier papers were marred by a failure to appreciate the reason for Keynes's break with the quantity theory which this paper attempts to establish. I thank for their comments Nancy Wulwick, Geoff Harcourt, John Crow, Marc Lavoie, Mario Seccareccia and, in particular, Peter Howitt.
2. The Bank of Canada came to believe that *the* only thing it could affect was the rate of inflation: see Rymes (1986a).
3. Even Friedman has recoiled from this modern extremity of view; cf. A. Schwartz and M. Friedman (1986).
4. See Rymes (1985, 1986b, 1986c) for attempts in this direction.
5. The signs below the arguments in the production function indicate the value of the second partial derivatives.
6. Just as the services of waiting are the primary inputs associated with the services of reproducible capital, the services of the authorities stand behind the services of real fiat money balances.
7. The policy is the same if the authorities engineer a rate of change of the money supply such that a rate of deflation equal to the steady-state rate of return is confidently expected to prevail.
8. If the $\dot{K} = 0$ locus were vertical, then money would be superneutral in Sidrauski's (1967) sense.
9. The assumption of stability is the source of the modern discussion to the effect that modern monetary theory is an arbitrary artefact, that central banks are fifth wheels and that full general economic equilibrium, with private production of transactions and portfolio services of 'money', could exist (see Fama, 1983; Hall, 1982).
10. Instability, in this sense, could be generated by postulating myopic expectations (see Grandmont, 1983). Here, however, technical conditions in monetary production are postulated such that:

$$\frac{\partial^2 C}{\partial K^2} \cdot \frac{\partial^2 C}{\partial M/P^2} < \frac{\partial^2 C}{\partial M/P \partial K}$$

References

Ascheim, J. and Talvas, G.S., (1979), 'On monetarism and ideology', *Banca Nazionale del Lavoro Quarterly Review*, XXXII, June, 167–186.

Begg, D.K.H. (1982), *The Rational Expectations Revolution in Macroeconomics: Theories and Evidence*, Oxford: Philip Allan.

Brennan, G. and Buchanan, J.M. (1986), *The Reason of Rules: Constitutional Political Economy*, Cambridge: Cambridge University Press.

Davidson, P. (1972), *Money and the Real World*, London: Macmillan.

DeLong J.B. and Summers, L.H. (1986), 'Is increased price flexibility stabilizing?', Unpublished paper, Harvard University, 1986.

Dow, S.C. and Earl, P.E. (1982), *Money Matters: A Keynesian Approach to Monetary Economics*, Oxford: Martin Robertson.

Fama, E.F. (1983), 'Financial intermediation and price level control', *Journal of Monetary Economics*, XII, July, 1–28.

Friedman, M. (1968), 'The role of monetary policy', *American Economic Review*, March 1968 58, 1, pp 1–17; reprinted in *The Optimum Quantity of Money and Other Essays*, London: Macmillan.

Friedman, M. (1969), 'The optimum quantity of money', in *The Optimum Quantity of Money and Other Essays*, London: Macmillan.

Friedman, M. (1972), 'Comments on the critics', *Journal of Political Economy*, LXXX, September–October, 80, 5, pp 906–950.

Grandmont, J.-M. (1983), *Money and Value: A Reconsideration of Classical and Neoclassical Monetary Theories*, Cambridge: Cambridge University Press.

Hall, R.E. (1982), '*Monetary Trends in the United States and the United Kingdom:* a review from the perspective of new developments in monetary economics', *Journal of Economic Literature*, XX, December, 1552–1556.

Keynes, J.M. (1931), 'A monetary theory of production', *Der Stand und die nächste Zunkunft der konjunkturforchung*; Reprinted in the *Collected Writings of John Maynard Keynes Volume XIII*, (ed.) D.E. Moggridge, London: Macmillan.

Keynes, J.M. (1936a), *The General Theory of Employment, Interest and Money*; reprinted in the *Collected Writings of John Maynard Keynes Volume VII*, (ed.) D.E. Moggridge, London, Macmillan.

Keynes, J.M. (1936b), 'The theory of the rate of interest', *The Lessons of Monetary Experience: Essays in Honour of Irving Fisher*; reprinted in *The Collected Writings of John Maynard Keynes Volume XIV* (ed.) D.E. Moggridge, London: Macmillan.

Keynes, J.M. (1937), 'The general theory of employment', *Quarterly Journal of Economics*, VI, February, 209–223: reprinted in *CW*, XIV, 109–123.

Klein, B. (1978), 'Money, wealth and seigniorage', in K.E. Boulding and T.F. Wilson (eds) *Redistribution through the Financial System*, New York: Praeger.

Kregel, J.A. (1985), 'Hamlet without the prince: Cambridge microeconomics without money', *American Economic Review Papers and Proceedings*, May, 133–139.

Lerner, A.P. (1952), 'The essential properties of interest and money', *Quarterly Journal of Economics*, LXVI, May, 172–193.

Lucas, R.E., Jr (1968), 'Principles of fiscal and monetary policy', *Journal of Monetary Economics*, XVII, January, 117–134.

Minsky, H.P. (1975), *John Maynard Keynes*, New York: Columbia University Press.

Nell, E.J. (1983), 'Keynes after Sraffa: the essential properties of Keynes's theory of interest and money: comment on Kregel', in J. Kregel (ed.), *Distribution, Effective Demand and International Economic Relations*, London: Macmillan.

O'Donnell, R.M. (1982), 'Keynes's philosophy and economics: an approach to rationality and uncertainty', PhD dissertation, University of Cambridge.

Rotheim, R.J. (1981), 'Keynes' monetary theory of value (1933)', *Journal of Post Keynesian Economics*, III, 568–585.

Rymes, T.K. (1985), 'Inflation, nonoptimal monetary arrangements and the banking imputation in the national accounts', *Review of Income and Wealth*, XXXI, March, 85–96.

Rymes, T.K. (1986a), 'Does the Bank of Canada matter?', in M. Prince (ed.), *How Ottawa Spends*, Toronto: Methuen.

Rymes, T.K. (1986b), 'Further thoughts on the banking imputation in the national accounts', forthcoming in *Review of Income and Wealth*.

Rymes, T.K. (1986c), 'On the neoclassical theory of the efficiency of banking', Carleton Economic Papers 86–03.

Rymes, T.K. (ed.) (1986d), *Keynes's Lectures, 1932–35, Notes of Students*, Chapter C3, Notes of Robert B. Bryce, Ottawa: Department of Economics, Carleton University.

Schwartz, A. and Friedman, M. (1986), 'Has government any role in money?', *Journal of Monetary Economics*, XVII, January, 32–62.

Sheffrin, S.M. (1983), *Rational Expectations*, Cambridge: Cambridge University Press

Surveys of Economic Literature.

Sidrauski, M. (1967), 'Inflation and economic growth', *Journal of Political Economy*, LXXV, December, 796–810.

Talvas, G.S. (1981), 'Keynesian and monetarist theories of the monetary transmission process: doctrinal aspects', *Journal of Monetary Economics*, VII, 317–337.

Townshend, H. (1937), 'Liquidity-premium and the theory of value', *Economic Journal*, XLVII, March, 159–169.

14 Money, interest and rentiers: the twilight of rentier capitalism in Keynes's *General Theory*

Marc Lavoie and Mario Seccareccia[1]

Introduction

To most contemporary economists who have never read Keynes, Keynesian policy views emerging from the *General Theory* can be appropriately summarized by the original Hicksian IS/LM cross with the usual liquidity trap-cum-wage rigidity litany and an emphasis on activist fiscal policy.[2] The view which we intend to convey in this chapter is quite different from this stereotyped caricature of Keynes's policy perspectives. Because of his concern with the study of an advanced monetary economy in which the process of production is its most vital characteristic, Keynes's theoretical analysis led him to contemplate several radical steps in the direction of a more profound and integrated view of public policy.

In what follows we shall underline some of these radical implications of Keynes's analysis, in particular, that part of his monetary theory which is opposed to the classical quantity theory of money or to modern monetary theory of the Patinkinesque variety. Beginning with this analysis of a monetary ('entrepreneur') economy in which production is its most essential process, Keynes was to sweep away much of the explicit hypotheses that continue to constitute the foundation of today's most 'advanced' research programme. In addition to questioning the postulates of the received theory of employment and criticizing the logical fallacy of the orthodox view of the saving–investment causality, Keynes was categorically opposed to the explicit dichotomy in neo-classical monetary theory of treating the rate of interest as a real phenomenon and price formation as a process driven forward by exogenous disturbances in the quantity of money. To establish more clearly the implications of Keynes's monetary theory for public policy, it will first be necessary to discuss briefly his monetary framework which placed much emphasis on the institutional characteristics of the economy. This analysis will be accompanied by a discussion of Keynes's support for a low interest rate policy, whose ultimate impact would be to reduce the

significance of the rentier share of income – a process elegantly described by Keynes as the euthanasia of the rentier class. We conclude
with an analysis of the importance of distribution policy in Keynes's
work and the empirical significance of this distributive transfer mechanism over the business cycle.

Some aspects of Keynes's monetary theory

As is well known, Keynes's analysis of a monetary production economy
was based on the principle of effective demand. Even when short-term
expectations are fulfilled at the point of effective demand, Keynes
argued, the existence of uncertainty explains the fluctuations of
investment (the most volatile component of effective demand) and
the difficulty of attaining higher long-term levels of employment. This
indeed was reiterated and emphasized in his famous *Quarterly Journal
of Economics* article of 1937 (*CW*, XII, pp. 109–23).

In his two main articles for the *Economic Journal*, in 1937, Keynes
justified how investment precedes saving from a logical and a chrono-
logical point of view, through the introduction of the finance motive and
the theory of endogenous money that was contained therein (*CW*, XIV,
pp. 201–23). The finance motive was the necessary connecting link that
brought together his monetary theory with his theory of capital formation. As it has been cleared up since by Graziani (1984), the finance
motive points out that *all* production requires preliminary finance (or, to
use Graziani's expression, *financement*) , that is independent of the level
of saving, and that consumption spending as well as the financial acquisition of stocks and bonds by households provide firms with most of the
necessary long-term finance. Thus the role of the rate of interest cannot
be to bring to equality the desired flows of saving and investment in the
capital markets since all types of income and expenditure flows both
require and provide finance. Rather the rate of interest is a monetary
phenomenon, linked to the ease with which the banking system is
willing to grant initial finance or loans.

Since money is created in response to the public's demand for credit,
and hence its existence being a mere consequence of the loans initially
awarded, Keynes deduces from this that inflation cannot be a monetary
phenomenon in the sense understood within the confines of the quantity
theory. Inflation, of the traditional type resulting from excessive monetary demand, could occur either as a consequence of temporary bottle-
necks or of global scarcities, but such states of affairs were less common,
according to Keynes, and he believed that economists knew how to deal
with them. Instead Keynes was concerned with inflation under conditions of affluence (almost à-la-Galbraith) in which firms and trade

unions alike struggle over output through a policy of 'administered or monopoly prices' (*CW*, VII, p. 270). In the mechanism of the upswing where there are no restraining forces working to contain the escalation of labour and user costs (as each individual group seeks to maintain its *relative* position), inflation becomes an institutional phenomenon arising quite independently of monetary demand, and which he dubbed 'semi-inflation' to distinguish it from the less common 'true inflation' emerging out of conditions of global scarcity (*ibid.*, p. 301).

In Keynes's monetary framework the rate of interest is set by the central bank in the purely Wicksellian sense. It is true that both the term and risk structures of interest rates depend on the expectations of the dominant group dealing in the financial markets – the rentiers; however, in all cases the central bank retains its price leadership role (*ibid.*, p. 203), in that the 'monetary authorities can have any rate of interest they like' (*CW*, XXVII, p. 390). Although this was the crucial message of Keynesian monetary theory, there were subtleties in that message.

The rate of interest appears to Keynes also as a 'highly psychological phenomenon' (*CW*, VII, p. 202), crystallizing dominant perceptions in the financial markets of which the central bank is but one participant. The ease with which the central bank can set the rate of interest or influence the structure of various rates depends in effect on its past behaviour, on the level of rates abroad and also on the public sentiment towards holding liquid assets. As was pointed out very early by H. Townshend (1937), the rate of interest can be considered as 'an independent variable in the scheme of economic causation', but one that is heavily dependent upon conventions almost in the Veblenesque sense (*CW*, VII, p. 203).[3] With the rate of interest not being a real phenomenon, it follows that there cannot be a natural rate corresponding to some situation of full employment. Keynes at one point, however, did consider the concept of an optimum rate of interest that can be likened to the Wicksellian natural rate and which depends on how much investment is technically necessary to attain full employment and on 'how much reward to saving is socially desirable' (*CW*, XXVII, p. 390). Here again we can see that conventions take the centre-stage in his consideration of the determinants of the rate of interest.

Keynes's support for a low interest rate policy

The most striking recommendation arising out of Keynes's monetary theory is his insistence on continuous cheap money policy. It is true that on some occasions Keynes agrees that 'to raise the rate of interest during a boom may be, in conceivable circumstances, the lesser evil' (*CW*, VII, p. 322). But these circumstances may only be relevant if fiscal policy and investment planning are impossible, and if the boom induces disappointed expectations and waste.[4]

Keynes is unquestionably opposed to high rates of interest. There is a complete set of reasons presented by Keynes which form a coherent whole. The most obvious reasons arise out of chapters 11 and 17 of the *General Theory*. In chapter 11, Keynes introduces his well-known concept of the marginal efficiency of capital with the associated negative relationship between the level of investment and the rate of interest. Chapter 17, on the other hand, contains a more comprehensive analysis. In this chapter, Keynes claims to have shown that as a consequence of the essential properties of money, particularly its low elasticity of production, the money rate of interest sets the pace for all other own-rates of interest, hinders the production of commodities and removes the possibility of attaining full employment.[5] However, for those who remain unconvinced by the analysis of chapter 17, an exposé of the other reasons compelling Keynes to argue in favour of a cheap-money policy is required.

High interest rates are usually recommended nowadays by those who are afraid of the potential inflationary consequences of a boom or by those who want to relieve the economy of existing inflationary pressures. As we have underlined it above, however, Keynes does not believe that inflation is a monetary phenomenon. Consequently, a restrictive monetary policy can have only indirect effects on inflation. First, restrictions on credit 'withdraw from employers the financial means to employ labour at the existing level of prices and wages' (*CW*, IX, p. 218). Producers are forced to cut down on production and employment because of lack of adequate working capital (initial finance). Secondly, as a result of high interest rates, investment projects become non-profitable or too risky and thus must be abandoned, with all the multiplicative effects on output and employment. Inflation will recede only if it were of the scarcity variety, or if the increased unemployment allows the system to reach a point of discontinuity in the wage–price inflation of the affluent type.

Keynes believed that inflation could be brought under control with means that are less barbarian than planned unemployment.[6] He proposed schemes designed to restrain the probability of inflation, such as the use of buffer stocks for commodities traded on international markets, some kind of income and price controls to lower existing inflation (*ibid.*, IX, pp. 228–9) and possibly accompanied by some form of investment planning.[7] In addition to the fact that restrictive monetary policy basically affects inflation by creating unemployment, Keynes thought that it was utterly inefficient in the neo-classical sense. First, restrictive monetary policy negatively affects mainly those that are not powerful, have not yet established long-term relations of confidence with their bankers or happen to be in a short-run liquidity squeeze rather than those that are inefficient producers. Secondly, the increase in interest rates initially discourages those projects that have been prepared by entrepreneurs for production purposes, while speculative financial acquisitions would continue unabated (*CW*, VII, p. 323). In modern parlance, when interest rates are hiked up, the valuation ratio of most corporations drops below unity. It thus becomes less profitable to build new plants than to buy existing ones from rivals.[8] As a result, takeovers become the only acceptable investment activity to be financed by banks.

Indeed, even when inflation is of the excess-demand type, Keynes remains opposed to a policy of high interest rates, favouring instead taxation policies and possibly investment planning (*CW*, XXI, p. 390). From this, Keynes notes that small changes in the level of interest rates are usually without effect in restraining entrepreneurs. Only large increases in interest rates can make a serious dent on the level of spending. Yet there appears in this connection a structural asymmetry. Although it is easy for the central bank to raise the level of the complete vector of interest rates, it is much more difficult to get back to previous low levels, especially for long-term rates. In short, the upward trend cannot be easily reversed and hence 'a low enough long-term rate of interest cannot be achieved if we allow it to be believed that better terms will be obtained from time to time by those who keep their resources liquid' (*ibid.*, XXI, p. 389). The psychological and conventional aspects of the interest rate thus play an important role. From this analysis it ensues, therefore, that those members of the community who participate in the financial markets may have the ability to dampen the efforts of the central bank to lower interest rates and re-establish prosperity.

Keynes's opposition to rentier capitalism
It is because of the powerful stranglehold secured by this group of actors in the financial markets that Keynes is so much opposed to the rentier class, who in his eyes obtain returns on usury (*CW*, XXI, p. 412). On several occasions he recommends or predicts the euthanasia of the rentier class (*CW*, VII, pp. 221, 376). Financial rentiers are likened to the land rentiers of the Ricardian model. Both were responsible, in Keynes's eyes, for the relative scarcity of accumulated capital and to the relative impoverishment of much of mankind (*ibid.*, p. 242). Interest rates are high, according to Keynes, because rentiers manage to extort a premium, similar to land rent, on the scarcity of capital. This unor-

thodox belief was related to the conviction that ultimately capital will become abundant in an advanced society.

Keynes, however, builds up his case against the rentiers in a manner that far exceeds the Ricardian precepts. Rentiers are, above all, part of the class of speculators who, according to Keynes, tend to destabilize the economy by their irrational behaviour on the stock market. Through their strong preferences for liquidity rentiers could thus generate cumulative movements that often lead entrepreneurs to forestall or misdirect their investments (*ibid.*, pp. 158–61).

In spite of this destabilizing role, however, Keynes's case against the rentiers has to do with the negative consequences of high interest rates. Because of rentier reaction, high interest rates tend to feed on themselves and fuel still further increases in the rates of interest. Facing declining investment and rising unemployment, governments may decide to counter this tendency by a discretionary increase in the budget deficit. Under certain conditions an increase in the government deficit could generate an increase in the rate of interest, but this would be true only for psychological reasons due to the reaction of the rentiers (*CW*, IX, pp. 353–4). Similarly, increases in government expenditures may be perceived as a threat to businessmen which then lead to a decline in confidence and to a further fall in private investment (*CW*, VII, p. 162).[9] This phenomenon had also been pointed out in 1943 by M. Kalecki (1971) in a well-known article on the politics of full employment. Also emphasized by Kalecki was the fact that rentiers could become 'boom-tired' when price increases accompany upswings. This rentier resistance to full employment was thus a further reason for Keynes to oppose the rentier class and to hope for its disappearance.[10] Keynes was well convinced that rising commodity prices lead to a negative reaction from the rentier class whose income is largely fixed in money terms. (Unexpected) inflation leads to a transfer of income from rentier lenders to other classes of income recipients, and as a consequence it would be presumed that rentiers would pressure for anti-employment policies. Rentiers appeared in this light to constitute a class in itself whose interests were diametrically opposed to those of the active and more dynamic classes of entrepreneurs and workers. Moreover, given this rentier fear of inflation, their opposition would turn out to be the primary obstacle to the adoption of a full-employment policy (*CW*, XXVII, p. 37). This was for Keynes an unwelcome conclusion, for he knew that under the past and present institutional arrangements inflation was the ineluctable consequence of full employment.

Still more important, however, the weight given by Keynes to the speculative activities of the rentiers in both restricting finance and affecting enterpreneurial perceptions of future returns had enormous implications for the attainment of the full-employment goal. As the proportion of the equity of enterprises falling into the hands of the rentier class had grown over time, investment spending on the part of firms had become progressively vulnerable to what he described as 'the mass psychology of a large number of ignorant individuals' (*CW*, VII, p. 154) whose main preoccupation in the capital market was to remain liquid. With the decay of productive entreprise under a rentier capitalism that was unwilling to direct itself towards long-term investment prospects, the only viable solution appeared to be the collective commitment of a State that purposely becomes engaged in long-term investment planning. In essence, the socialization of investment becomes the only viable long-term solution to the critical problems posed by the strong attenuating influence rentier behaviour has on the 'spontaneous optimism', or animal spirits, of entrepreneurs.

Distribution policy and the postwar experience
Unlike Keynes's *Treatise* whose underlying 'widow's cruse' theory of distribution became popular during the 1950s through the work of Kaldor and Robinson, the *General Theory* has had little impact within this areas of economic analysis. Yet income distribution was a major concern to Keynes, especially in evaluating the effects of public policy. Indeed this was a major preoccupation to the extent that Keynes initially wanted to dedicate a complete chapter to the 'Influence of Changes in the Distribution of Income between the Rentiers and Earners' in his early drafts of the *General Theory* (*CW*, XXIX, p. 63).

   Much of this concern with the problem of distribution arises out of his monetary theory. This is because changes in the rate of interest have both a direct and indirect impact on the distribution of income between rentiers and the 'active earning class' of workers and enterpreneurs. First, an increase in the rate of interest can be perceived as a direct levy imposed on the productive system in proportion to the stock of interest-bearing debt and accruing to the rentier sector in the form of increased interest income. Secondly, through its effect on the cost of initial finance and, consequently, on the desire of firms to expand production and employment, the levels of wages and profit could also be indirectly affected by the upward movement in the rate of interest. That is to say, the ensuing depressed conditions in the product and labour markets cannot be assumed to be distributionally neutral on the wage–profit relationship.

   However, the full effect of this redistribution of income could only be understood when taking into consideration its impact on another important component of aggregate spending, consumption. Keynes writes, for instance,

> The transfer from wage-earners to other factors is likely to diminish the propensity to consume. The effect of the transfer from entrepreneurs to rentiers is more open to doubt. But if rentiers represent on the whole the richer section of the community and those whose standard of life is least flexible, then the effect of this also will be unfavourable. (*CW*, VII, p. 262)

It can be deduced from Keynes's arguments that changes in the share of rentier income is not only important to an understanding of the long-period composition of aggregate spending, as Joan Robinson was to work out in great detail in her *Accumulation of Capital* (1956, p. 253), but also of the cyclical fluctuations arising from these relations between income shares and spending. In short, accompanying any increase in the bank rate, there will occur a massive transfer of income from the industrial to the rentier sector which then brings about a cumulative process of contraction in both the levels of consumption and investment expenditures. These changes in the distribution of income between rentiers and the 'active earning class' were thus of crucial importance to Keynes in explaining the depressed state of economic activity during the 1930s.

Furthermore, while the high degree of stickiness of money wages was construed to have a stabilizing effect on economic activity, the low degree of sensitivity of nominal interest rates to both changes in prices and output over the cycle was an important factor contributing to greater amplitudes of cyclical fluctuations (*CW*, VII, pp. 232–3). Although at times he goes so far as to suggest that a negative interest rate would not be undesirable for a community (*ibid.*, pp. 221, 234), the existence of a floor of zero for nominal interest rates is a factor guaranteeing a positive net transfer of income to the rentier sector in times of recession.

How important was this transfer of income during 1930s and was there a recurrence of this phenomenon during the postwar period and, in particular, during the 'Great Recession' of the 1980s? In order to answer these questions a relevant indicator of this transfer of income had to be selected. Following L.L. Pasinetti (1981, chapter 8), we shall choose as an index of this transfer the difference between the real rate of interest [r] and the growth rate of output g (or productivity of labour, ϱ, as effectively specified by Pasinetti).[11] Whenever $r - g > 0$, there exists a net transfer of income from the industrial to the rentier sector. Conversely, a period of prosperity would be associated with $r - g < 0$, and involving a declining share of rentier income.[12]

Figure 14.1 presents the Canadian time-series data for the period

1927–39.[13] As one would expect, during the growth years prior to 1929 and after 1933 (excluding the recession year, 1938), the index is strongly negative. On the other hand, for the deep depression years, especially 1931 and 1932, the index reached positive levels that have not been reached again historically. These strong negative values confirm the massive transfer of income and wealth towards the rentier sector that Keynes discussed and found unacceptable for the British economy.

Figure 14.2 is important for our purpose since it tries to provide an empirical analogy of the intensity of the transfer during the Great Depression of the 1930s with that during the 'Great Recession' of the 1980s. The reference year 0 on the horizontal axis was the point of the highest transfer of income towards the rentier sector, and which turned out to be 1931 and 1982 for the two respective periods. Data for the four years prior to and following these two reference points were then plotted on the graph and superimposed. The evidence shows that, while the 1980s recession followed a scenario not unlike that of the 1930s, the transfer was somewhat lower but, at the same time, seems to have persisted longer than that of the 1930s (as the evidence for year 3, 1985, on the graph suggests).

Finally, Figure 14.3 presents data for the complete postwar period, but using as indicator the difference between the real rate of interest and average labour productivity growth.[14] This index fits most closely the original Pasinetti proposal and it is analogous to comparing the growth in real wages with the growth in productivity on the labour-market side when seeking some measure of the movement in the share of labour. The evidence displayed in the graph is of particular interest since in observing these deviations between the real rate of interest and productivity growth there appears an almost perfect symmetry with our cursory knowledge of the reference cycle in Canada. It is found that whenever the difference is *becoming* positive, the Canadian economy is normally headed towards a recession as was, for instance, the case during the late 1950s and early 1960s. However, the deviations need not be positive to be associated with a recession, as in 1974. As long as the direction of the drift is towards a net transfer away from the industrial sector, the result is normally a mild recession.

Moreover, Figure 14.3 allows us to situate better the experience of monetarism of the last decade in Canada. Unlike the previous high growth era of much of the postwar period associated with a negative value of $r - \varrho$, the monetary gradualism of the Bank of Canada now appears in its true colour. From the late 1970s and onwards there has been an immense transfer of income towards the rentier sector, accompanied by overall conditions of stagnation, especially in investment spending.

Figure 14.1　Percentage deviations between the real rate of interest and the rate of growth of output, Canada, 1927–39

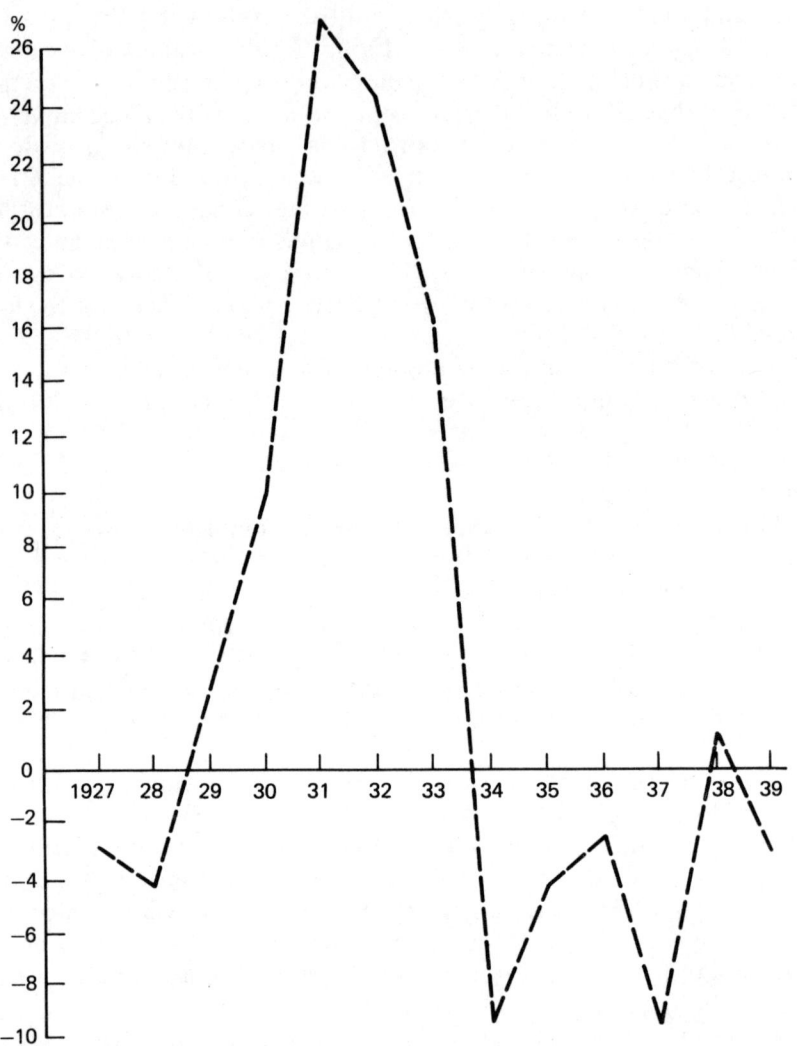

Source:　*Canada Year Book* (selected issues); Statistics Canada, Cat. no. 13–531; and *Historical Statistics of Canada* (2nd edn), 1983.

Figure 14.2 A comparison of the intensity of the redistribution in Canada between the Great Depression of the 1930s and the 'Great Recession' of the 1980s

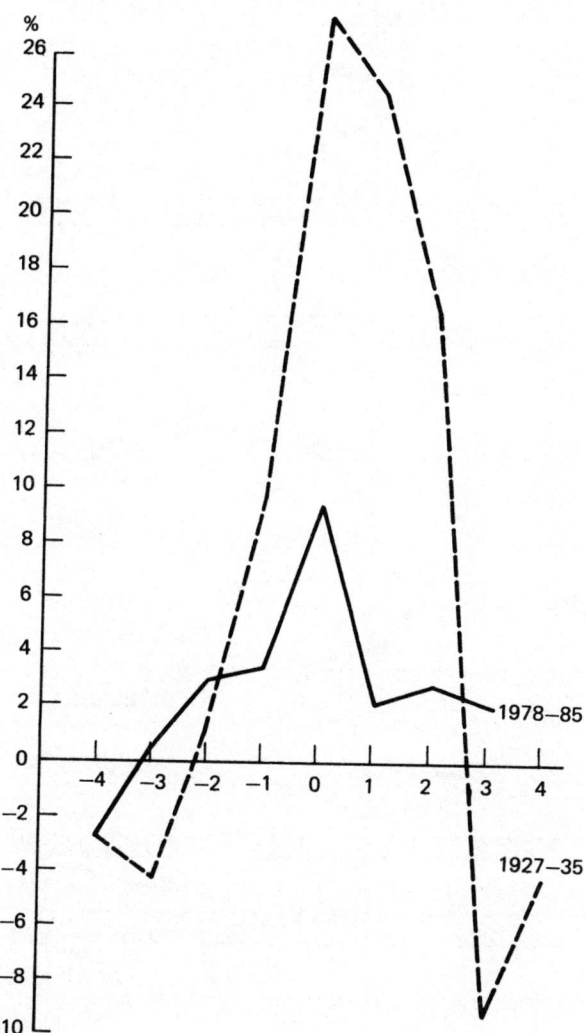

Source: *Canada Year Book* (selected issues); Statistics Canada, Cat. nos 13-201, 13-351 and 62-001; *Historical Statistics of Canada* (2nd edn), 1983; and *Bank of Canada Review* (selected issues).

Figure 14.3   Percentage points deviation between the real rate of interest and the rate of growth of average labour productivity, Canada, 1947–85

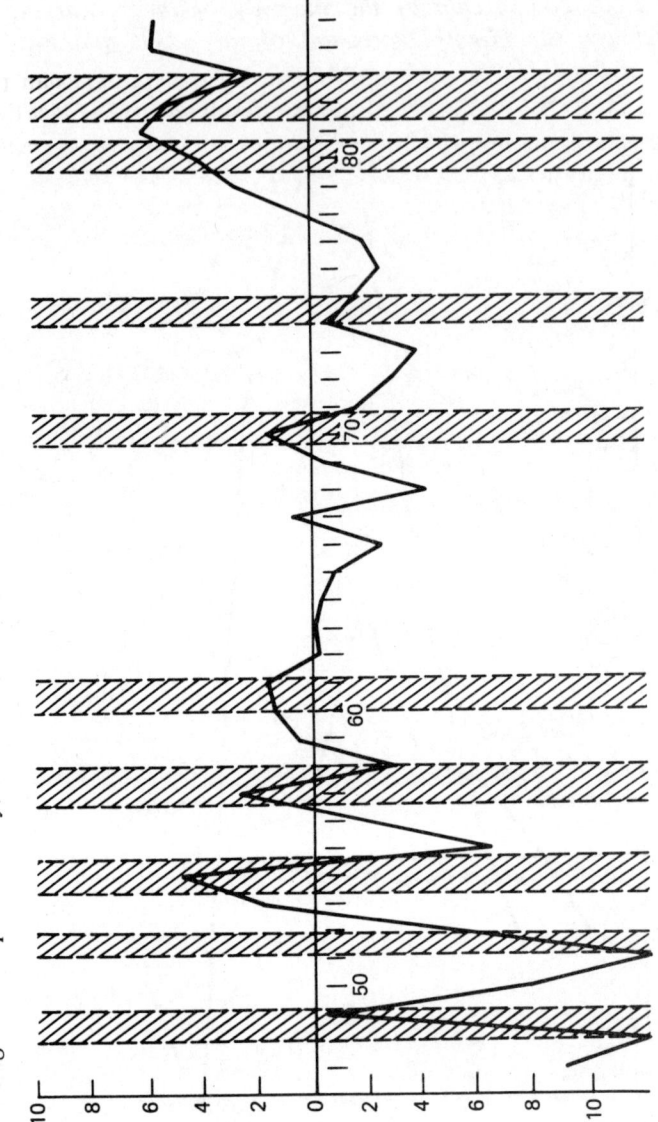

Note: The shaded bands refer to periods of recession as normally defined in accordance with the Canadian reference cycle. It should be noted, however, that though not officially declared as years of recession, 1967 as well as the complete period of the late 1970s and 1980s are examples of years of slower growth and relative stagnation. This is well confirmed by the data series plotted in the above chart.

From all this empirical evidence it would not be inappropriate to conclude, as Keynes did during the 1930s, that the primary obstacle to economic expansion is the interest burden. A truly Keynesian policy must thus be one that seeks to counter the tendency of the last decade through an activist monetary-cum-investment policy by short-circuiting the current institutional arrangements in the financial capital markets. As Joan Robinson (1937, p. 251) put it so succinctly, 'when capitalism is rightly understood, the rate of interest will be set to zero, and the major evils of capitalism will disappear'.[15]

Notes

1. The order is simply alphabetical. The authors would like to thank Basil Moore, Alain Parguez, Michael Perelman and Tom Rymes for their comments. The usual disclaimers apply.
2. About the famous liquidity-trap, Keynes wrote that he knew 'of no example of it hitherto', (*CW*, VII, p. 207). Also, contrary to conventional wisdom, wage-rigidity does not arise out of any questionable assumption about workers' money illusion in Keynes's analysis, as explained in M. Lavoie (1985, p. 178).
3. It should however be emphasized that the decisions of the central bank tend to have an impact primarily on short-term rates, while long-term yields on financial assets are more of a 'conventional' nature.
4. See Keynes's analysis of the Hayekian austere policy of high interest rates (*CW*, VII, pp. 326–7). His overall position can be characterized by the following two sentences: 'Thus the remedy for the boom is not a higher rate of interest but a lower rate of interest!' (*ibid.*, p. 322). 'Thus it is a fatal mistake to use a high rate of interest as a means of damping down the boom' (*CW*, XXI, p. 389).
5. G.C. Harcourt (1986), on p. 97, writes: 'Sraffa may have been unhappy with the use which Keynes made of Sraffa's construct of own rates of interest in Chapter 17 of the *General Theory*. Sraffa employed the construct in order internally to criticize the argument of Hayek's *Prices and Production* rather than to provide an integral part of a positive theory of the operation of capitalist markets.'
6. In this context we borrow the term used by Rostow (1983) to designate modern austerity policies.
7. For further details on the necessity of investment planning to control inflation see M. Seccareccia (1984), pp. 208–16.
8. This point has been made by economists such as Robin Marris and Richard Kahn (see S.J. Moss, (1978, p. 317). Takeovers have been a major activity in Canada in the early 1980s.
9. Keynes was quite opposed to the Treasury View, which relied for its intellectual pedigree on the writings of F. Hayek, and which constituted the initial version of our modern crowding-out theorem. Keynes only conceived of a 'psychological' crowding out, unless there was full employment (cf. *CW*, IX, p. 115 ff.).
10. In this connection it may be noted that, if Keynes favoured the euthanasia of the rentiers, he also thought that the rentier class performed a unique and useful civilizing role (see Robert Skidelsky's contribution in Volume I of this work). It was suggested to us by Michael Perelman that Keynes may have reconciled in his own mind the divergent economic and cultural roles of the rentier class by imagining that the proposed investment planning agencies would be run by the bankrupted rentiers. Deprived of their interest income, they would then make a positive contribution to both the social and economic spheres.
11. Keynes had no difficulty in using Fisher's concept of the real rate of interest.

However, in the *Treatise*, he was critical of the use made of this concept in explaining the so-called Tooke–Gibson paradox (Cf. *CW*, V, p. 197).

12.   Our indicator, in many ways, is a far better measure of the magnitude of the transfer than merely observing the relative share of rentier income in the national accounts. This is because the relative share is determined by at least two factors that have no significant bearing on our index. First, the share of rentier income is affected not only by changes in the rate of interest, as our measure is, but also by the flow of saving in the system over time (while our indicator is not). Secondly, the relative share from the national accounts is influenced significantly by a number of structural changes occurring in the rentier sector that our index is not affected by. In particular, we know that during the Great Depression while numerous rentier shareholders were wiped out, the remaining rentiers holding financial assets were to benefit greatly from the situation. Our measure would thus be insulated from such offsetting compositional changes that would render the national accounting measure more equivocal. Canadian data show that while the fluctuations of these variables are in the same direction, the amplitude of the fluctuations of our indicator far exceeds that of the relative-share time-series.

13.   The data series used on output and prices were obtained from the *Historical Statistics of Canada* (2nd edn) by Statistics Canada. As to the interest rate series, since no data on Treasury Bill rates was available officially prior to 1934, nor on business prime lending rates prior to 1935, an average interest rate (at 31 March of each year) on bonds, debentures and Treasury Bills was published during selected years in the *Canada Yearbook* for the complete period 1913–52. The time-series found to follow closely this earlier series for the period during which the two series overlapped is the business prime lending rate published by the Bank of Canada. This was the rate used to calculate the values of the deviations in Figures 14.2 and 14.3.

14.   While the time-series on interest rates was identical to that used in the previous diagram for the 1970s and 1980s, the aggregate productivity measure is that provided by Statistics Canada Cat. No. 14-201.

15.   This quote was brought to our attention by Bill Hixson.

References

Graziani, A. (1984), 'The debate on Keynes's finance motive', *Economic Notes*, 5–33.

Harcourt, G.C. (1986), 'On the influence of Piero Sraffa on the contribution of Joan Robinson to economic theory', *Economic Journal*, supplement, 96–108.

Kalecki, M. (1971), 'Political aspects of full employment', in *Selected Essays on the Dynamics of the Capitalist Economy*, Cambridge: Cambridge University Press.

Keynes, J.M. (1971–), *The Collected Writings of John Maynard Keynes*, ed. D. Moggridge, London: Macmillan.

Lavoie, M. (1985), 'Inflation, chômage et la planification des récessions: la "Théorie Générale" de Keynes et après', *L'Actualité Economique*, June, 171–199.

Moss, S.J. (1978), 'The post-Keynesian theory of income distribution in the corporate economy', *Australian Economic Papers*, December, 303–322.

Pasinetti, L.L. (1981), *Structural Change and Economic Growth*, Cambridge: Cambridge University Press.

Pigou, A.C. (1950), *Keynes's 'General Theory': A Retrospective View*, London: Macmillan.

Robinson, J. (1937), *Essays in the Theory of Employment*, London: Macmillan.

Robinson, J. (1956), *The Accumulation of Capital*, London: Macmillan.

Rostow, W.W. (1983), *The Barbaric Counter-Revolution*, London: Macmillan.

Seccareccia, M. (1984), 'The fundamental macroeconomic link between investment activity, the structure of employment and price changes: a theoretical and empirical analysis', *Economies et Sociétés*, April, 165–220.

Townshend, H. (1937), 'Liquidity-premium and the theory of value', *Economic Journal*, March, 157–69.

15 Money and interest rates: a comment

Nancy J. Wulwick

I comment here on the chapters by Tom Rymes and Basil Moore. Both consider that a central problem of the *General Theory* is the determination of the rate of interest. Moreover, both consider that a Keynesian analysis calls for a discretionary monetary policy. However, in terms of their theoretical elaboration, no two essays could be more distinct.

Rymes's paper is stated in terms of neo-classical monetary theory. It purports to present a *temporary general equilibrium* analysis of asset rates of return, like that of chapter 17 of the *General Theory*. Yet chapter 17 does not show that all rates of return are determined simultaneously, but rather that the rates of interest on non-money assets adjust to the money rate of interest. In particular, this rate, defined by the liquidity premium of money, sets a floor on all other rates of return. Therefore, it is the money asset that 'rules the roost' (see *General Theory*, p. 223). In any event Rymes, not unconventionally, does not present a general but a *partial* equilibrium model in which the rates of return on one commodity – capital – and real-money balances are equalized. Moreover, a main interest of the paper is to generate a *steady state* as well as a temporary equilibrium model. Yet chapter 17 states that the marginal efficiency of investment is influenced by the state of business confidence, a changing psychological phenomenon. As a result, Keynes's investment demand function is unstable, which precludes discussion of a steady-state equilibrium. Thus it appears that the paper actually does not elaborate upon the *General Theory*'s chapter 17.

Nor does this approach, in my view, promise a fruitful analysis. The identity of money is confined to mere fiat money. The monetary authority stabilizes the value of fiat money and charges a premium for the service. This 'liquidity premium' reflects the community's confidence in the ability of the monetary authority to stabilize the price level. But surely an analysis of a modern monetary economy mainly concerns bank money? Moreover, central banks to my knowledge do not levy a charge on fiat money, and I am not sure what one would identify as a service charge on bank money. And though in the postwar period central banks have often been 'concerned with price stability', they have not succeeded in anything like stabilizing the price level and several countries have experienced hyperinflation. There seems little point in elaborating a model that generates such unrealistic results that must be, *ad hoc*, explained away.

The rest of my comments are addressed to Moore's chapter. This lies in the tradition of the *Treatise on Money*. There Keynes stated that '[t]he Banking System has no ... *direct* control over the quantity of money ... [T]he governor of the whole system is the rate of discount. For this is the only factor which is directly subject to the will and fiat of the central authority' (see Vol. II, p. 211). This means, Keynes continued, that the central bank's influence over demand inflation is exercised through its influence over the rate of investment. Here we have the starting-point of Moore's impressive post-Keynesian manuscript, 'Horizontalists and Verticalists'. His Conference paper forms the appendix to Chapter 9, 'The Determination of Interest Rates'.

This paper reformulates the definition of equilibrium in the investment market. Equilibrium occurs when the marginal efficiency of investment equals the ex-ante real money rate of interest. This equals the nominal rate of interest set by the central bank minus the *expected* rate of inflation. But the introduction of the expected rate of inflation into the post-Keynesian model must affect how the interest rate control is designed to work. Say, during a boom inflationary expectations are high. Meanwhile, the central bank is pursuing a countercyclical monetary policy. Will the bank be able to influence investment by controlling the nominal interest rates? Perhaps not. For in this case short-term ex-ante real rates of interest may well be negative and the corresponding long-term rates may well fall below the marginal efficiency of investment. Such a case would call for direct control over bank credit, a control to which Basil does refer in the main part of Chapter 9. Of course, if inflationary expectations are high during stagflation, assuming that loan expenditure is interest responsive, a monetary policy based on the interest rate control indeed would be efficient.

My last remark concerns the importance of the *General Theory* in the context of a post-Keynesian theory of money. Chapter 17 of the *General Theory* defined three properties of money: (1) the elasticity of supply in respect to private demand is nearly zero and the elasticity of employment is zero; (2) the price elasticity of substitution between money and real durables, which have a high elasticity of production, is nil, except during hyperinflation; and (3) money is the standard in which wage contracts are set and wages tend to be sticky in terms of money. These three properties make money that asset with the highest liquidity premium. As Moore writes, "these arguments were all designed to show why, for money alone, its marginal efficiency need not fall in response to an increase in demand'. Yet are the first two properties relevant in a theory of endogenous credit money? The second property about price substitution becomes irrelevant. In regard to the first property, the elasticity of supply in respect to private demand becomes unity, though the elasticity of employment naturally remains zero.

16 Keynes and money: a comment

M.L. Burstein

I look at 'Keynes and money' in a certain way. The principal discriminant between 'classical' and Keynesian economics is based on this query: 'Do you accept monetary theories of the real rate of interest; or are real rates of interest determined by real causes?' So, for me, the Appendix to chapter 14 of the *General Theory* is most a propos – especially the discussion of an extract from Ricardo's *Principles*. The 'classical' tradition Keynes confronted was that of Ricardo, Senior (*The Cost of Obtaining Money*), J.S. Mill, Marshall and Pigou and Hayek. Milton Friedman the monetarist is not centrally important here; but his précis of Knight's accumulation model (Friedman, 1962) and his presidential lecture (1968), including its critique of bond-support operations, are useful to a proper critique of 'Keynes and Money'.

T.K. Rymes's paper on this subject is technically accomplished and can be summarized in the following way. Along lines familiar since Hahn (1966), profiles of integrations of dynamic models including asset markets display saddlepoint (in)stability. Since Rymes does not belong to the lunatic fringe of new classical macroeconomics, he relies on external intervention to assure attainment of the convergent arm, namely, the intervention of a monetary authority, described in real-monetary balances/real-capital space, but the analysis is essentially neo-classical and I find nothing in Keynes's monetary theory that informs, or illuminates, this line of attack. For example, references to the *marginal physical product of capital* are improper to a Keynesian analysis. Suffice it to say that the marginal efficiency of investment is a subjective idea, brilliantly elucidated in chapter 12 of the *General Theory*.

Rymes's diagram (see Figure 1) shows that his analysis is a variant of the Hahn problem. But Keynes's monetary theory is irrelevant in this paradigm, in which the theory of money concerns the process of assuring attainment of the convergent arm.

Consideration of 'Keynes and Expectations', instead of 'Keynes and Money', would have been highly relevant for the sort of problem Rymes wants to study. Thus chapter 12, 'The State of Long Term Expectation', of the *General Theory* and its parable about a newspaper contest, choosing the prettiest faces according to average opinion, is central for

Townsend (1978) and the studies collected in Frydman and Phelps (1983) – including those of Phelps, Frydman, Townsend, Radner and Hahn. The following remarks of Hahn would have been especially helpful:

> If you decide that one should and can study an economy as if it were always in Walrasian equilibrium, then you had better be prepared to justify this on the basis of first principles or you should keep silent on Keynes. For, plainly, once the hypothesis is granted, Keynes makes no sense at all. (Hahn, 1983, pp. 223–4).

What *is* the theory of money of the *General Theory*? In chapter 13, Keynes categorically endorses the idea that the real rate of interest is determined by the quantity of money – and so loses ground attained in the *Treatise* (1930); see his interesting analysis of the Gibson paradox (chapter 10), leading to what Friedman and Schwartz (1982) call the Wicksell–Keynes hypothesis[1].

Keynes's theory of *liquidity preference* supposedly links up the nominal quantity of money and the real rate of interest. But it has long been established that liquidity motivation can be satisfied by many assets (see e.g. Chang *et al.*, 1983). And Keynes deals more satisfactorily, in chapter 15 of the *General Theory*, with the causes of sticky long rates: see especially the bootstrap theory stated at pp. 202–3. The dénouement of chapter 13, 'The General Theory of Interest', is starkly plain. Keynesians must live with it: '[I]n fact [interest] is the reward for not hoarding' (Keynes, 1936, p. 174).

In the very interesting Appendix to chapter 14 of the *General Theory*, Keynes captures the pith of the classical theory of interest: its invariance against the quantity of money or banking policy. And in the following he is acutely sensitive to the way money supply becomes a residue of interest rate targeting instead of a product of a Fisherine aggregate-determinate process of the sort that dominates the *General Theory*, but not the *Treatise* (see Professor Moore's Glendon discussion of a related point):

> If Ricardo had been content to present his argument solely as applying to any given quantity of money created(*sic*) by the monetary authority, it would still have been correct on the assumption of flexible money wages. (Is this not a stupendous admission?) ... But,if by the policy of the monetary authority we mean the terms on which it will increase or decrease the quantity of money, i.e. the rate of interest at which it will ... increase or decrease its assets ... then it is not the case either than the policy of the monetary authority is nugatory or that only one policy is compatible with long-period equilibrium ... [t]he terms on which the monetary authority will change the quantity of money enters(*sic*) as a real determinant into the economic scheme. (*ibid.*, p. 191)

Here Keynes regains the ground of proper high theory. The analysis originates in the work of Ricardo, Thornton, J.S. Mill, Wicksell, Hayek, Robertson[2] and the Keynes of the *Treatise*. And Keynes may well be quite right: it may be impossible to establish neutrality, let alone super-neutrality, of money in 'bank rate' modelling (see Cagan, 1972, for an excellent discussion). But it cannot much comfort Keynesians that the correct content of Keynes's theory of interest boils down to a qualification of the classical theory of interest on a front commanded by contemporaries like Hayek and Robertson.

Notes

1. Ingrid Rima called my attention to the relevance of the Gibson Paradox for this discussion. Friedman and Schwartz (1982) conclude that the implications for real interest rate behaviour of the Wicksell–Keynes hypothesis are inconsistent with relevant data, but are quite respectful of the construction which is indeed ingenious – I should say several cuts above the interest rate theory of the *General Theory*.
2. See especially *Banking Policy and the Price Level* (1926).

References

Cagan, P. (1972), *The Channels of Monetary Effects on Interest Rates*, New York: Columbia University Press/NBER.

Cagan, P. (1980), 'Comment', in S. Fischer (ed.), *Rational Expectations and Economic Policy*, Chicago: University of Chicago Press.

Chang, W., Hamberg, D. and Hirata, J. (1983), 'Liquidity preference towards risk is a demand for short-term securities – not money', *American Economic Review*, 73, 420.

Friedman, M. (1962), *Price Theory: A Provisional Text*, Chicago: Aldine Press.

Friedman, M. (1968), 'The role of monetary policy', *American Economic Review*, 58, 1.

Friedman, M. and Schwartz A.J. (1982), *Monetary Trends in the United States and the United Kingdom*, Chicago: University of Chicago Press/NBER.

Frydman, R. (1983), 'Individual rationality, decentralization and the rational expectations hypothesis', in R. Frydman and E.S. Phelps (eds), *Individual Forecasting and Aggregate Outcomes: 'Rational Expectations' Explained*, New York: Cambridge University Press.

Frydman, R. and Phelps, E.S. (eds) (1983), *Individual Forecasting and Aggregate Outcomes: 'Rational Expectations' Explained*, New York: Cambridge University Press.

Hahn, F. (1966), 'Equilibrium dynamics with heterogeneous capital goods', *Quarterly Journal of Economics*, 80, 4, pp 633–46.

Hahn, F. (1983), 'Comment', in R. Frydman, and E.S. Phelps (eds), *Individual Forecasting and Aggregate Outcomes: 'Rational Expectations' Explained*, New York: Cambridge University Press, p. 223 ff.

Hayek, F.A. (1939), 'Price expectations, monetary disturbances and malinvestments', in *Profits, Interest and Investment*, London: Routledge; reprinted in *Readings in Business Cycle Theory*, Philadelphia, Pa.: American Economic Association, 351–365.

Keynes, J.M. (1930), *A Treatise on Money*, 2 vols. London: Macmillan.

Keynes, J.M. (1936), *The General Theory of Employment, Interest and Money*, London: Macmillan.

Mill, J.S. (1862), *Principles of Political Economy*, 5th edn, London: Parker, Son and Bourn, Book 3, ch. 23, para. 4.

Phelps, E.S. (1983), 'The trouble with "rational expectations" and the problem of inflation stabilization', in R. Frydman and E.S. Phelps (eds), *Individual Forecasting and Aggregate Outcomes: 'Rational Expectations' Explained*, New York: Cambridge University Press, 31 ff.

Radner, R. (1983), 'Comment', in R. Frydman and E.S. Phelps (eds), *Individual Forecasting and Aggregate Outcomes: 'Rational Expectations' Explained*, New York: Cambridge University Press, 133 ff.

Ricardo, D. (1951–5), *The Principles of Political Economy and Taxation*; reprinted in P. Sraffa and M. Dobb (eds), *The Works and Correspondence of David Ricardo*, Cambridge: Cambridge University Press.

Robertson, D. (1926), *Banking Policy and the Price Level*, London: P.S. King.

Rymes, T.K. (1986), 'Keynes and stable money', paper presented at the Conference on Keynes and Public Policy After Fifty Years, Glendon College, York University, Toronto, September 1986.

Senior, N. (1830), *The Cost of Obtaining Money*, London: London School of Economics; reprinted as No. 5 in Scarce Tract series.

Thornton, H. (1939), *An Enquiry into the Nature and Effects of the Paper Credit of Great Britain*, ed. F.A. von Hayek, London: Allen and Unwin; originally published, 1802.

Townsend, R.M. (1978), 'Market expectations, rational expectations and Bayesian analysis', *International Economic Review*, 19, 481.

Townsend, R.M. (1983a), 'Forecasting the forecasts of others', *Journal of Political Economy*, 91, 546.

Townsend, R.M. (1983b), 'Equilibrium theory with disparate expectations: some issues and methods', in R. Frydman and E.S. Phelps (eds), *Individual Forecasting and Aggregate Outcomes: 'Rational Expectations' Explained*, New York: Cambridge University Press, 169.

Wicksell, (1907), 'The influence of the rate of interest on prices', *Economic Journal*, 17, 213.

Wicksell, K. (1936), *Interest and Prices*, London: Macmillan, trans. by R.F. Kahn, *Geldzins und Güterpreise*, Jena: Gustav Fischer, 1898.

PART V

INTERNATIONAL
TRADE AND FINANCE

17 Keynes and the question of tariffs

Bernard M. Wolf and Nicholas P. Smook[1]

Introduction

It was fitting for the Conference to address Keynes's views on tariffs since there is a distinct possibility that a new wave of protectionism reminiscent of the period 1930–2 may soon be unleashed. This chapter traces Keynes's attitude towards tariffs from his initial position as a free trader in the 1920s to his later stance as a pragmatic protectionist. His views on the question of tariffs are certainly relevant to contemporary issues of protection and free trade. In the last section of the chapter an attempt will be made to determine what Keynes might have said on these issues.

Keynes, the free trader

During the election debate of 1923, Keynes made his position as a free trader quite clear by denouncing Conservative Prime Minister Baldwin's call for Britain to retreat from its long-standing free trade position. Here he continued the free trade views which he held in his student days when he was secretary of the Cambridge University Free Trade Association (Skidelsky, 1983, p. 241). Resting his case on classical economics, Keynes argued for free trade on two counts: on the gains from international specialization based on comparative advantage, and on the belief that 'an artificial interference with imports must either interfere with exports or involve an artificial stimulation to capital to leave the country', neither of which he thought was desirable (*CW*, XIX, p. 148). However, Keynes did recognize exceptions to the principle of free trade in the cases of dumping, infant industries, overdependence on foreign supplies in key industries and the encouragement of such socially desirable industries as agriculture. Further, he acknowledged that import duties might be levied when a country wished to give preference to one source of supply over another, to obtain trade concessions from a trading partner in return for their removal or to improve the terms of trade (*ibid.*, XIX, p.150). Keynes clearly considered that these exceptions would occur rather infrequently.[2]

It was the issue of the effects of a tariff on employment over which

Keynes disagreed most emphatically with protectionists. In December 1923, he strongly argued that:

> For if there is one thing that protection cannot do, it is to cure unemployment, . . . There are some arguments for protection, based upon its securing possible but improbable advantages to which there is no simple answer. But the claim to cure unemployment involves the protectionist fallacy in its grossest and crudest form. (*ibid.*, pp. 151–2)

In fact, Keynes maintained that the tariff could make matters worse: first, it would raise the cost of British manufactures with imported inputs, and secondly, by limiting access to sterling, Britain's trading partners would not have the wherewithal to purchase its exports. As he saw it, unemployment was to be reduced through increased exports rather than decreased imports. He cited the cases of the USA and France as evidence that a tariff would not be effective in generating employment.

Keynes advocates a revenue tariff

By July 1930, Keynes's attitude towards protection had changed dramatically due to Britain's changing circumstances. In a memo to Prime Minister Ramsay MacDonald, Keynes noted that he had 'become reluctantly convinced' (*CW*, XX, p. 378) that some protectionist measures should be introduced by Britain. He had already hinted at his change of view in testimony to the Macmillan Committee (on Finance and Industry) on 28 February 1930 (*ibid.*, p. 115).

Keynes's advocacy for a substantial revenue tariff was publicly revealed in an article entitled, 'Proposals for a Revenue Tariff', published in the *New Statesman and Nation* on 7 March 1931, and in a more popular version entitled, 'Put the Budget on a Sound Basis: a Plea to Lifelong Free Traders', which appeared in the *Daily Mail* on 13 March 1931. Although his apparent conversion to protectionism created a sensation, Keynes himself did not consider his move from a free trader to an advocate of tariffs to be that radical.[3] He still favoured free trade under normal circumstances as the best policy, but Britain's predicament in 1931 did not fulfil free trade's necessary conditions. In fact he characterized the situation as an 'emergency' calling for drastic measures (*CW*, IX, p. 238). This emergency situation stemmed in part from the consequences of Britain's return to the gold standard at the prewar parity of US $4.866 in April 1925.

Keynes's views on the gold standard and the return to prewar parity changed between 1922 and 1925. At the Genoa Conference of April 1922 he advocated a return to the gold standard (in the form of a gold bullion standard) for countries whose exchange rates were within 20 per cent of prewar parity. He declared:

> If gold standards could be reintroduced throughout Europe, we all agree that this would promote, as nothing else can, the revival not only of trade and of production but of international credit and the movement of capital to where it is needed most. One of the greatest elements of uncertainty would be lifted. (*CW*, XVII, p. 360)

For Britain he proposed an exchange rate US $4.20 for the pound, with a 5 per cent difference between the buying and selling prices for gold, so that exchange rates could fluctuate within a wider band than under the old gold points (*ibid.*, pp. 354–69). Furthermore, he advocated a crawling peg by which central banks, if they wished, could raise the exchange rate up to 0.5 per cent per month. Therefore, if conditions warranted, sterling could be back to the prewar parity in twenty months.

By 1923, in *A Tract on Monetary Reform*, Keynes revised his position about returning to the gold standard and called it 'a barbarous relic' (*CW*, IX, p. 179). He now worried that the gold standard would not provide internal price stability. He felt that the prewar system was incapable 'of dealing with large or sudden divergencies between the price levels of different countries as have occurred lately' (*ibid.*, p. 172). In particular, he noted that with the existing distribution of gold a return to the gold standard would mean that Britain would surrender its regulation of the internal price level to the Federal Reserve Board of the USA.

When Britain returned to the gold standard in 1925, Keynes vehemently attacked the decision in the pamphlet, 'The Economic Consequences of Mr Churchill'. He saw the overvaluation of sterling as the main obstacle to achieving full employment since it meant that prices and money wages in Britain had to fall in order to obtain a balance-of-payments equilibrium. The chief means available which could accomplish this task was the restriction of credit and the maintenance of a high bank rate by the Bank of England. Keynes saw tight money as having the effect of deliberately intensifying unemployment:

> The object of credit restriction, in such a case is to withdraw from employers the financial means to employ labour at the existing level of prices and wages. This policy can only attain its end by intensifying unemployment without limit, until the workers are ready to accept the necessary reduction of money wages under the pressure of hard facts ... It is a policy ... from which any humane or judicious person must shrink. (*CW*, IX, p. 218).

Instead he suggested that the appropriate strategy was a policy of easy credit:

> We want to encourage business men to enter on new enterprises, not as we are doing, to discourage them. Deflation does not reduce wages automatically. It reduces them by causing unemployment. The proper object of dear

money is to check an incipient boom. Woe to those whose faith leads them to use it to aggravate a depression! (*ibid.*, p. 220)

However, by 1931, he had become convinced that a devaluation, given Britain's 'special circumstances' (*CW*, XX, p. 495) would have more disadvantages than advantages. In fact he took the stance that Britain's 'exchange position should be relentlessly defended today' (*CW*, IX, p. 236). More specifically, he had in mind Britain's role as an international banker and the large debts owed to it fixed in terms not of gold, but sterling. He felt that the maintenance of the pound's value was essential if Britain was to 'resume the vacant financial leadership of the world which no one else . . . [had] the experience or the public spirit to occupy' (*CW*, IX, p. 236). Therefore, he sought a policy instrument which would achieve effects similar to a devaluation in terms of money wages and prices but which 'would leave sterling's international obligations unchanged in terms of gold' (*CW*, XX, p. 296).

Ruling out a devaluation, Keynes identified two possible alternative policy options for Britain to consider: either the cost of output could be reduced ('the contractionist cure') or the demand for output could be increased ('the expansionist cure') (*CW*, IX, p. 236). He ardently rejected the former, as he had done in 1925, because it involved a drastic general reduction in money wages leading to 'social injustice and violent resistance since it would greatly benefit some classes of income at the expense of others' (*ibid.*, p. 235).[4] Moreover, he thought that it would have the effect of diminishing domestic demand. Hence a policy of contraction sufficiently drastic to do any good might have been quite impractical. In fact, Keynes worried that it could begin a "disastrous process of competitive international wage cutting' (*loc. cit.*). If this occurred, then even foreign demand for British exports might not increase.

Instead, Keynes embraced the expansionist policy. However, he had to 'neutralize its dangers' (*ibid.*, p. 236) by finding a substitute for a lower value of sterling, which would still allow a relatively easy credit policy. Without the substitute, he felt that the expansionist policy would have put too large a burden on the trade balance, the budget and business confidence.

The revenue tariff which Keynes proposed was to cover as wide a range of goods as possible. He suggested as a possibility a 15 per cent duty on all manufactured and semi-manufactured goods and a 5 per cent duty on all foodstuffs and some raw materials; other raw materials would be exempt (*CW*, XIX, p. 237). Along with the tariff, Keynes called for a subsidy on exports. He argued, in the *Addendum to the Macmillan Committee Report* of May 1931, that for protection to have the desired equivalence to a devaluation both 'a tariff of the same percentage on all imports' and 'an equal subsidy on all exports' was required (*CW*, XX, p. 296). He was not too explicit on the implementation of these export bounties, but rather he concentrated on arguments for the tariff, suggesting that it was 'probably much easier to restrict imports than to augment exports' (*CW*, XX, p. 378).

To the extent that the tariff did not curtail imports (and it was, of course, for the most part not a prohibitive tariff) it would raise revenue. Hence, Keynes termed his proposal a 'general revenue tariff'. The revenue aspect he saw as a benefit since it would help balance the budget at a time when he felt that other taxes could not be raised because of the low level of incomes and profits. He thought that a lower budget deficit would contribute to the restoration of business confidence and thereby lead to greater domestic investment. An added bonus was that part of the revenue would be paid by foreigners through an improvement in the terms of trade.[5]

Unlike his views on tariffs during the 1923 election debate, Keynes now saw them as an intricate part of the expansionist scenario. He had come to the conclusion that when a country is facing a high and persistent level of unemployment, '. . . a tariff may bring about a net increase of production and not merely a diversion' as it would in the case of full employment equilibrium (*ibid.*, p. 298). More specifically, Keynes now claimed that:

> Free trade is profoundly based on the assumption of equilibrium conditions and in particular that wages always fall to their strict economic level. If they do not, and if for several reasons we do not desire them to, then it is only by means of a tariff that the ideal distribution of resources between different uses, which free trade aims at, can be achieved; and there is an unanswerable theoretical case for a countervailing import duty (and also for an export bounty) equivalent to the difference between the actual wage and the economic wage. (*ibid.*, p. 379)

For Keynes in 1930–1, an equilibrium was still only possible at the full employment level, although he saw that an economy might not be 'in sight of equilibrium' for large periods of time (*ibid.*, p. 398). He had not yet formulated the revolutionary notion of an equilibrium at less than full employment (*ibid.*, p. 504).

Britain, in 1931, was faced with an unemployment rate of about 25 per cent (*CW*, IX, p. 231), and there were no apparent means to achieve an automatic restoration of a full employment equilibrium. Therefore, there was not much point in prescribing policies designed for the long run, especially when other countries were targeting short-run objectives:

> Ever since 1918 we, alone amongst the nations of the world, have been the slaves of 'sound' general principles regardless of particular circumstances.

> We have behaved as though the intermediate 'short periods' of the economist between our position of equilibrium and another really were short, whereas they can be long enough – and have been before now – to encompass the decline and downfall of nations. (*CW*, XX, p. 379)

Undoubtedly, Keynes's views were influenced by the rising protectionism elsewhere in the world, particularly the USA's imposition of the infamous Smoot-Hawley tariff in June 1930.

Keynes also suggested (perhaps somewhat too optimistically) that while the tariff would initially curtail imports, it would eventually lead to their increase as the British economy expanded and, in addition, it would provide funds to finance loans by London to debtor countries. The temporary reduction in imports was clearly preferable to a persistently low level associated with high unemployment (*CW*, IX, p. 237–9).

With respect to the impact which an import tariff would have on exports, Keynes had altered his earlier view by now postulating that there was no 'direct and simple relationship between the volume of exports and the volume of imports' (*CW*, XX, p. 503). It depended upon current circumstances and, in this case, he thought exports would not decline precipitously because two favourable forces were at work. First, a tariff by initially improving the trade balance would allow a lower bank rate which would permit more lending to foreigners, and hence greater purchasing power abroad. Secondly, the 'large surplus capacity of men and plant' might allow 'a substantial increase in output for use at home ... without the reaction on the price of our exports which might be expected if we had no surplus capacity' (*ibid.*, p. 505). Moreover, it must also be kept in mind that Keynes intended exports to be subsidized where feasible. What he seems to have ignored, however, is the reduction of exports which occurs when tariffs rise worldwide as countries retaliate against escalating protection elsewhere. Perhaps he overlooked this because Britain's major trading partners had already erected extremely high tariff barriers which were not likely to go much higher.

Finally, Keynes surmised that by 1930 the case for specialization in manufacturing based on comparative advantage was not as strong as earlier, so that a tariff would not result in a serious cost penalty. (He did not seem to place much emphasis on scale economies or product differentiation as a basis for international trade.) He also argued that (*CW*, 111, p. 193): 'now that nearly all the manufacturing countries of the world have decided on a certain measure of self-sufficiency, a country which does not follow suit may pay a much greater price in instability than it gains through specialisation.' His conclusion was that if wages or the exchange rate were not at their equilibrium levels, so that industries such as motor vehicles, iron and steel and, especially, agriculture were temporarily uncompetitive, they should be protected (*CW*, XX, p. 350).

In summary, during 1930–1, Keynes saw the tariff as 'a crude departure from laissez-faire whch we have to adopt because we have no better weapons in our hands' (*ibid.*, p. 495). Ultimately the tariff by expanding effective demand would provide the 'breathing space and margin of financial strength' necessary to make an 'assault against the spirit of contraction and fear' (*CW*, IX, p. 238).

The abandonment of the gold standard

One week after Britain suspended the gold standard, Keynes withdrew his support for the tariff. If the exchange value of sterling could adjust to make British wages and prices competitive again, there would be no need for the revenue tariff (Moggridge and Howson, 1974, p. 237). On 28 September 1931 he declared:

> Until recently I was urging on Liberals and others the importance of accepting a general tariff as a means of mitigating the effects of the obvious disequilibrium between money costs at home and abroad. But the events of the last week have made a great difference. At the present gold value of sterling British producers are probably in many directions among the cheapest in the world. In these circumstances we cannot continue as if nothing had happened. It is impossible to have a rational discussion about tariffs so long as the currency question is altogether unsolved. For until we know more about the probable future level of sterling in relation to gold and, above all, until we know how many other countries are going to follow our example, it is impossible to say what our competitive position is going to be (*CW*, IX, p. 243)

Once again, by November 1932, Keynes's sympathy for protection was on the rise. He claimed to have considerable regard for both the pros and cons of tariffs. On the con side he acknowledged the benefits of specialization and as well now admitted that the use of tariffs to generate employment was in fact a beggar-thy-neighbour policy since it shifted to other countries some part of Britain's unemployment burden (*CW*, XXI, pp. 204–7); on the pro side he was particularly disposed to tariffs, in what he viewed to be key industries. As in 1930–1, he identified motor vehicles, steel and agriculture as candidates for protection. Motor vehicles he saw as a new industry which provided attractive jobs and was one in which, in the long run, Britain ought to have a comparative advantage. In the case of iron and steel he wanted a regeneration of the industry because he saw immense social and economic costs of its collapse. Here, as well as in the case of agriculture, Keynes was unwilling to allow the forces of comparative advantage to work fully. He

made it quite plain that 'a country which cannot afford art or agriculture, invention or tradition, is a country in which one cannot afford to
live' (*ibid.*, p. 210).[6] Keynes summed up his position in November 1932
as follows:

> Neither free trade nor protection can present a theoretical case which entitles
> it to claim supremacy in practice. Protection is a dangerous and expensive
> method of redressing a want of balance and security in a nation's economic
> life. But there are times when we cannot safely trust ourselves to the blind-
> ness of economic forces; and when no alternative weapon as efficacious as
> tariffs lies ready to our hand. (*ibid.*, p. 210)

The tariff was thus an instrument to be used, but no longer a primary
weapon. It was to be employed selectively rather than across-the-board.
In March 1933 (in 'The Means to Prosperity') the beggar-thy-neighbour
consequences of tariffs and devaluations accompanied by retaliation
further soured him on these instruments. He turned his attention once
again to obtaining cheap credit on a worldwide scale (*CW*, IX, p. 252).
With sufficient liquidity, he argued that 'tariffs and quotas imposed to
protect the foreign balance, and not in pursuance of permanent national
policies, should be removed' (*ibid.*, p. 361).

In July 1933, writing in the *New Statesman and Nation* (*CW*, XXI, pp.
233–46) on 'National Self-Sufficiency', Keynes continued to push for 'a
mutual reduction of tariffs' (p. 244). At the same time, he expressed a
desire to lessen 'economic entanglement between nations':

> Ideas, knowledge, art, hospitality, travel – these are things which should of
> their nature be international. But let goods be homespun whenever it is
> reasonably and conveniently possible; and above all, let finance be primarily
> national. Yet, at the same time, those who seek to disembarrass a country of
> its entanglements should be very slow and wary. It should not be a matter of
> tearing up roots but of slowly training a plant to grow in a different direction.
> (*CW*, XXI, p. 236)

During the latter half of the 1930s, Keynes did not devote much of his
public and private correspondence to the issue of tariffs. However, in
the *General Theory*, chapter 23, 'Notes on Mercantilism, etc.' he makes
clear his policy prescription on general tariffs:

> There are strong presumptions of a general character against trade restric-
> tions unless they can be justified on special grounds. The advantages of the
> international division of labour are real and substantial, even though the
> classical school greatly overstressed them. A policy of trade restrictions is a
> treacherous instrument even for the attainment of its ostensible object, since
> private interest, administrative incompetence and the intrinsic difficulty of
> the task may divert it into producing results directly opposite to those in-
> tended. (*CW*, VII, pp. 338–9)

The concluding chapter 24 of the *General Theory* maintains that if full employment could be achieved by domestic policies following Keynesian principles, then international trade could be further liberalized (*ibid.*, pp. 382–3).

In assessing Keynes's views on the tariff in the interwar period, one sees that depending on circumstances he moved from being generally opposed to them with certain rare exceptions to being temporarily in favour of them on an across-the-board basis and, finally, to support tariffs only in chosen industries. When he perceived tariffs to assist the attainment of his goals, he willingly embraced them, otherwise, he rejected them as 'a first-class curse' (*CW*, XXI, p. 103).

Keynes and planning for the post-World War II period
Keynes's views on commercial policy for the post World War II period were a continuation of those he held in the mid-1930s. He stated in his 'Clearing Union' proposal of 1941–2 that 'the plan aims at the substitution of an expansionist, in place of a contractionist, pressure on world trade' (CW, XXV, p. 176). However, he still proposed that a country, which found itself to be an aggregate debtor 'should be allowed to adopt special expedients as a temporary measure to assist in regaining equilibrium in its balance of payments, in spite of a general rule not to adopt them' (*ibid.*, p. 80). Moreover, his plan allowed for protection to serve as a necessary safety valve to industries 'which for special reasons ought to be maintained for domestic purposes only' (*ibid.*, p. 81). In his criticism of the majority report issued by the Overton Committee on Commercial Policy, in December 1942, he was particularly concerned with the case of Britain, which was likely to find itself in a debtor position in the postwar years.[7] While he thought that Britain should be 'willing to accept any ceiling for tariffs, however low, which ... [was] found to be generally acceptable for incorporation in a multilateral agreement' (*ibid.*, p. 259), Keynes was unwilling to abandon non-discriminatory quotas until it was clear that Britain could afford to do so and this was unlikely to be the case in the near future (*ibid.*, p. 260).

Thus he was now (1943–4) convinced that import quotas on a temporary basis were the necessary protectionist vehicle and superior to tariffs or a depreciation. He expected that sterling would start out at a very low value after the war but later its 'optimum' value would be higher (*CW*, p. 284). Hence there was not much point in a temporary depreciation. As well he was pessimistic that the elasticities would not be high enough to improve the balance of payments and that 'where wages are closely linked with the cost of living, the efficacy of exchange depreciation may be understandably reduced' (*ibid.*, p. 289).

Quantitative regulation of imports Keynes saw as needed to support the degree of national planning he envisioned for the post World War II period (*ibid.*, pp. 258, 306–7).[8] He thought that for key manufactured products, particularly newer industries (*CW*, XXIV, p. 329), capacity would be generated in a planned way. He was confident that Britain would be represented in all key manufacturing industries without a loss of comparative advantage, still clinging to the notion that 'a great many manufactured products can be produced with almost equal efficiency in any industrial[ized] country' (*CW*, XXVI, (p. 264). Once capital was sunk in these areas, quotas would be the most effective and sensible way of limiting imports to 'the excess of our demand over what we are in a position to supply' (*CW*, XVI, p. 263). Agriculture would also be assured a guaranteed portion of the home market (*CW*, XXVI, p. 285).

After negotiating the Anglo-American Loan Agreement in December 1945, Keynes reported to the House of Lords that he saw the postwar currency and commercial proposals as a package:

> devised to favour the maintenance of equilibrium by expressly permitting various protective devices when they are required to maintain equilibrium and by forbidding them when they are not so required. [He emphasized that] the outstanding characteristic of the plans is that they represent the first elaborate and comprehensive attempt to combine the advantages of freedom of commerce with safeguards against the disastrous consequences of a laissez-faire system which pays no direct regard to the preservation of equilibrium and merely relies on the eventual working out of blind forces. (*CW*, XXIV, p. 621)

The multilateral clearing system would allow Britain to offset its likely balance-of-trade deficit with the USA through a surplus with the rest of the world. This trade surplus would be derived from the restoration of non-discriminatory multilateral trade, which he saw to be more advantageous to British commerce than a hostile world of separate economic blocs (*ibid.*, p. 623). Overall, Britain required 'a strong expansionist stimulus throughout the world' (*CW*, XXV, p. 137) in order to provide 'willing markets for a largely expanded volume of [its] exports' (*ibid.*, p. 137).[9] Keynes's optimism for an expansion in world trade was generated by his perception of a change in US policy away from a protectionist stance (*CW*, XXIV, p. 263): 'For the first time in modern history the United States is going to exert its full, powerful influence in the direction of reduction of tariffs, not only of itself but by all others.'

Thus, by 1945, Keynes was looking forward to trade liberalization in the postwar period, but he wanted assurance that potential deficit countries such as the UK would have protectionist instruments available as temporary expedients if they found themselves in balance-of-payments difficulties. But in an article published posthumously, 'The Balance of Payments of the United States', which appeared in the *Economic Journal* of June 1946, he also recognized that import tariffs and export subsidies should not progressively offset the classical medicine which he thought would ultimately correct balance-of-payments problems given the nature of the proposed postwar international monetary system (*CW*, XXVII, pp. 444–5). At this point, he no longer talked explicitly about protecting specific key industries, perhaps because he expected them to do well in the liberalized trading environment and, of course, he was trying to convince the British government of the merits of multilateral trade.

In summary, Keynes certainly held different views on the desirability of tariffs and other protectionist devices as policy instruments at various times depending upon economic circumstances.[10] At any particular moment, he weighed the benefits and costs of protection. In the end, he was neither a strong free trader nor a staunch protectionist, but he tended more towards free trade than protection. For him, following expansionist policies towards full employment in the world and keeping Britain a strong economic power were the overriding objectives; he saw protection as a means to those ends, sometimes.

Keynes and contemporary protectionism

The last section of this paper deals with what Keynes would likely have said about commercial policy in the period after his death in 1946. This is, of course, only speculation since on the issue of protection he was by no means doctrinaire. Yet it is interesting to see what views he might have held on a few important issues such as European economic integration, the GATT tariff-cutting rounds, Nixon's 1971 US tariff and the current trend towards protectionism.

First, when it became clear that the International Monetary Fund was not going to play a key role in the early post World War II reconstruction, Keynes would have likely subscribed to the idea of a regional Clearing Union in Europe (the European Payments Union) since at least it would help to get Europe on its feet and it was, of course, patterned after the global Clearing Union which he advocated at the Bretton Woods Conference. Moreover, given the difficulty of global trade liberalization and the fragility of the European economies in the mid-1950s, he probably would have abandoned his hostility towards separate trading blocs and accepted some form of regional free trade area in Europe just as he outlined after World War I in 'The Economic Consequences of the Peace' (*CW*, II, p. 189). Whether, in 1957, Keynes would have leaned towards the European Free Trade Area model or the European Economic Community model is difficult to say.

When it came time for the various GATT tariff-cutting rounds, Keynes probably would have wholeheartedly endorsed them since they provided for a gradual decline in protectionism combined with some machinery for temporary protection.[11] They seem to fit his inclinations in 1944 when he drafted the 'Principles of British Commercial Policy':

> Great Britain both by tradition and self-interest is concerned with the removal of obstacles to international trade and, in particular, the moderation of tariffs ... Nevertheless, her prospective trade position after the war means that safeguards for the balance of trade are indispensible to her. (*CW*, XXVI, p. 305)

In the case of Nixon's 10 per cent tariff of August 1971, which was instituted by the USA when it closed its gold window to central banks, Keynes might have been sympathetic since it was a temporary expedient designed to press the rest of the world into adopting more realistic exchange rates through which the USA was supposed to achieve a balance-of-payments equilibrium. Keynes, both in 1931 (after Britain's abandonment of the gold standard) and in 1944 (while the post World War II currency and commercial proposals were being formulated), had indicated that tariffs and currency depreciations had to be viewed together since they were alternatives in many cases (*CW*, IX, p. 243, and XXVI, p. 5).

Finally, in terms of the early to mid-1980s, it is useful to consider whether Keynes would have opted for protection as a solution for the overvalued US dollar. While the overvalued US dollar has had a similar impact on the USA's exports and import competing industries as did prewar parity upon those of Britain from 1925 to 1931, our view is that he would not have joined the cry for protection as the remedy this time. Rather he is likely to have been critical both of the US government's monetary–fiscal policy mix, involving excess monetary restraint coupled with fiscal ease, and of the combination of tight fiscal and tight monetary policies in other major industrialized countries. He would have probably opted for an easier monetary policy in order to stimulate investment both in the USA and abroad. The effect would have been a lower US dollar, smaller US trade deficits and less unemployment worldwide.

The value of the US dollar has finally come down (at least against the German mark and the Japanese yen), but its effects may be too late to stop an impatient and protectionist-minded US Congress.[12] For the US to follow a protectionist policy at a time when an immobile overvalued dollar no longer exists, Keynes would surely have seen as another instance of the USA abdicating its world leadership role, as it did in the interwar period when it sharply curtailed its lending to the rest of the world.[13,14] His advocacy of general tariffs for the UK in 1930–1 was mainly in reaction to an unviable level for sterling which he did not think could be altered and to significant protection already adopted elsewhere. In his later years, Keynes spoke out against rounds of protection followed by retaliation which end up strangling world trade and, ultimately, paralysing the world economy.

Notes

1. Helpful comments on an earlier draft of the paper were made by Robert Dimand, Omar Hamouda, Donald Moggridge, John Smithin and Lorie Tarshis. References to Keynes's writings are cited from his collected writings showing the appropriate volume and pages, e.g. *CW*, XXVI, p. 307.
2. Nicholas Kaldor (1982) is incorrect when he says that in 1923 Keynes had 'an uncompromising attitude to free trade with no exceptions' (p. 5).
3. His conversion to tariff advocacy in 1930–1 was neither as revolutionary nor as permanent as implied by Joan Robinson (1962, p. 86): 'In some way the unkindest cut of all [against *laissez-faire*] was Keynes' repudiation of the doctrine that tariffs must be harmful to the country that imposes them.' The fact that his strong pro-tariff stance was short lived is presented in this chapter.
4. Later in chapter 19 of the *General Theory* (1936) he even questioned whether a reduction in money wages would increase employment. Instead he suggested 'a stable general level of money wages is the most advisable policy provided that equilibrium with the rest of the world can be secured by means of fluctuating exchanges' (*CW*, VII, p. 270).
5. Of course, this improvement in the terms of trade made foreigners less able to purchase British goods, a point Keynes failed to recognize.
6. Since this paper was presented, an article by Barry Eichengreen (1984) has come to our attention. In the article, Eichengreen makes the useful distinction between Keynes's views on how protection affects employment and how it affects industrial policy (what Keynes called 'planning').
7. Already, in July 1941, Keynes opposed Britain's acceptance of article VII of the Land Lease Agreement in which the US proposed that the two countries agree not to discriminate after the war 'against the importation of any produce originating in the other country' (*CW*, XXIII, P. 175). He argued that the UK could not abandon Imperial Preference or fail to take into account the postwar international economic position of the UK which might require less than free trade (*CW*, XXIII, pp. 194–6, 225–8).
8. As early as March 1931, Keynes had said (*CW*, XX, p. 495): 'But if I look into the bottom of my own heart, the feeling which I find there is, rather, that a tariff is a crude departure from laizzez-faire . . . but that it will be superseded in time, not by a return to laissez-faire, but by some comprehensive scheme of national planning'. By national planning, Keynes may have had in mind the type of planning undertaken by the Japanese which encouraged the growth of capacity in industries only to what the Ministry of International Trade and Investment thought was an optimal size or he may have had in mind an even looser form of industrial policy.
9. Harrod (1963) seems to have correctly characterized Keynes as an internationalist, who 'had only despaired of a revival of greater freedom of trade because he judged that other nations would be unco-operative' (p. 609).
10. Our interpretation of Keynes's changing views on tariffs is essentially in accord with

that of Williamson (1983, p. 89), and Eichengreen (1984).

11. However, he might have had some difficulty with the most-favoured nation clause (which is at the heart of GATT) as he did when he criticized the Lend Lease Agreement in 1941 (*CW*, XXIII, p. 178).

12. Of course, the Congress is also frustrated by the protectionist stance of some of the USA's trading partners. Especially irritating is the European Community's policy affecting agricultural imports.

13. In a commentary on a paper by Edward M. Bernstein, 'Keynes and US Foreign Economic Policy', delivered after this paper was presented, Samuel I. Katz agrees with Bernstein that Keynes would have sanctioned protection at the end of 1986 (Katz, 1986, p. 6). Whether Katz and Bernstein or the authors of this paper are correct about what would have been Keynes's view on the use of protection by the US depends in parts on whether Keynes would have thought that the US dollar had depreciated sufficiently enough against other key currencies and on his assessment of the damage US protection would inflict on the world economy.

14. Keynes also would have been troubled by the stance of the USA (and other industrialized countries) on the current debt situation of the LDCs since he would have perceived parallels with America's withdrawal of credit in the early 1930s; but that is the subject of another paper.

References

Eichengreen, B. (1984), 'Keynes and protection', *Journal of Economic History*, XLIV, June, 363–373.

Harrod, R.F. (1963), *The Life of John Maynard Keynes*, New York: St Martin's Press.

Kaldor, N. (1982), 'Keynes as an economic advisor', in A.P. Thirlwall (ed.), *Keynes as a Policy Advisor*, London: Macmillan: 2–37.

Katz, S.I. (1986), 'Commentary on "Keynes and U.S. Foreign Economic Policy" by Edward M. Bernstein', presented at the American Economic Association Meetings, New Orleans, 28 December 1986, mimeo.

Keynes, J.M. (1971–), *The Collected Writings of John Maynard Keynes*, Vols I–XXX, London: Macmillan Royal Economic Society.

Moggridge, D.E. and Howson, S. (1974), 'Keynes on monetary policy', *Oxford Economic Papers*, XXVI, July, 226–247.

Robinson, J. (1962), *Economic Philosophy*, Chicago: Aldine Press.

Skidelsky, R. (1983), *John Maynard Keynes: Hopes Betrayed 1883–1920*, London: Macmillan.

Williamson, J. (1983), 'Keynes and the international economic order', *Keynes and the Modern World* (Proceedings of the Keynes Centenary Conference, King's College, Cambridge), eds. D. Worswick and J. Trevithick, New York: Cambridge University Press, 87–113.

18 The international debt of the LDCs

Lorie Tarshis

What may well be the most threatening of today's economic problems –
that posed by the international debt of the less developed countries
(LDCs) – is very much like the problem that Germany (and her
creditors) faced when she was obliged to pay reparations at the end of
World War I. In this examination of the international debt of the Third
World, I intend to follow the lead offered by Keynes in his writings on
'Reparations and the Peace Treaty' (*CW*, II, III, XII and XVIII).[1] But
while these problems have many features in common, in others, such as
size, they are worlds apart. The total bill for reparations that was placed
before Germany, came to from $5 to $8 billion. (Germany was never
informed about the *total* sum she was to pay. Instead she was told to pay
$x million annually, and x was revised downwards several times between
1922 and 1932.) Then with financial collapse everywhere, Chancellor
Bruning announced that Germany would pay no more, and nobody
seemed to notice. The international debt of the LDCs has now passed $1
trillion, or from 125 to 200 times as high as Germany's 'debt'. Keynes
urged the victors to cancel their claims for reparations; he saw
economic disaster for both sides if they did not. A very strong case can
be made for at least the partial cancellation of today's claims for, if not,
why not the same? But nobody seems to be concerned that, since the
crisis surfaced in 1982, their debt has climbed from $730 billion to $1
trillion, and still it rises.

While Germany was forced to pay reparations by the victors of the
war, the obligations now borne by the LDCs were accepted 'voluntarily'.
On the surface this seems to constitute a second real distinction; however, there was more in common between Germany's agreement to pay
reparations and the Third World's agreement to service its debt than
appears at first glance.

Turn the story back 130 years. The United States was then the major
'developing economy'. It had been borrowing heavily for a few decades,
mostly from Britain, and had used the funds it received to finance the
purchase of various goods and services needed for the economy's
development. The more the U.S. borrowed, the more rapidly could her
development proceed and, therefore, the faster would be the growth in

the economy's output at capacity. Such a growth in output made the payment of interest easier – always provided that foreign markets for part of the output could be found. And it seemed likely that the larger were the imports of technically advanced machinery and equipment, the more successfully would US producers compete abroad. In fact the USA had no real difficulty in servicing her international debt, except for short periods of crisis.

This story of development financed by foreign borrowing was, of course, repeated, with Canada, Italy, Russia, Japan and later with South Korea, Taiwan, Singapore and Hong Kong in leading roles. And in such a scenario there could be no strong objection to paying interest on one's debt because the loans that created the debt clearly contributed to the growth of the economy and to its ability to produce and pay interest, with something still left over for domestic use.

Germany's reparations obviously represent a special and different case. Losing the war added nothing to her capacity to produce. Indeed since she lost men and women, land, labour skills and capital assets, her productive capacity by 1920 had fallen below its 1912 level. She was compelled to pay reparations not because she gained from the war, but because her warlike acts had damaged the victors' economies. I would not argue that she should have been excused from that obligation; only that because her ability to respond to it had surely fallen, her creditors would be bound to hear her appeals for mercy, and perhaps to be persuaded that the interests of the whole European community might be furthered by responding to her appeal.

Germany's exports, from the time she began to pay reparations, were never large enough to cover her bills. She had to borrow the difference and in order to appeal to potential lenders, she had to keep interest rates in Germany higher than they were in other developed economies. She was also forced to curb government extravagance and raise taxes, apparently because it was felt that only if she were *to be seen* to be suffering would her credibility, probity and certificate of merit be high enough to allow her to enter the kingdom of borrowers. At first Germany's loans took the form of *ad hoc* delays in her scheduled repayments. Later she was required to raise the hard currency needed by getting loans from investors, speculators (who were looking for the mark to appreciate), and housewives and nannies, in Britain, the USA, etc. Still later, banks in the USA and UK added their funds – mostly loaned short term – to the stream that poured into Germany.

Midway through the process, Keynes described it as follows: 'For five years Germany's victors have squeezed the lemon with both hands, have heard the "pips squeak" and felt their own hands ache, have seen a trickle flowing into the bowl – only to discover in the end that every drop has come, not from the lemon, but from the hands themselves' (*CW*, XVIII, p. 245). Generally the proceeds of loans to Germany were recycled directly back as reparations, but meanwhile Germany's international debt grew steadily, though faster from late 1925 to mid-1928.

It was all, of course, a vast charade in which the payer pretended to pay from his own pocket and the recipients smacked their lips as they relished what they were receiving from the payer – but really from themselves. It lasted only until someone whistled the end of the game; had no one ever whistled, the process would still be underway – though many thousand times bigger! But it ended and the real troubles began.

Whether the monetary and fiscal policies forced on Germany helped her to pay is questionable, but clearly they did press Germany, without mercy or sense, into an ever deepening deflation. Keynes described the situation in 1932:

> Germany today is in the grip of the most terrible deflation that any nation had experienced ... The result reaches, or goes beyond, the limit of what is endurable. Nearly a third of the population is out of work. The standards of life of those still employed have been cruelly curtailed ... The growing generation is without the normal incentives of bourgeois security and comfort. Too many people in Germany have nothing to look forward to – nothing except a 'change', something wholly vague and wholly undefined, but a *change*. (*ibid.*, p. 366)

Six years earlier, describing the first manifestations of deflation, he wrote:

> The worm of deflation gnawed his way through. The Reichsbank's policy of credit restriction gradually became fully effective ... Governor Schacht has topped his million unemployed in Germany by the remorseless working of the same beautiful and reliable technique by which Governor Norman had previously achieved a comparable figure in England. Now to put 10 per cent of the working population of Germany on to the relief fund does not help reparations. (*ibid.*, pp. 274–5)

The present situation of Third World debtors is less clear-cut. Obviously much of their borrowing before 1972 contributed to the development of their economies. But afterwards, borrowing – which was greatly accelerated – was mostly required to keep their economies from collapse. Crude petroleum, whose price in the next nine years rose by a factor of 13 times, was essential as a source of power, heat, light and transportation. Dollars were needed to pay the bills.

With no matching increase in the proceeds from LDC exports, a steady flow of imports could only be financed through such massive borrowings of US dollars. But there is no evidence that the dollars were used to build up significantly the stock of capital assets; instead they were used also to support an active exodus of private wealth to safer havens in the USA, Canada, and so on, and of course to pay the much higher prices demanded by OPEC, etc.

The piracy of private interests, who succeeded in moving their fortunes abroad, and of OPEC, must have required all the dollars raised by LDC-borrowing. Their exports of goods and services were approximately equal to non-petroleum imports; the enormous increase in Third World international debt from 1972 to, say, 1980 made almost no contribution to their development. And this implied that the ability of the borrowers to service their growing debt scarcely grew at all. After 1980, the situation deteriorated still further. The LDCs were even short of the dollars they needed to pay interest to their creditors, and from then on, despite some growth in their exports, they had to borrow even to continue servicing their debt. The increase in their international debt already noted – from $730 billion in 1981 to more than $1 trillion in 1986 – reflected their desperate efforts to avoid default as well as the continued high price, to 1985, of crude petroleum, etc. And as we shall see shortly, the frantic efforts of their creditors to save their debtors, and hence themselves, are also reflected in the increase.

Today's game, though different from Germany's in origin, is likewise a vast charade, and vastly destructive. With the debtors now obliged to pay out roughly $95 billion in interest on their $1 trillion debt, with their aggregate balance on current account showing about $350 billion in receipts from their sales to developed economies and with their purchases, including the interest due on their debt, amounting to about $390 billion, it is evident that in order to pay they must borrow dollars – at least $40 billion worth a year, and bound to rise unless interest rates drop. The hands that are squeezing the debtors are supplying the funds that the debtors pay out to those same hands. And every party pretends that a real transfer is taking place. Again, though it is all make-believe, its consequences have been very real and they promise to be increasingly sinister for debtor and creditor. Their borrowing, like Germany's fifty years earlier, was unproductive in the extreme.

But another difference between the arrangements for reparations and for the servicing of LDC debt must also be noted. The suppliers of loan funds for most of the reparations-era borrowing before 1926 were the many private investors and speculators who were attracted by the higher interest rates or were ready to bet on the mark and Germany. Because no one (or very few) of the creditors had a big stake in Germany's debt, no one was likely to feel responsible for the ability or willingness of the debtor – Germany – to service it. Obviously each creditor would want the debt to be serviced, but if he judged the prospects to be poor, he would, if possible, withdraw his funds from Germany before the market had become as keenly aware of the situation as he was. He would clearly have no reason to hesitate – hoping, for instance, that if *he* showed patience, Germany would try even harder. After that date and for three years, large banks supplied an increasing share of the funds, but by the end of 1928 there was no single bank which had loaned enough to Germany to cause it to feel responsible for Germany's servicing the whole debt. As a result, each lender was concerned only with *its* interest, and if pessimism swept the market all creditors would be moved to get out while they could. And they did!

The LDCs, after 1960, borrowed much less from private investors than Germany had done forty years earlier; they turned instead to the larger banks. They were the more willing to turn to such banks because by that time they could borrow more cheaply from Eurodollar banks than from other lenders. And after 1972, these banks found themselves awash in US dollars. In order to turn a decent profit they had to lend the dollars they had been so successful in buying as quickly as possible. Even though these leading banks offered participations to other, smaller, banks, they usually reserved the lion's share for themselves. As a result, the ownership of the LDCs loan certificates tended to concentrate in a comparatively few banks.

Any one bank with a relatively large participation would naturally feel itself to be in some degree responsible for the viability of any debtor signalling that it needed help, and also that if help were not provided, it might have to default. Moreover, each of the major creditors would surely realize that its refusal to join in a rescue operation would be communicated to the other chief participants and no good would come to it if that happened. This situation was one in which the pressure to cooperate in any bail-out would keep a debtor alive – though perhaps only because, if unaided, it would have died.

Related to that, the bankruptcy of an LDC-debtor would have led to a concentration of losses among the larger banks. By contrast, when Germany declared that she would pay no more reparations and, a year later, that she would not service any debt owed abroad, there were, of course, serious losses: first, to the several governments that claimed reparations, then to the thousands of private investors and, finally, to banks – but the share of any bank or individual in the losses was comparatively small, though large enough to force some banks that had already grown weak into bankruptcy. Still, the concentration of losses was insufficient to provoke the losers to take strong measures.

The debtors are now allowed to play this same game but only so long as they observe a set of rules, established by the IMF, which helps to further the illusion. They must curtail their imports, adhere to a tight money policy, curb governmental extravagance and raise taxes. In short, they must follow the very deflationary programme that failed so miserably for Germany, sixty years earlier. All this to convert a deficit of $40 billion into a surplus. Never have so many had to pay so much for so little. And no one can doubt that the conditions laid down by the IMF are creating a deflation in Mexico, Brazil and most of the other heavily indebted countries at least as severe as Germany's. And to no better purpose.

Now deflation is often an effective prescription for a single economy that seeks an improvement in its balance of payments so it can pay off some of its debt. But its efficacy falls away sharply when it is employed by a group of countries with a very large aggregate deficit. They can only pay back debt, in the aggregate, if they can convert their aggregate deficit into a surplus – a surplus that has to be large if they aim to pay back large chunks of debt. With the international debt of the LDCs over $1 trillion, debtors could pay it off in ten years if for that period they could convert their present aggregate deficit of, say, $60 billion a year into a surplus of $100 billion. Easily said, but if it is to be done, it demands that the creditor economies – assuming that they are also the surplus economies (the surplus economies include the major oil producers) – must consent to the transformation of their surpluses into deficits aggregating $100 billion. There are two difficulties to plague any such effort. First, most of the creditor economies would resist surrendering any of the markets for their products to debtor economies and, for the most part, poor economies. Their governments would certainly feel that it was one of their holy missions to protect the jobs of their working men – especially if it could be done at the expense of the foreigner! A whole armoury of 'Buy American Acts', 'Canadian Content Rules' and 'Agriculture Protection Acts' lies waiting to be rushed into the breach. And there is a second difficulty. The heavily indebted LDCs have already been forced to cut their imports savagely. As a result, shortages of every kind abound and the normal poverty of all but the richest families is compounded several times over. Once their country begins to have a surplus in its balance of payments, domestic pressures to relax restrictions on imports would be overwhelming. (A country in deficit can plead its inability to finance the purchase of more imports, but how could a country with a large surplus find a persuasive excuse for continuing to hold down imports?) Yet, if it gives in, its ability to repay debt vanishes.

The sufferings of debtors, which became all too obvious in the period 1922–32 and seem to have been confirmed since 1982, were not limited to them. Creditors in the 1920s suffered too; in the course of an interview that Irving Fisher conducted with Keynes in March 1929, Keynes showed why deflation in the debtor country tends to spread. After pointing out that Germany's ability to pay reparations depends upon her ability to expand her exports, while restricting her imports, Fisher asks: (*ibid.*, pp. 316–17) 'If putting pressure on Germany to pay a large sum means strengthening her competitive power, how do you think this will affect British interests?' Keynes replies:

> Very adversely indeed. It becomes a question of how far Great Britain wants to force down German wages in order that Germany may steal her export industries (*sic*) away from her ... Great Britain does not want to press down the German standard of life so as to compete with her own exports because she is quite sure that it would finally have the effect of driving down her own standard of life. [This was no zero-sum game!]

It should be apparent that Keynes, by 1929, had neither read nor anticipated his own *General Theory*. Had he faced these questions after 1936, he would have seen more clearly that the link between deflation in Germany and deflation in Britain was no absolute. It could be modified. A decline in Britain's exports would not necessarily have led to decline in Britain's output and employment level; after all, his own theory showed that the aggregate demand function could be maintained by fiscal or monetary measures, despite falling exports.

The fact that the bloom is now again leaving the boom in the advanced economies as the result of declines in their exports to the LDCs (with damaging consequences for the efforts of the LDCs to expand *their* export proceeds) suggests that the *General Theory* has been neither read nor understood in Britain, Germany, Canada, etc. What tragedies are born of ignorance! And to note that one of Keynes's most important creations – the IMF – has been in the lead in generating this tragedy!

It must be emphasized that the international debt of the LDCs cannot be repaid, or even stopped from growing, unless the developed economies manage to maintain themselves, *for years*, in a state of high prosperity accompanied by serious payments deficits. If they do, the LDCs can hope to earn enough US dollars to cover not only hard-currency purchases, but also the servicing of their debt, and have dollars left over to pay off some of it. But if the developed countries fail, debt repayment by the LDCs becomes impossible, though no doubt some of the less seriously indebted of them could manage to repay theirs; while those whose debt had been heaviest would find it continuing to grow.

In this connection, it is easy to see that if interest rates could be sharply reduced, the debt problem would be eased, though only slowly. However, the LDCs have no handle they can move to bring interest rates down – and, in particular, they have no lever by means of which they can lower rates on *US funds*. The responsibility for reducing interest rates must be for the advanced economies. And *they* too must be responsible for maintaining high prosperity and very high payments deficits. The IMF has made, up to now, a fetish of 'conditionality' for debtors. Actually there is very little that debtors can do except control their own imports and capital flights. The IMF should consider rewriting its clauses on conditionality to apply to *creditors*: and then see to it that creditors actually follow its rules.

It seems all too clear that the major debtors are incapable of paying off their international debt without a substantial change in the macro-economic policies of creditor or developed economies. This lesson could have been inferred from Germany's experience after World War I; it has been demonstrated again between 1982 and today. By now, it seems obvious that the major creditor countries are unwilling to learn that lesson, despite the enlightened (but late) pressure of the USA for such a change. Britain, West Germany, Canada, France, Japan and even Italy have strongly resisted every such move. The picture this presents is of a small and foundering lifeboat filled with a representative from each of these countries all crowded into the bow, while the USA is working hard to close a tremendous hole in the stern. When asked for help, they answer: 'Why should we be bothered? The leak is at your end of the boat.'

In our imperfect world there seems to be but one option left – an option less attractive than the best, but it seems unlikely that the best can be implemented. To avoid real catastrophe creditors will have to cancel great chunks of debt. Much has to be forgiven, cancelled or for the sake of appearance refinanced at zero interest and to mature at the option of the debtors. The remainder, which should be serviced in the normal way, must be low enough to be serviced without imposing an excessive burden on debtors. Creditor countries must take the initiative in formulating and offering this option to the debtors in order to ease the gales of ill-will that the present arrangement is generating. (If, to punish the LDCs, the advanced economies were to agree to keep them out of world capital markets, they would in effect be creating the dreadful fate that these moves were designed to avert.)

The strongest argument for this option is that no one need lose and most would gain. Creditors lose no more than has already been lost because they cannot hope that most of their claims against their debtors will be fully satisfied. Debtors, released from the pressures created as they try to achieve the impossible, gain – indeed gain doubly – because they would then be able to turn their energies to their major task, to encourage the development of their economies. And the threat of sickening, counterproductive deflation would be eased. Moreover, if creditors accepted the initiative, *they* would be able to choose the time and have a voice in determining the extent of the cancellations. If they do nothing, the debtors' situation will deteriorate rapidly, and a Debtors' Strike will become a fact. Debtors will determine the time and extent of the settlement. What hope could creditors nourish then?

Defaults by debtors – especially by international debtors – have, in recent years, come to be regarded as a capital sin, no doubt reflecting the incredible size of their debts. I dare not question such a judgement, but it is important to note that, like all other sins, they have not been rare. Keynes, with his love for keeping score, wrote late in 1924:

> The record of defaults by foreign governments on their external debt are so numerous, and indeed so nearly universal, that it is easier to deal with them by naming those that have not defaulted than those which have. *All* foreign governments which have borrowed any considerable sum on the London market have been in default in whole or in part on the service of their external debt within the past twenty-five years, with the exception of Chile and Japan ... Other important defaulters within the past twenty-five years include ... Mexico, China, Egypt, Turkey, Greece, Spain, Portugal, Russia, Austria, Hungary, Bulgaria and Roumania. (*ibid.*, p. 263)

Keynes, of course, wrote this before Germany's defaults in 1932 and 1933, and those of central and Eastern Europe after 1946.

In recent years most central banks have accepted for themselves a relatively new role, as 'lenders of last resort' to their banks. In effect, they agree to supply funds, if needed, to keep their major banks open for business. But these commercial banks would be in serious difficulties if they were to forgive much of their outstanding claims against LDCs. The source of their problem consists in the nature of their liabilities. Corresponding to their large holdings of dollar-denominated assets, they are liable to their depositors and other banks, for very large sums also denominated in US dollars. *Their* creditors – e.g. their depositors – if they choose to exercise their claims will want, and have the legal right to demand, *dollars* in payment. But their central banks, except for those of the US Federal Reserve system, do not hold enough dollars to enable them to bail out their desperate banks. The Bank of England can supply British commercial banks with sterling. The Bank of Canada can lend or grant Canadian dollars. And because the private banks' holdings of assets denominated in US dollars are the very ones that are being

questioned, these assets will *not be* useful. If the Bank of Canada or the
Bank of England are to serve in this new role, they will have to acquire
US dollars. And the best and only source would be to use a line of credit
that the central bank had established with the Federal Reserve.

With that line of credit, the Bank of Canada could supply US dollars
to any of its private banks that had made large US dollar loans to LDCs.
Should, then, the Federal Reserve collect interest on their loans to the
Bank of Canada or another? I believe not. If it recognized the dangers
to its own banks from the bankruptcy of some of Canada's, it would
surely see gains from loans by it to the Bank of Canada. Moreover, the
case would be even more persuasive if, to match the US dollar loan to
the Bank of Canada, there were an equal Canadian dollar interest-free
loan to the Federal Reserve by the Bank of Canada. And likewise for
the other major central banks.

There is no good reason why anyone but the shareholders of the
various banks should lose from this 'mess'. No one can doubt that many
of the banks loaned far more than was prudent and their shareholders,
therefore, were partly responsible for this, but not fully. For one thing,
banks were generally under heavy pressure from national governments
and international agencies to assist in recycling petrofunds. Secondly, it
is widely recognized that most banks must be kept alive and functioning;
their role in domestic economies is too vital to allow them to disappear.
It follows that the stockholders of most banks should get partial protection.

What this means is that each central bank would have to establish a
compensation rule for the LDC debt to be cancelled, such as: 'for every
$100 million of write-offs (at face value), compensation of, say, $70
million in either US dollars or domestic currency, should be provided'.

Most governments apparently do not understand that all these
transactions are merely bookkeeping transfers. But they are. And so
there is *no* reason why taxes have to be raised or other government
expenditures must be curtailed 'to pay for' such transfers for compensation. However, each bank that receives compensation, in keeping with
the government's goal of saving it from oblivion, should be *required* to
make new loans to LDC's, but this time far more cautiously than before.

Readers of this proposal may believe it to be too ambitious and not
called for by the gravity (mild, they say) of the situation. They may be
correct, but it should be obvious that the real gravity of any such
situation can never be seen when it is being covered over by a flood of
loan money. Keynes, in April 1929, while a replacement plan for the
Dawes Plan was under discussion, wrote: 'The difficulty in formulating
revisions is that Germany having paid hitherto by means of borrowed

money, we really have no more evidence as to her capacity to pay than we had when the Dawes Committee met five years ago' (*ibid.*, p. 326).

There have been too many instances in recent history in which optimism has blinded judgement and few were prepared for the disaster into which the world was dashing. Unfortunately, days of panic are unlikely to provide the atmosphere in which sensible measures can be devised. But it must be granted that the 'solution' – cancellation of the debt by creditors, with compensation for them by the various central banks – is not the best of all possible solutions. It would be better for all parties if debtors were able to pay off their debts, but only if that could be achieved without forcing the debtor economies into serious depression, and no less emphatically, without blocking their development. So far as I can see there is only one path to that idyllic land. The developed economies have to undertake a programme that gives top priority to securing uninterrupted prosperity for all of them; and to be prepared for their balance of payments on current account to be in serious deficit, year after year – *and even to welcome that development.* After all, there is no other route that would enable the major debtors to repay some of their debt.

Keynes in the 1920s insisted that Germany could not meet its reparations obligations, and the allies would have to cancel them or accede to German forfeiture. It is difficult to see for those years any other answer – but the delay in reaching it was almost fatal. The same response appears to be appropriate in regard to the international debt of the LDCs. Its effects on debtors and creditors seem to be similar to, but stronger than, those caused by the mess of reparations. However, this time, there is an 'out': something that could destroy the link that in the 1920s was responsible for multiplying the direct destructive consequences by much more than one. However, with Keynes's analysis of the macroeconomy so out of favour, it seems only prudent to put forward a second-best solution, for now. After all, if a start is made and then the virus of uncommon sense sweeps through the developed economies, these first steps can be withdrawn, without any real cost.

Note

1. *CW* refers to *The Collected Writings of John Maynard Keynes*, ed. D.E. Moggridge, London: Macmillian, 1971–

19 The international debt problem and the 'Clearing Union'

Bernard Schmitt

In this short chapter we shall briefly deal with the core of a large subject, involving the future of international financial capitalism; we are here concerned with the dollar standard and our argument will apply to the exchange rate mechanism. We shall attempt to prove an utterly strange proposition, whose truth value has hitherto, to our knowledge, never been assessed: *the dollar standard exchange mechanism is fundamentally flawed at least in one important respect and puts a break on the development of international economic relations; the disorder lies in the fact that whenever a country services its external debt, it is invariably burdened with exactly the same debt all over again*, so that the external debt is in fact an eternal debt. In support of this point of view we shall advance a very simple argument (I). In (II) we shall draw the logical consequence: if external debts were positively repayable, indebted countries would stand to gain cumulatively in their own currencies the whole amount of their disbursements in earned foreign exchange. The way capable of leading the world out of the deadlock depicted in (I) is the implementation of an improved 'Clearing Union' (III).

I *Under the dollar-standard the external debt is a phoenix, perpetually rising from its own ashes* Country X has built up an external debt to the amount of x dollars (including interest). Suppose that X achieves a current trade surplus, equal to y dollars. Barring outgoing financial capital, y is available for servicing the external debt, at least in interest payments. Therefore, x should be diminished by y; this desirable condition is taken for granted. As a matter of fact, though, it does not obtain: *under the automatic rule of the dollar standard, x − y is equal to x, notwithstanding the fact that y is positive.*

It is important to bear in mind that (capital flight being nil) the whole amount of the trade surplus is actually disbursed by the indebted country, for suppose that y is used to build up exchange reserves (private or official) in the indebted country. Even then, the credit thus gained must be set against, and thus exerts a negative influence on, the overall external debt. So in no conceivable circumstance could it be validly argued that y is withheld from foreign creditors in general. It would seem, therefore, that x − y, and certainly not x, is, whatever happens to the trade surplus, the resulting sum of the external debt. All the same, *the correct answer is x and not x − y.*

Under a true 'system' of international payments the logic of debt servicing would be exactly the same whether borrowing was external or internal. Suppose, then, that the 'dollar standard' is such a 'system'. The argument then runs as follows: the net flow of incoming dollars, equal to y, is matched by an equal outflow, which diminishes the global debt of country X. Current net imports of goods and services from country X imply a positive excess demand of money X in terms of dollars; conversely, in order to service their external debt, borrowers in country X (State, firms, households) exercise an excess supply of money X in terms of dollars; the excess demand is equal to −y; the contemporaneous excess supply is equal to +y; and as a consequence, the excess demand is equal to zero. This is as it should be since the simultaneous (i.e. occuring in the same period) receipt and outlay of y dollars by country X should not elicit any *asymmetry* in the foreign exchange markets. Schedules of supply and demand of foreign exchange drawn in the textbooks conform to this requirement.

Yet, however perplexing, such an *asymmetry* precisely does in fact arise under the present arrangements of international payments. Note the steps in the correct argument.

1. Inflowing dollars do not necessarily transit via the exchange markets; imported commodities may instead be directly paid for in dollars.
2. On the other hand, imports from country X may be payable in money X. On the face of it, (a) in the diagram (Figure 19.1) is a transaction in the exchange markets, while (b) is a transaction in the market for commodities. But let us look more closely into the matter. In

Figure 19.1

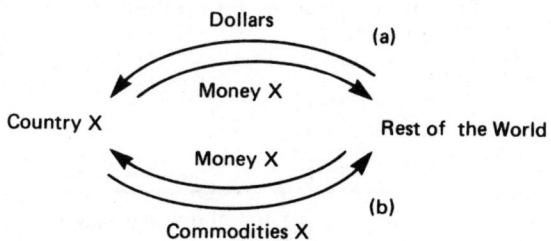

the given circumstances, money X is not bought for its own sake, as a *final good*, that is, to be added to the portfolio of assets held in the Rest of the World; money X is only a means of purchasing commodities X (sold by country X). So how are we to define the excess demand exercised by the Rest of the World: is it an excess demand for *money X* or an excess demand for *commodities X*? Surely, it cannot be one and the other at the same time since, in the given experiment, the total amount of excess demand is only equal to −y dollars and not to −2y dollars. The logically correct conclusion states that the relevant excess demand is defined in terms of *commodities* X and not of *money* X.

It could still be argued that the exchange market is held in complete ignorance as to the 'end' of the transaction and that it can register no difference whatever according to whether money X is purchased as a final good or merely as a means of payment. Consequently, (a) appears to be a fully fledged transaction in the exchange markets after all. But this would be a mind-boggling inference leading to an unwarranted excess demand equal to −2y dollars.

What really happens is quite simple. True, the exchange markets sell money X to the amount of y dollars; but in the same process the exchange markets sell the y dollars to banks in country X (Figure 19.2). *Money creation by banks X* is thus a key adjunct to the depicted experiment: the exchange market is nothing more than an *intermediary*. Finally, common sense is restored in its rights; equal to −y dollars, the relevant excess demand is defined in terms of *commodities X* and not of *money X*.

3.   Exactly the same conclusion applies when the net exports of country X are directly payable in dollars (as in 1, above). Again, money X brought forth by the sale to banks X of the dollar receipts is created *ad hoc*. We have arrived at the heart of the matter because we now know that, within the given experiment, the excess demand of money X is identically zero. This conclusion obviously holds when the dollar receipts are not converted at all. *Money X cannot possibly be in excess demand since it is either not demanded at all or, if demanded, it is newly created.*

4.   Should the same type of analysis be applied to the sum of dollars

Figure 19.2

Banks in country X

Assets	Liabilities
y dollars	equivalent sum in money X

which flow out of country X in servicing its debt? It may well be surmised that debtors in country X purchase newly created dollars from banks in the outside world. It would follow, then, that the excess demand of dollars in terms of money X is equal to the excess demand of money X in terms of dollars both being nil. Accordingly, most writers in the field remain constant to the view that, given the overall balance of positive (export surplus) and negative (debt payments) monetary flows between country X and the outside world, the relative value of currency X remains unchanged; but the majority view overlooks the crucial conjucture, namely, the fact that the outflow of money X is a *financial flux*, while the inflow of dollars defines a *commercial flux*. Clearly, if each side achieved equal commercial inflows and outflows or equal financial inflows and outflows, logic would ratify the majority view. But as things are, the indebted country takes in 'commercial money' and hands out 'financial money', so that the real difficulty is evaded when economists jump to the conclusion that money X retains in full its (previous) external value.

If we may timidly proffer a minority view, what really happens runs:

(i) either the debtors in country X purchase y dollars in the exchange markets;

(ii) or the debtors in country X convert into newly created dollars a sum of money X equal to y dollars.

Logically case (ii) leads exactly to the same result as case (i), at one remove. The issuing banks in the Rest of the World now hold money X and use it to repurchase the y dollars held by banks in country X. The line of thought is strictly equivalent in both cases: in spite of the fact that country X currently earns y dollars in its trade surplus, all the same, its residents (State, firms, households) cannot meet their dollar liabilities unless they *purchase* the y dollars earned in exports.

But what if the same body, say the State, earns the dollars in its exports and spends them in its own debt repayments? Even then, the asymmetry is still there: the dollars flow in against an additional creation of money X; the dollars flow out against an equivalent destruction of money X; and the symmetry of events seems perfect but how delusive. Inflowing dollars encounter no pre-existent units of money X; but when the newly created sum of money X is destroyed in purchasing the net dollar receipts, these receipts owing their existence to another 'cause', namely, the trade surplus, are already *given* (and certainly not created *ad hoc*) when they are bought and spent in servicing external debts (Figure 19.3).

Note that (a) *is not a transaction in the exchange markets*; banks in

Figure 19.3

Banks in country X

Assets	Liabilities
(a) Trade surplus $	money X
(b) Payment of external debts − $	− money X

country X supply money X *ad libitum*: they simply create in their own currency whatever sum is required, at the *given exchange rate*, to offset dollar intakes.

Contrariwise, (b) undoubtedly *is a transaction in the foreign exchange markets*: here we see the expenditure (and destruction) of a sum of money X used to 'demand' dollars held in the accounts of banks within country X. In other words, transaction (b) *defines a positive excess demand of dollars in terms of money X.* Since (a) exerts no counter-balancing effect whatever, the excess demand defined in (b) is entirely *net*:

> *This fundamental asymmetry has the effect of penalizing indebted nations with excess exports: their currencies depreciate, entailing a proportionate negative change in relative product values between the indebted countries and the outside world; the adverse effect on the 'terms of trade' translates into the unavoidable and complete 'revival' of an external debt, as soon as it is repaid (in interest or amortization).*

Let us now turn our attention to the logical inference that pertains to the point we have just made.

II   *There is only one logical way by which external debts can be diverted from their present course of perpetual renewal: before being passed on to creditors in the outside world, foreign exchange earned in commercial exports of indebted countries should never be allowed to transit via the exchange markets* (Figure 19.4)   Under the new scheme it must be

Figure 19.4

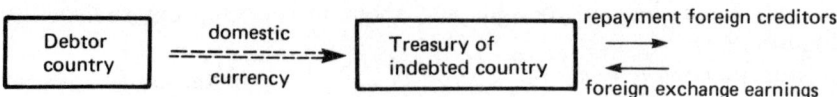

Figure 19.5

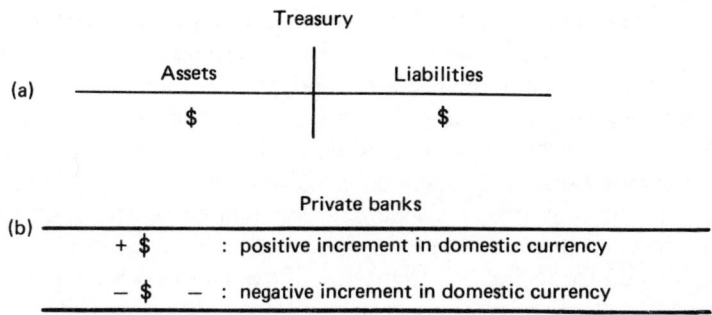

understood that in dealing with foreign exchange the Treasury keeps it entirely out of domestic banks. As a result, no increment of domestic money is created when foreign currency flows into the country. The Treasury balances its external accounts in dollars (foreign exchange) exclusively (Figure 19.5).

Transactions (b) are thus shunted or short-circuited. How can we ascertain that method (a) is novel and fruitful and does not reduce to a device or a trick? A very simple criterion is on hand: residents (State, firms, households) currently relinquish a fraction of their money income in servicing their external debts; let y' (= y dollars) be the amount of *domestic* currency surrendered in this way. Now the aforementioned criterion reads as follows: the new scheme is workable if and only if y' *accrues to the Treasury of the indebted country.*

Remember that under the dollar standard y' is entirely lost: it is *spent* or *used up* in the exchange market. By selling y dollars domestic banks destroy the corresponding amount in their own national currency, y' (at the initial exchange rate). Nobody can possibly recoup y', for whatever is destroyed is simply annuled and abolished and can no longer go the rounds. This incontrovertible fact provides the clue: by servicing its external debt a country invariably weakens its currency. *There is a direct correlation between the loss of y' and the proportionate loss in value of the domestic currency.*

Clearly, if the new plan obviates the loss of y', then it correlatively ensures the full value preservation of the domestic currency.

But that is precisely what the new arrangements bring about: instead of being destroyed in purchasing foreign exchange, y' *now accrues to the Treasury.* Does the outside world suffer a corresponding loss? By no means, for creditors still receive y dollars. What difference does it make to them when they receive the y dollars directly and no longer via the exchange markets?

The next step in the argument should be devoted to combating all forms of sophistry that the new plan may conjure up. In particular, it is not true to say that the net gain of the Treasury is really nil; yet it would seem to be absorbed in the payment of net commercial exports. *But this is not so*. Even under the dollar standard, y' in no way pays for exports; it is simply wiped out in the exchange markets. It logically follows that by saving y' the new plan yields a *net gain* reaped by the Treasury in each indebted surplus country. Explaining how net exports are to be paid for would take us beyond the scope of this chapter. Suffice it to say that the amount of domestic currency allowed to by-pass the foreign exchange markets is thereby perserved from destruction, i.e. *saved* within the indebted country, where it is used either to scale down the outstanding *internal* public debt or for some other budgetary appropriation. The proposals for the establishment of an 'International Clearing Union' are an important step towards the new international order.

III *Implementation of an improved 'Clearing Union'* There is no need for a newfangled international money unit like the bancor devised by Keynes. A basket of national currencies is all the world requires to restore the *system* of payments between nations. But the fulfilment of one precondition cannot be dispensed with if the plan is to achieve its end. A basket of moneys is of no avail unless it is currently 'issued' or 'emitted' by a newly founded International Bank.

We do not intend here to analyse money emissions, a question which we have carefully studied in several publications. We merely propose to conclude this short chapter by showing how the activity of the International Bank will automatically result in breaking the deadlock between debtor countries and their creditors which strengthens its grip as the foreign debt of the developing countries is approaching $1 trillion.

The International Bank will take care of all external payments of member *countries*. Central and commercial banks will continue to deal in individual national currencies only. In each member country the Treasury will be the only partner of the International Bank.

Consider an indebted country achieving a current trade surplus equal to y dollars and assume that 1 international unit (IU) is equivalent to 1 dollar. The diagram in Figure 19.6 depicts the logical process of international debt payments.

The International Bank will be functioning in all conceivable cases but we entreat the reader to focus his or her attention on the particular instance which we have endeavoured to highlight throughout, namely,

Figure 19.6

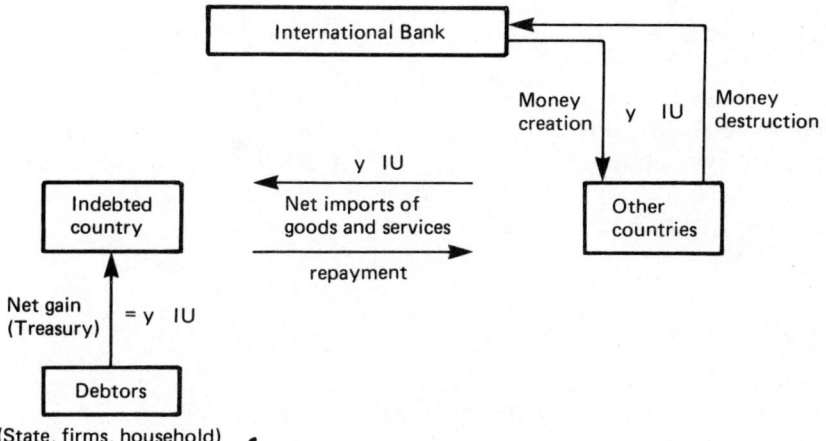

the undeserved lot of indebted countries and the bad omen attaching to it as to the future of international capitalism. The dollar standard inflicts an infuriating illogicality on international relations; an orderly system will never deprive indebted countries of even the smallest amount of their dearly earned trade surpluses. If, say, Mexico is to repay over the years $1 billion, the Mexican 'Hacienda' will, over the same period of time, reap exactly the equivalent amount in pesos, a decisive contribution to Mexico's development.

PART VI

POSITIONAL GOODS AND GROWTH: ANALOGIES TO KEYNESIAN ECONOMICS

20 Stagflation for our grandchildren

Omar F. Hamouda and Lorie Tarshis

(This chapter is based on the paper read by Professor Tibor Scitovsky in September 1986 at the Glendon College Keynes Conference, 'Keynes and Public Policy after Fifty Years'. An earlier commitment by its author stood in the way of its being published as a companion to the other papers presented here. The following summary of his argument was prepared by Professors Omar Hamouda and Lorie Tarshis to enable readers of the collected papers of that Conference to place his contribution in context. While we have not sought his approval for this version, he supported our plan, and we believe we have been generally faithful to his essay. Any one who wants to read it in its entirety will find it in the *Lloyd's Bank Review* for January 1987. It is also to be published in a collection of the various lectures delivered to honour the memory of the late Professor F.C. Hirsch, to be issued later in 1987 for the Twentieth Century Fund, New York.)

One of the major contributions of Keynes's *General Theory* was to question the validity of the widely held belief that market forces would, on their own, push an economy that had fallen into a recession back into full prosperity. In his attack on that belief, Keynes's first target was Say's law. His *General Theory* was formulated on the assumption that it was inapplicable to modern market economies.

Scitovsky's intention here was not to question that argument. Instead he chose to examine another overoptimistic assumption, that when labour's productivity rises, workers, made temporarily redundant, would find new jobs, as the income of the still-employed workers would rise with their growing productivity, and their spending, as a result, would rise too. Is that certain or even likely?

There had been good reasons for such a belief in the past. People spent *more* as their earnings grew; and when their incomes grew very rapidly not only were they able to afford larger and more sumptuous banquets, more horses, more luxurious carriages, more rooms in their villas, etc., but they were eager to acquire most everything they could afford. There seemed to be no limit to the amount they would purchase probably because in their contest to win the approval of society, any of their competitors would, if he could, buy more esteem by buying more, bigger, richer, greater, etc. Staying ahead was then part of the competitive struggle. Conspicuous consumption was then the weapon.

Recently, however, there has been a shift in the symbols that indicate a person's worth. More is no longer better. There are now different ways of indicating one's social worth which have come to be preferred.

The possession of goods that are unique, beautiful, tasteful, elegant and exceptional has now become the most effective symbol of one's quality, and the consequence is that as income and wealth grow, an increasing proportion of the spending of the very rich is being directed to the acquisition of such goods. Because of their role as symbols of the social position of their owners, these are called 'positional goods'; other outputs which are wanted because they keep one warm, fed, comfortable, etc. are called 'material goods'.

'Positional goods' owe their efficacy largely to their uniqueness. To own an original Van Gogh – and still better a particular one – is to own a *unique* work, while to own even a precise reproduction of the same gives its owner no social standing; indeed it suggests that he is one of the *nouveaux riches*, who deserves pity rather than esteem. Most 'positional goods' by their very nature cannot be reproduced. A choice site in the mountains, a Frank Lloyd Wright house, an ancient castle, a rare Cape of Good Hope stamp, even the only gown of its kind created by one of Rome's most admired designers offer other examples. Most 'positional goods' are unique because they cannot be multiplied; not surprisingly, because their creators may no longer be living, and even if they are, they have surely learned that scarcity creates value. Owning one of them reduces the probability that another seeker can compete along the same line because there are so few just like it.

An increase in the demand for material goods will normally lead to an increase in their output – and probably no significant rise in their price. But an increase in the demand for a positional good, because the elasticity of its supply is low, or even zero, will have little effect on its output; though its price is likely to go on rising.

As wealth and income in an economy increase and as the demand for positional goods becomes more important (if the newly rich seek to imitate the old-rich), the output of most positional goods will, at best, increase slowly; but their prices will rise ever more rapidly. In such a society it follows too that the demand for '*material* goods' will normally increase less quickly; after all, an increasing share of the purchasing power of the heavy spenders is likely to be siphoned off in the effort to acquire the *ne plus ultra* of 'positional goods'. As a result, the output of 'material goods' will rise less quickly than it would have done in earlier times.

The net effect of this is (1) that the rise in overall output will be sluggish, (2) that the number of jobs offered, reflecting the increase in labour productivity may not rise at all and (3) that prices of 'positional goods' will rise swiftly.

In some ways, the effect on output resembles that predicted in the writings of Alvin Hansen on 'secular stagnation'. But as Scitovsky pointed out, the two explanations for it are quite different. For Scitovsky, the demand for 'positional goods' and money – another symbol of its owner's worth – will grow faster than the demand for 'material goods'; for Hansen, the demand for investment and consumer goods is likely to lag; and the case is strengthened by the fact that as interest rates drop, further declines in the demand for 'positional goods' become more and more unlikely.

Scitovsky puts his hypothesis forward as the single most persuasive *secular* explanation for stagflation, but he is careful not to claim that it is the only explanation. Moreover, he qualifies his analysis by pointing out that the supply of some positional goods (for example, household services) is quite elastic.

Price increases, possibly limited at first to 'positional goods', are likely in turn to spread throughout the economy. The mechanism for this process is activated by the frustration of those who would have been able to purchase some positional goods had their prices not risen; not surprisingly, they will do all they can to have their pay raised, to enable them to keep up. Their example is likely to be followed by others who don't want to fall behind in their standing in the pay scale. As pay raises become more general, price rises will spread throughout the economy, even if demand remains sluggish. (Prices of cars rise steadily, even though the demand for them is slack; and as car prices are raised, workers try hard to get their pay raised to match increases in the prices of what they buy.)

One should note an important distinction pointed out by Scitovsky in his analysis. While the demand for material goods may become sated, the demand for positional goods is likely to become *unfillable*. The effort to come first cannot succeed for most because success by one implies a lower place for all the rest. If one owns the best building-site on the West Coast, it condemns all others to sites, at best, no better than second. The desire for positional goods may promote demand for them, but there is no danger that it can be fully satisfied; indeed it is likely to intensify.

What can be done about this secular tendency for the number of jobs created over time to fall behind the number of women and men who want jobs? The author is not at all optimistic about programmes to encourage the demand for investment goods by varying taxes and the supply of money. Nor is he hopeful that government can raise its purchases from the economy by enough to absorb the widening gap between what the economy can produce when operating at capacity and the amount its public wants to purchase.

Obviously, as an economy becomes richer, it has more opportunity to produce to satisfy the needs of the disadvantaged and destitute at home and abroad. This is true, physically, but it does not follow that arrangements to provide these goods to those in need will be politically possible.

In short, the growth in society's demand for 'material goods' may reach a limit well short of its ability to supply that output. If so, there may be nothing left but to try to persuade those who now want full-time jobs and the pay they would yield to be content with less and somehow to handle the psychological and sociological difficulties created when too many have too little to do. Education would then have to change its goal from preparing us to produce to preparing us to consume and to enjoy leisure.

Name index

Abouchar, Alan 49
  Pricing Highways 55
Ackerlof, G.A. 117
Allen, R.G.D. 19
Ascheim, J. and Talvas, G.S. 130
Asimakopulos, A. 70, 73, 74

Baldwin, Stanley 169
Barber, Clarence L. 35
Begg, D.K.H. 137
Belesley, D.A., *et al.* 27
Benassy, J.P. 81
Bernstein, Edward M.: 'Keynes and
      US Foreign Economic Policy'
      182n
Bodkin, Ronald G. 3
  et al. 12, 23, 24, 25, 28, 30
Boltho, Andrea 38
Brennan, G. and Buchanan, J.M.
      131
Bresciani-Turoni, C. 46
Brown, A.J. 4
Bruning, Chancellor 183
Burns, Arthur and Mitchell, Wesley:
      Measuring Business Cycles 18
Burstein, M.L. 162

Casarosa, L. 74
Caskey, J. and Fazzari, S. 68n
Chang, W. *et al.* 163
Christ, C.F. 18
Clark, Colin 4, 9n
Cook, R.D. and Weisberg, S. 27
Cowles, Alfred 7, 17, 18

Davidson, Paul 81, 85, 86, 87, 130
  and Davidson, G.S. 85
  and Smolensky, E. 81
Debreu, G. 83
DeLong, J.B. and Summers, L.H.
      68n, 140
Dhrymes, P.J. 25
Dimand, R.W. 20n, 121, 124, 126

Dow, S.C. and Earl, P.E. 130
Dupuit, J. 54, 55

Eichengreen, Barry 181n, 182n

Fama, E.F. 142n
Fisher, Irving 17, 130, 157n, 189
  theory of depressions 68n
Frank, R.H. 117
Friedman, Milton 19, 130, 135, 141,
      142n, 162
  and Schwartz, A.J. 163, 164n
Frisch, Ragnar 12, 14, 17, 24
Frydman, R. 163
  and Phelps, E.S. 163

Glass, D.V.: on declining population
      in 1930s 36
Glenday, R.: 'Business
      forecasting . . .' 20n
Goldberger, A.S. 25
Grandmont, J-M. 81, 142n
Graziani, A. 146
Griliches and Intriligator: *Handbook
      of Econometrics* 24

Haavelmo, Trygve 16, 17, 23, 28, 29,
      30
  view of testable hypotheses 29
Haberler, G. 15
  Prosperity and Depression 14
Hahn, F. 162, 163
Hall, R.E. 142n
Hamouda, Omar F. 205
Hansen, Alvin 37, 207
Harcourt, G.C. 157n
Harrod, Roy 20n, 22, 26, 40n, 73,
      91n, 181n
  'Essay in Dynamic Theory' 37
  on Tinbergen's work 15
Hawtrey, R.G. 71
  'The Monetary Theory of the
      Trade Cycle and its statistical

test' 20n

Hayek, F.A. von 157n, 162, 164
  Prices and Production 157n
Hendry, D.F. 23
Hicks, Sir John 8n, 19, 20, 45, 93,
    127, 128
  *Crisis in Keynesian Economics,
    The* 93, 101
  interpretation of Keynes's
    wage-theorem analysed 93–101:
    General Theory as foundation
    for wage-theorem 99–100;
    inflation, importance of 97–9;
    Keynes's belief in wage-
    theorem holding true 97;
    Keynes's theory of prices 97;
    Keynes's wage-unit measures
    94–7; theorem defined 93–4;
    theorem stated to be central to
    General Theory 94
  IS/LM analysis 126, 127, 128, 145
Hirsch, Prof. F.C. 205
Howitt, Peter 61

Jain, R. 24
Johnston, J. 25
Judge, G.C. *et al.* 25

Kahn, Richard 8n, 15, 46, 78n, 157n
Kaldor, Nicholas 151, 181n
Kalecki, M. 150
Katz, Samuel I. 182n
Keynes, J.M. 7, 84, 86, 90n, 91n
  aggregate demand function
    developed 70, 74, 78, 82, 87
  aggregate supply function
    developed 70–3 *passim*, 78, 82,
    87–8, 89
  'Balance of Payments of the
    United States, The' 179
  belief in: post-WWII trade
    liberalization 178–9; stationary
    population 36–7
  'Can Lloyd George Do It?' 7, 10n
  'Clearing Union' proposal,
    (1941–2) 177, 179
  'co-operative economy',
    description 70
  econometric analysis, doubts
    about 12–13, 14, 16

econometrics, contribution to 24
'Economic Consequences of
  Mr Churchill, The' 100, 171
'Economic Consequences of the
  Peace, The' 179
*Economic Prospects for our
  Grandchildren* 103
'entrepreneur economy',
  description 70, 75
Essays in Persuasion 98
*General Theory of Employment,
  Interest and Money, The* 3, 4–5,
  9n, 12, 20, 24, 35–40 *passim*,
  53, 55, 57, 70–5 *passim*, 78,
  79n, 87, 93, 94, 96–101 *passim*,
  121, 123–8 *passim*, 130, 131,
  132, 145, 148, 151, 159, 160,
  162, 163, 177, 181n, 189, 205:
  automatic recovery from
  recession questioned 205; Book
  III, 'The Propensity to
  Consume' 4, 36; Book IV, 'The
  Inducement to Invest' 4; Book
  V, 'Money-Wages and Prices' 4;
  'Classical Theory of the Rate of
  Interest, The' (chapter) 121;
  'Essential Properties of Interest
  and Money, The' (chapter) 123;
  'General Theory of Interest,
  The' (chapter) 163; 'Notes on
  Mercantilism, etc.' (chapter)
  176; 'State of Long Term
  Expectations, The' (chapter)
  162
'General Theory of Employment'
  lectures 130
heart attack, (1937) 4
'How to Pay for the War' 7, 10n
income distribution, concern with
  151–2
inflation 146–7, 148–9
international debt defaults 191
involuntary unemployment,
  definition 102, 105; equilibrium
  with 70, 71, 74–6
Keynes-Tinbergen exchange
  23–30: Keynes's criticisms of
  Tinbergen's study 5–6, 14–16,
  23–30 *passim*
main strands of General Theory 70

'Means to Prosperity, The'
(article) 176
'money did not matter' myth
concerning 130
National Debt Inquiry minutes
128
'National Self-Sufficiency' (article)
176
negotiates Anglo-American Loan
Agreement, (1945) 178
'Newton the Man' 16
opposition to rentier capitalism
146, 149–51, 157n
'Principles of British Commercial
Policy' 180
'Proposals for a Revenue Tariff'
(article) 170
purchasing power of money,
preservation of 98
'Reparations and the Peace
Treaty' 183
Say's law 82, 87, 205
'Some Economic Consequences of
a Declining Population' lecture
37
theory of prices 97
Tract on Monetary Reform 98, 171
transition from *Treatise on Money*
to *General Theory* 71–4
Treatise on Money 12, 41, 43, 45,
71, 74, 98, 125, 140, 151, 160,
163, 164
Treatise on Probability 13, 15, 20
unemployment's non-
attributability to wage
inflexibility 61
value, modern theory of 53
wages 103
wage-theorem concept, *see* Hicks,
Sir John
see also Econometric analysis,
Interest, Investment,
Macroeconomic modelling,
Microeconomics, Money,
Replacement investment,
Tariffs, Unemployment, and
Wage flexibility and
employment, which all set out
Keynes's views, subject index
Klant, J.J. 6, 9n, 23

Klein, B. 135
Klein, Lawrence R. 3, 9n, 12
'The Use of Econometrics Models
as a Guide to Economic Policy'
19
Kmenta, J. 25
Knight, Frank 14, 18, 19
Kolm, S.-C. 102
Koopmans, T.C. 14, 16, 23, 24, 26,
30
'Measurement without Theory' 18
Kregel, J.A. 130
Kuznets, Simon 4

Lange, Oskar 19
Lavoie, Mark 145, 157n
Lawson, T. 6, 9n, 23
Leamer, E.E. 23
Leontief, W. 12
Lerner, A.P. 81, 88, 141
Lucas, Robert 8n, 9n, 131, 135

MacDonald, Ramsay 170
Maddala, G.S. 25
Maddison, A.: *Economic Growth in
the West* 40n
Malinvaud, E. 25
Marget, Arthur 20n
Marme, Christopher 93
Marris, Robin 157n
Marschak, Jacob 18, 24
Marshall, Alfred: 'The New
Generation of Economists and
the Old' 8n
Marwah, Kanta 3
Meade, J.E. 8n
Menger, Karl 13, 18
Mill, J.S. 162, 164
Modigliani, F. 81
Moggridge, D.E. 8n, 23
and Howson, S. 175
Moore, Basil J. 121, 159, 163
comment on chapter by 160–61
'Determination of Interest Rates'
160
'Horizontalists and Verticalists'
160
Morganstern, Oskar 13, 20n
Holmes-Moriarty example 13
Theory of Games and Economic

Behaviour, The (with J. von
Neuman) 14, 16
Wertsschaftsprognose 13, 20n
Mundell, R. 64

Nell, E.J. 130

O'Donnell, R.M. 131

Parrinello, S. 74
Passinetti, L. 127, 152
Patinkin, Don 3–4, 7, 8n, 9n, 12, 23,
25, 68n, 72
Perelman, Michael 41
Pesaran, H. and Smith, R. 6, 10n, 23
Pratt, Edwin: *History of Inland
Transportation and
Communication in England* 54

Quesnay, François 10n
tableau économique 8, 10n

Radner, R. 163
Reder, M.W. 19
Ricardo, David 90, 123, 163, 164
on interest 122
Principles 122, 162
Rima, Ingrid H. 13
Robertson, D.H. 44, 73, 81, 164
Banking Policy and the Price Level
164n
Robinson, Joan 72, 151, 157, 181n
Accumulation of Capital 152
Roos, Charles 17
Rostow, W.W. 157n
Rotheim, R.J. 130
Rowley, Robin 23
and Jain, R. 24
Rymes, T.K. 130, 142n

Sargent, T.J. 8n
Schmitt, Bernard 194
Schultz, H. and Goodrich, C. 72
Schumpeter, Joseph 14
Schwartz, A. and Friedman, M.
142n
Scitovsky, Tibor 205
demand, for more material goods
206, 208

demand, to 'positional goods' 206,
207
ever-rising employment via more
consumption question 205–6
explanation for stagflation 207
'Keynes and Public Policy after
Fifty Years' 205
Seccareccia, Mario 145, 157n
Shackle, G.L.S. 121
Sheffrin, S.M. 137
Sidauski, M. 142n
Sims, C.A. 8n
Skidelsky, R. 157n, 169
Smith, V.L.: on Keynes's conditions
for modelling 27–8
Smook, Nicholas P. 169
Sraffa, P. 44, 46, 157n
Stone, Richard 3, 7, 9n, 23
Szilard, L. 18

Talvas, G.S. 130
Tarshis, Lorie 79n, 183, 205
Taylor, J.B. 68n
Terborgh, G. 42
Theil, H. 25
Tinbergen, J. 7, 9n, 14, 16, 24
*Business Cycles in the USA,
1919–32* 3, 14
*Economic Approach to Business
Cycle Problems, An* 9n
efforts to test theories of business
cycle 2
Keynes-Tinbergen exchange 23–
30: Keynes criticisms 5–6,
14–16, 23–30 *passim*;
Tinbergen's study for League of
Nations 5, 14–16, 30
*Method and Its Application to
Investment Activity, A* 14
Tobin, J. 68n
Townsend, R.M. 163
Townshend, H. 141, 147
Tyler, Mr 24, 26, 29

Vining, Rutledge 18
Von Neumann, John
'Theory of Games' 13
*Theory of Games and Economic
Behaviour, The* (with
O. Morganstern) 14, 16

Wald, Abraham 17
Weintraub, E.R. 20n
Weintraub, S. 81, 82, 88, 89
Weitzman, M.L. 78
   Share Economy The, 76
   share economy concept 76–8, 79n,
      81–2, 86, 90n, 91n, 92n:
      aggregate supply function 87–9;
      assumptions regarding
      perishability and demand 82–6;
      common features with Keynes's

ideas 76, 78; departures from
   Keynes's views 76, 77;
   technology's independence of
   compensation system, question
   of 86–7; wage system vs share
   system 90
Wells, Paul 93
Williamson, J. 182n
Wolf, Bernard M. 169
Wulwick, Nancy J. 159

Subject index

American Economic Association 130
American Society of State Highway
    (and Transportation) Officials
    (AASH(T)O) 51, 52

Bank of England 191, 192
Bretton Woods Conference 179

Cambridge University Free Trade
    Association 169
Canada 153
    Bank of Canada 136, 142n, 153,
        158n, 191, 192
        Review 155, 156
    Bovey Commission 51
    Canada Year Book 154, 155, 158n
    Canadian Bankers' Association
        136
    confounding prices and taxes in
        51, 52
    deviations between real rate of
        interest and growth of
        productivity, (1947–85) 153,
        156
    deviations between real rate of
        interest and rate of growth,
        (1927–39) 152–3, 154
    Historical Statistics of Canada 154,
        155, 158n
    Statistics Canada 154, 155, 156,
        158n
    transfer of income during
        depressions of 1930s and 1980s
        153, 155
Chicago: Harris Foundation lectures
    71
Cowles Commission 17–18, 19, 20,
    23, 25–6, 28, 30

Daily Mail 170

Econometric analysis 12, 19–20
    business cycle predictions 12, 13, 14

controversies 18–19
    Keynes's doubts about 12–13, 14,
        16
    pioneer work 14, 16–17
    probability approach 17, 18
Econometric Society 7, 17, 20, 20n
Econometrica 20n
Economic Journal 16, 22, 146, 179
Eugenics Society: Galton lecture 37
European Payments Union 179

General Agreement on Tariffs and
    Trade (GATT) 179, 180

Interest
    classical theory 122, 163
    Keynes's treatment of 121–8, 157,
        157n, 158n: attempts to refute
        'classical' view 121–3;
        determinants of marginal
        efficiency of money 126; efficacy
        of monetary policy 124; liquidity
        preference theory 126, 128;
        'liquidity trap' 124–5, 157n; rate
        of interest and unemployment
        123, 147; rates determined by
        supply of and demand for
        liquidity 121; rejects loanable
        funds theory 121; support for
        cheap money policy 145, 147–9,
        157n
International debt 184
    defaults 191
    German reparations, 1920s 183,
        184–5: borrowing needed 184,
        192–3; Dawes Plan 193–4;
        Germany stops payment 183,
        187; Keynes on 183, 184–5, 189,
        192–3; lenders to Germany
        186–7
    less developed countries' 183:
        bank problems re cancelling
        debts 191–2; borrowing to

prevent collapse 185–6; charade
of 186; IMF rules for debtors
190; interest payments 186;
lenders 187; need to cancel large
amounts of debt 190–1, 193;
repayment doubtful 189–90;
size of debt 183
need for creditors to transform
surpluses into deficits 188
problem of perpetuation
of external debt under
dollar-standard 195–8: logical
consequences 198–200; solution
via improved 'Clearing Union'
200–1
spread of deflation to creditors 189
US borrowing, 19th c. 183–4
International Monetary Fund (IMF)
131, 179, 188, 189, 190
Investment
Keynes's views 35–40 *passim*
see also Replacement investment

League of Nations 14
Lend Lease Agreement 181n
Lloyd's Bank Review 205

Macmillan Committee on Finance
and Industry 170
Addendum to Report 172
Macroeconometric modelling 3–8
antecedents 3
General Theory as antecedent
3–4, 7
Keynes's attitude to 5–7, 8n, 9n,
10n
papers showing developing field of
20n
Microeconomics 57
cost theory 53–5
Keynes's influence in public sector
investment 49–50, 53, 54, 55
central role of interest rate 54
labour input vs employment
creation 55–6, 57
public sector expenditure as
cyclical policy 50–3
Money
distribution policy and postwar
experience 151–7

Keynes's monetary theory 130–1,
159, 160, 162–4: aspects 146–7;
stable money 130–1; theory of
discretionary services on
monetary authorities 131–4
liquidity premium 140–2
neo-classical theory 131, 145;
non-discretionary sources of
monetary authorities 134–6
problem of instability and
discretionary policy 136–40
quantity theory 131, 145

National Bureau 18
National Institute of Social and
Economic Research:
'Cambridge Research Scheme' 7
New Statesman and Nation 170

Organization for Economic
Cooperation and Development
(OECD) 38
Organization of Petroleum
Exporting Countries (OPEC)
186
oil price increases 38
Overton Committee on Commercial
Policy 177

Post-WWII period
baby boom 37–8
decline in growth from 1970s 38–9
'Great Recession', 1980s 152, 153
increase in productivity 38
oil price increases, 1973 38

Quarterly Journal of Economics 20n,
130, 146

Replacement investment 41
basic principles 42
Keynes and q-theory of
investment 46–8
Keynes's treatment of 41, 43–6
normal backwardation and market
for capital services 42–3
*Review of the International Statistical
Institute* 19

Say's law 82, 83, 85, 87, 90, 90n,

127, 205
Stagflation 205–8

Tariffs, Keynes's views 169, 175–7,
181n, 182n
  after abandonment of gold
    standard 124, 175–7
  free trader in 1920s 169–70
  Keynes and contemporary
    protectionism 179–81
  planning for post-WWII period
    177–9
  revenue tariff, advocacy of 126,
    170–75, 181
  views on gold standard 170–1
Times, The 124

Unemployment
  British, (1931) 173
  'classical' reason for 102
  involuntariness 104–6: imperfect
    competition, problems of 105
  Keynes's definition of involuntary
    102
  model relating wages,
    unemployment and fiscal policy
    106–8: efficiency of global
    balanced fiscal policy 113–15;
    labour demand 110–11; labour
    supply 108–10; optimality
    111–13; tax-subsidy solution
    115–16
  norm and status economy 116–17
  preferences on prices and wages
    102–4, 107
  'social multi-level voluntariness'
    105

United States of America
  borrowing, 19th c. 183–4
  confounding prices and taxes in
    51, 52
  Federal Reserve 191, 192
  heavy-vehicle road damage 51
  'nickel tax' on motor vehicle fuel
    51
  pricing public sector activities 51
  problems of dollar 180–1
  rapid replacement of capital,
    reason for 47–8
  Smoot-Hawley tariff, (1930) 174
  weak equity prices during inflation
    of 1970s 46

Vienna Circle (Colloquium) 13, 18

Wage flexibility and employment
  61–4
  employment and wages 65–7
  Keynes's ideas 61, 62: increased
    wage flexibility making
    employment more variable 62,
    63, 66, 68n; wage reduction
    effect of reducing employment
    62, 63, 65, 68n
  model 62, 64–5
Wages
  importance of relative wages 103
  labour markets 107–8
  question of social status or norms
    103–4, 116–17
Walrasian-Paretian models 3, 7
  conception of mutual
    interdependence 17